THE

EVERYTHING®

VEGETARIAN COOKBOOK

300 healthy recipes
everyone will enjoy

Jay Weinstein

Adams Media Corporation
Avon, Massachusetts

EDITORIAL
Publishing Director: Gary M. Krebs
Managing Editor: Kate McBride
Copy Chief: Laura MacLaughlin
Acquisitions Editor: Bethany Brown
Development Editor: Michael Paydos

PRODUCTION
Production Director: Susan Beale
Production Manager: Michelle Roy Kelly
Series Designer: Daria Perreault and Colleen Cunningham
Layout and Graphics: Paul Beatrice,
Brooke Camfield, Colleen Cunningham,
Daria Perreault, Frank Rivera

An Everything® Series Book.
Everything® is a registered trademark of Adams Media Corporation.

Published by Adams Media Corporation
57 Littlefield Street, Avon, MA 02322 U.S.A.
www.adamsmedia.com

ISBN: 1-58062-640-8
Printed in the United States of America.

J I H G F E D C B A

This publication is designed to provide accurate and authoritative information with regard to
the subject matter covered. It is sold with the understanding that the publisher is not engaged
in rendering legal, accounting, or other professional advice. If legal advice or other expert
assistance is required, the services of a competent professional person should be sought.
     —From a *Declaration of Principles* jointly adopted by a Committee of the
American Bar Association and a Committee of Publishers and Associations

Cover illustrations by Barry Littmann.
Technical illustrations by Eulala Conner.

This book is available at quantity discounts for bulk purchases.
For information, call 1-800-872-5627.

Visit the entire Everything® series at everything.com

Acknowledgments

Thanks to Jasper White and the many other chefs who have helped, taught, cajoled, and inspired me, especially Mark Cupolo, Stan Frankenthaler, Graeme Bent, Bruce Putney, Claudio Papini, Eric Ripert, Dona Abramson, Mark Baker, Michael Kornick, Uwe Hestnar, and Fritz Sonnenschmidt.

Thanks also to the friends and family who have encouraged me in both the kitchen and the writing room: Pearl and Seymour Weinstein, Naomi Dreeben, Tuan Pu Wang, Douglas Bailey Clark, Josh Martin, James Moses, Todd K. Snyder, Kevin Mulcahy, Paul Tarantola, and other important people too numerous to mention.

V : This symbol indicates that the recipe is vegan. Veganism takes vegetarianism to the next level. A vegan recipe has no animal products at all—including dairy, honey, and ingredients derived from animal byproducts (such as gelatin).

Contents

Introduction

These are great days to be a vegetarian. There's no such thing as "Mad Tofu Disease," there haven't been any outbreaks of "Sprout-in-Mouth Disease," and *60 Minutes* hasn't run an exposé about the dangers of undercooked carrots. The variety of healthful, dynamic, fresh, and wholesome vegetarian options in mainstream U.S. food markets and restaurants has never been better!

Even Europe, where classical chefs once looked down their noses at vegetarian dining, is abloom in splendid meat-free cafés, restaurants, and markets. I spent several months in Berlin recently, expecting to find menus of meat accompanied by meat with a sidedish of meat. Imagine my surprise when I stumbled on the upscale, mostly vegetarian Café Abendmahl only a few steps from the door of my Kreuzberg apartment! Wandering through the "strasses" and "platzes" on day two, I came upon a restaurant whose specialty was spinach pancakes. Blocks away was a thriving vegetable market along the Landwehrkanal stretching for block after city block, with more choices than I'd ever seen in a

lifetime of A & Ps. A recent trip to Paris revealed a similar botanical bounty.

With celebrities like Alec Baldwin, Melissa Etheridge, Brooke Shields, Drew Barrymore, and Brad Pitt proudly proclaiming their flesh-free proclivities, today's vegetarianism is not just ethical, it's chic. When bodybuilders, triathletes, and marathon runners eschew meat and win events, who can deny the strength-giving character of their balanced diets?

On our shrinking planet, arguments for vegetarianism are as close as the front page of the newspaper. Every day, articles feature stories of famine, while livestock consume enough grain to feed millions. Horrific tales of herbivorous sheep and cows being forced to eat the ground-up remains of their unfortunate brethren as "feed" have sent shockwaves through the meat-consuming public. And the near-annihilation of many fish species due to over-fishing has become routine. Just cutting down on the amount of meat and fish in your diet is something to feel good about.

With proper balance and, in some cases, judicious use of dietary supplements like B vitamins, the vegetarian lifestyle can lead to better heart health, clearer skin, longer life, and fewer disease threats without any deficiencies. The first thing critics of the meat-free diet cite is a supposed dearth of protein. But nutritionists agree on two things: Americans grossly overdose on protein, and the right combination of vegetarian foods gives us more than enough building blocks to complete our protein needs. The pages of this book overflow with all the delicious ways you'll need to enjoy food in a whole new way.

Complete Proteins

The building blocks of protein (of which our muscles, bones, hair, and fingernails are made) are called amino acids. Most of the twenty amino acids humans need are produced by our bodies naturally. But we must consume nine essential amino acids in the form of food.

All nine of these amino acids exist in meat, so nonvegetarians simply eat meat to fulfill their bodies' need for these vital building blocks. The good news for vegetarians is that the essential amino acids also exist in abundance in the plant kingdom. But vegetarians must draw on several different foods to build the same protein a nonvegetarian gets from meat. Since some but not all of the essential amino acids exist in certain foods, those foods are said to contain "incomplete proteins."

Whole grains such as rice, for example, contain incomplete proteins. Legumes contain other incomplete proteins. Between the two of them, you'll find all the amino acids necessary for the human diet; so a plate of rice and beans meets the same protein-building needs in your body as meat would. Another such combination is wheat and dairy. Macaroni and cheese is a complete protein.

Vegetarians must remain vigilant about consuming a diverse diet, containing the building blocks for protein. Without them, muscle loss and weakness will slow down their bodies, and make them susceptible to all kinds of illnesses. Until recently, it was believed that complementary foods had to be consumed at the same time in order to build complete proteins. That myth has been debunked. It's now known that the body stores incomplete proteins (amino acids), and combines them for complete proteins when complementary ones arrive in the system, even if it's hours or even days later.

A secret weapon vegetarians have on their side is a superfood that contains all of the essential amino acids in a vegetarian source: soy. Soy foods such as tofu, soy flour, whole soybeans, and tempeh (a textured soy protein) are the virtual protein equivalent of meat. That's why soy products are such an important part of the vegetarian diet.

Chapter One

Salads

Southeast Asian Slaw

This crisp, lightly spiced salad is fine enough to roll in Asian-inspired wraps, and combines beautifully with jasmine rice, cooked in coconut milk to make a unique taste.

Serves 4

¼ head (about ½ pound) Napa cabbage
½ carrot, grated
1 small red onion, julienne
1 small Thai "bird" chili **or** jalapeño pepper, finely chopped
¼ cup chopped cilantro
Juice of 1 lime
1 tablespoon rice wine vinegar
1 teaspoon sugar
1 teaspoon vegetable oil
A few drops sesame oil
½ teaspoon salt

1. Shred the cabbage as fine as you possibly can, using a knife, mandolin, or slicing machine. Combine with carrot, onion, chili pepper, and cilantro.
2. Dress with lime, rice vinegar, sugar, vegetable oil, sesame oil, and salt; toss thoroughly.
3. Refrigerate for at least 30 minutes before serving.

Tomato and Bread Salad (Panzinella) Ⓥ

Panzinella (bread salad) is a favorite side dish with sliced cheeses in Italy. Using both yellow and red tomatoes can make this a festive touch on your plate.

Serves 4 as an appetizer or side dish

2 cups diced (½-inch) ripe red tomatoes, any variety
¼ cup finely chopped red onion
½ teaspoon salt
1½ tablespoons extra-virgin olive oil
2 teaspoons fresh lemon juice
2 cups day-old country bread, cut into ½-inch cubes, air-dried
  *overnight **or** baked 20 minutes at 325 degrees*
¼ cup roughly chopped Italian parsley
Black pepper to taste

1. Dress tomatoes and chopped onion with salt, olive oil, and lemon juice.
2. Toss gently with dried bread cubes and parsley.
3. Season with freshly ground black pepper.

Read the Label

"Unlike wine, oil deteriorates," says chef and cookbook author Paula Wolfert, "The better oils give you the year it was produced." The shelf life for a really good extra-virgin olive oil is about two years. The label tells you a minimum of one important distinction: Extra Virgin. The International Olive Oil Commission (IOOC) has established that name to indicate that the oil was cold pressed, and that no chemicals were introduced to aid in extraction. It also indicates an acidity of less than 1 percent, which cannot be detected by taste. Oil must be analyzed in a laboratory to ascertain acidity level. "That's really important, because it means that the oil has all of its vitamins in it."

Salad of Celery Root and Pears

Wintertime in the Northeast brings basketfuls of celeriac (celery roots) to the produce markets. Their herby, vegetal flavor pairs perfectly with pears. Variations on this combination are popular all winter long.

Serves 6

1 medium celery root (about the size of a baseball), peeled
¼ cup mayonnaise (homemade is best, but any will do)
½ hard-boiled egg, chopped
1 tablespoon finely chopped Italian (flat-leaf) parsley
2 cornichons (little sour gherkins), finely chopped
2 tablespoons Dijon mustard
Juice of 1 lemon
2 ripe pears (Bartlett and Bosc are great, but choose your own variety)
2 tablespoons extra-virgin olive oil
Salt and freshly ground black pepper

1. Julienne (cut into very thin strips) the celery root. Combine mayonnaise, chopped egg, parsley, cornichons, mustard, and lemon, and toss with celery root. Season with salt and pepper.
2. Peel pears and slice into 6 to 8 wedges each. Divide dressed celery root into 6 portions, and garnish with pear slices.

How to "Chop" Eggs Through a Roasting Rack

Many racks intended for lining roasting pans are made as crosshatch weaves of thin steel rods spaced about a quarter of an inch apart. Not only are these excellent devices for roasting onions, mushrooms, and chili peppers, but they make great cooling racks for cakes and pies, too. But my favorite use for them is as a shortcut to chopping eggs. Simply place a peeled hard-boiled egg on the rack, and push it through with the heel of your hand. This method is a lifesaver when you're turning a few dozen eggs into egg salad for a picnic or luncheon.

Winter Greens Salad with Green Beans and Roquefort Vinaigrette

My mentor, Jasper White, introduced me to this type of salad, which, I think, highlights the fruitiness of blue cheese and the sweetness of the vegetables with the lightness of a vinaigrette dressing.

Serves 4

1 bunch watercress
2 heads Belgium endive
1 small red onion
½ pound green beans

Dressing:
⅓ cup balsamic vinegar
⅓ cup vegetable oil
⅓ cup extra-virgin olive oil
1 tablespoon chopped chives
*¼ pound Roquefort **or** other quality blue cheese*
Coarse (kosher) salt and freshly ground black pepper

1. Rinse watercress and break into bite-size pieces. Cut endives diagonally into 3 or 4 sections each, discarding cores. Slice red onion into thin rings.
2. In 3 quarts of rapidly boiling salted water, cook green beans in 2 separate batches until just tender, about 5 minutes, then plunge them into salted ice water to stop the cooking process. Combine with greens and onions.
3. Whisk together vinegar, vegetable oil, olive oil, and chives. Roughly break the blue cheese into dressing; stir with a spoon, leaving some large chunks. Season with salt and pepper. Dress salad with ⅓ cup of dressing. Remaining dressing will keep, refrigerated, for 2 weeks.
4. Arrange salad onto 4 plates, with onion rings and green beans displayed prominently on top.

Tatsoi Salad with Orange-Sesame Vinaigrette

Light, floral, and zesty, this salad pairs antioxidant-rich Japanese spinach (tatsoi) with springtime-fresh cross-cultural dressing. The salad works equally well with other types of spinach.

Serves 4

6 cups tatsoi (Japanese "baby" spinach leaves)
¼ cup orange-sesame vinaigrette (recipe follows)

½ cup red Bermuda onion, sliced paper-thin

1. Wash and spin the *tatsoi* leaves, then toss gently with one half of the dressing. Distribute onto 4 salad plates.
2. Arrange sliced onions atop each salad, and finish with a final spoonful of dressing.

Orange-Sesame Vinaigrette

Yields about 1¼ cups

Zest of ½ orange
Zest of ½ lime
1 pickled jalapeño pepper, and 1 tablespoon of the brine it came in (usually found near the olives in supermarkets), chopped
¼ cup Japanese rice wine vinegar

¼ cup orange juice concentrate
1½ teaspoons Dijon mustard
A few drops sesame oil (about ⅛ teaspoon)
¼ cup peanut oil
¼ cup olive oil
Salt and freshly ground black pepper

1. Combine zest, pickled jalapeño and brine, rice vinegar, orange concentrate, Dijon, and sesame oil in a blender.
2. Blend on medium speed, slowly drizzling in the peanut and olive oils. Season to taste with salt and pepper.

Madras Curry Dressing

Perfect as a dip for crudités or a spread on sandwiches, this dressing balances the sweetness of dried fruits with the complexity of Indian spices and light chili "heat."

Yields about 1¼ cups

1 tablespoon oil
1 small red onion, finely chopped
2 tablespoons chopped red bell pepper
1 teaspoon finely chopped and seeded jalapeño pepper
2 tablespoons Madras curry powder
1 teaspoon ground coriander
1 teaspoon ground turmeric
1 tablespoon raisins, soaked in ½ cup warm water
¼ teaspoon cayenne pepper (optional)
Juice of 1 lime (about 2 tablespoons)
1 cup mayonnaise
2 tablespoons chopped cilantro
Salt and pepper to taste

1. In a small skillet, heat oil over medium heat for 1 minute. Add onions, bell pepper, and jalapeño. Cook until onions are translucent, about 2 minutes; add curry powder, coriander, and turmeric. Cook 4 minutes more, stirring with a wooden spoon. Some of the spices may stick—this is not a problem. Remove from heat; allow to cool a few minutes. Drain the raisins.
2. In the bowl of a food processor, combine onion mixture and raisins. Pulse until smooth, scraping sides of bowl frequently. Add half of lime juice and the mayonnaise. Pulse to combine, then stir in cilantro. Adjust seasoning with salt, pepper, and remaining lime juice. Can be made up to 1 week in advance.

Potato Varieties

Red-Skinned New Potatoes
- Available full size, or as marble or golf-ball-sized "babies"
- Moist; sweet; lower in starch
- Best for boiling; mashed potatoes
- Won't become crisp when fried

Thin-Skinned Round White Potatoes
- Also known as Maine, Eastern, or Long Island potatoes
- Moist; low in starch
- Range from golf ball to softball size
- Excellent in casseroles and stews; for mashed potatoes; baked

Idaho "Russet" Potatoes
- Thicker, darker skin with distinctive web-like pattern; oblong shape
- High starch; drier, mealier texture
- Perfect for frying, chips, potato pancakes, hash browns—become crisp when browned, flavorful when baked
- Range from plum size to giant, one-plus pounds

Yukon Gold Potatoes
- Attractive golden color; small in size (usually four to five per pound)
- High starch; fragrant; potato-y flavor
- Versatile—crisp when fried, tender when stewed
- Thin-skinned

Fingerling Potatoes
- Trendy "heirloom" variety, a favorite of gourmet chefs
- Thin skin; waxy, moist texture; and pale to bright yellow color
- Long and narrow, small enough to fit several in the palm of your hand
- Best as a part of a stew or vegetable mélange, such as with string beans

Blue "Peruvian" Potatoes
- Another trendy "heirloom" variety, dark blue to purple in color
- Thick skinned; starchy; color lightens slightly when cooked
- Excellent for mashed potatoes; great visual appeal
- Descendants of first potatoes cultivated in the Andes, which conquistadors encountered in Peru in the sixteenth century

Classic American Potato Salad

Fourth of July picnics wouldn't be the same without this favorite. For an interesting twist, try making it with specialty potatoes, like slim "fingerlings," from your produce market.

Serves 8

¾ cup mayonnaise
1 teaspoon sugar
2 teaspoons Dijon-style mustard
Salt and white pepper to taste
2 pounds potatoes (any variety), boiled, skinned, and cut into
   chunks
1 small carrot, peeled and grated
1 tablespoon roughly chopped Italian parsley

Whisk together the first 3 ingredients in a small bowl. Add potatoes and carrots; toss them gently to coat. Season to taste. Garnish with chopped parsley.

Scrubbing Potatoes with an Onion Bag

Don't throw away that fishnet onion bag! Crumpled up into a ball, it's perfect for loosening stubborn bits of dirt from the nooks and crannies of potatoes when you scrub them. It's also useful when cleaning up flour from a work surface. Rather than ruining a perfectly good kitchen sponge with gummed-up wet dough, scrub with an onion sack, and discard it after use.

Asian Cucumber Salad

This refreshing, crisp dish is the perfect counterbalance with grilled tempeh, spicy corn fritters, and other hearty fare. I prefer European-style or "English" cucumbers which have a thin, edible skin.

Serves 4

¼ cup rice wine vinegar
1 teaspoon sugar
1 teaspoon chopped jalapeño pepper
1 European-style long cucumber **or** 1 large regular cucumber
Sesame oil

1. Whisk together rice vinegar, sugar, and chopped jalapeño. If using a European cuke, it is not necessary to peel, but if using an American cuke, peel it. Halve the cucumber lengthwise; remove seeds. Slice seeded cucumber very thinly into half-moons. Combine with dressing, drizzle in a few drops of sesame oil, and toss to coat.
2. Marinate for at least 10 minutes before serving.

Seeding Cucumbers

All cucumbers, even the thin-skinned "seedless" European-style cukes, have a watery seed bed inside that dilutes their flavor in salads. To remove this, the handle of an old-fashioned stainless steel swivel potato peeler works exceedingly well. Split the cucumber in half, lengthwise. Holding the peeler by the cutter end, lodge the handle in one end of the seed bed and drag it to the other end. The watery pulp should scoop out in one continuous ribbon, leaving the crisp cucumber flesh intact. If you do not have this type of peeler, a teaspoon will work, too.

Succotash Salad

In summer, any excuse to use sweet corn is welcome. In New England, fresh cranberry beans are in the market in June and July, and they are delicious in this complete-protein salad. This is a variation on a recipe from New England chef Jasper White. Use it in sandwiches and wraps, such as the Avocado-Beet Wrap, page 125.

Serves 8

*8 ears sweet corn, shucked (**or** 16 ounces top-quality frozen corn)*
*½ pound dried pinto **or** red kidney beans, cooked (see "Bean There," page 16, for cooking instructions) **or** 2 (16-ounce) cans, drained and rinsed*
*¼ cup champagne vinegar **or** rice wine vinegar*
¼ cup extra-virgin olive oil
¼ cup chopped chives
Salt and pepper to taste

1. Shave corn kernels from cob, shearing them from the stem end to the tip with a knife. Cook in rapidly boiling salted water for 1 minute.
2. Toss with beans, vinegar, oil, and chives; season to taste.

Seasonal Tip

During cooler, autumn weather, substitute chopped shallots for the chives, and add one teaspoon toasted ground cumin for seasonality. Serve warm or room temperature.

Buyers' Guide: Carrots

Loaded with beta-carotene, which is essential for healthy eyes, skin, and cell respiration, and has been linked in recent studies to lower lung and prostate cancer rates, carrots are a nutritional superfood that's cheap and available year-round. Always choose fresh carrots that are crisp and tight-skinned, not limp or marred or covered in brown blemishes. There are several different types of fresh carrots commonly available:

- **Cello carrots** come in plastic bags, and average seven or eight to the pound. These are general purpose carrots, and may have been stored for extended periods in a refrigerated holding facility. Their sweetness varies depending on their age.
- **Horse carrots** are much larger, usually two or three to the pound, and are juicier and sweeter, generally, than cello carrots. I prefer these in most preparations, since sweetness is one of the primary characteristics I look to carrots to provide. Since they are sold loose, they are also easier to inspect for freshness.
- **Bunch carrots** are sold with their stems and leafy fronds still attached, and are the easiest to check for freshness. Look for stiff, crisp stems and bright green, vital leaves. Wilted leaves or drooping stems mean they've sat around or been mishandled.

- **Cello prepeeled "baby" carrots** are not really baby carrots at all, but mature carrots, which have been tumbled in an abrasive drum which scrapes away skin and outer layers until the remaining pieces are bite-size. Without the skin, these are the most difficult to inspect for freshness, and are often flavorless. Since carrots, like all vegetables, lose their nutritional value the longer they sit in the market, these are a poor choice for people seeking maximum carrot performance.
- **True baby carrots** are sold with their greens still attached, and look like miniature bunch carrots. While the term "baby" is actually a misnomer (they're actually a different variety of carrots that is very small at maturity), they are very nutritious and make a beautiful presentation on the plate, especially when a small part of the green stem is left on for visual impact. Check them for freshness, as you would bunch carrots.

Summer Vegetable Slaw V

Bursting with summer's bounty, this slaw is a colorful fiesta. The best renditions of this summer harvest celebration, introduced to me by New England chef Jasper White, utilize whatever vegetables are freshest and best at the market—the more the better!

Serves 8

1 small head Napa cabbage **or** regular green cabbage (about
   1 pound)
1 large "horse" carrot, **or** 2 regular carrots, peeled
¼ pound snow peas
1 each red, yellow, and green bell peppers, seeded
12 green beans
1 small red onion
2 ears fresh sweet corn, shucked
½ teaspoon sugar
¼ cup cider vinegar
1 tablespoon vegetable oil (preferably peanut oil)
Pinch of celery seeds
Salt and black pepper to taste

1. Quarter and core the cabbage; slice as thinly as possible. Using a swivel peeler, shave carrot into as many paper-thin curls as you can. Discard or save remaining carrot for another use. Cut carrot curls, snow peas, bell peppers, green beans, and onion into fine julienne. Cut corn kernels from the cob.
2. Combine all vegetables in a large mixing bowl; dress with sugar, vinegar, oil, celery seeds, salt, and pepper. Allow to sit at least 10 minutes before serving. This is an excellent accompaniment to crispy fried foods like beer-battered onion rings.

Caesar Salad

Vegetarian Worcestershire sauce is now available in health food stores, and may be added for an additional dimension if you wish, but this vegetarian version of America's favorite salad is authentic in taste.

Serves 8

Dressing:
1 egg yolk
1 tablespoon Dijon mustard
Juice of ½ lemon (about
*   2 tablespoons)*
2 cloves garlic, finely chopped
½ cup vegetable oil (preferably
*   peanut oil)*
¼ cup grated Parmigiano Reggiano
*   cheese*

Pinch of cayenne pepper (optional)
Salt and pepper

Salad:
1 head romaine lettuce, washed,
*   torn into bite-size pieces*
1 cup croutons
1 small wedge Parmigiano Reggiano
*   cheese (optional)*

1. Make the dressing: In a mixing bowl or food processor, combine the egg yolk, mustard, lemon juice, and garlic. Vigorously whisk or process in the oil, starting just a drop at a time, and gradually drizzling it in a small stream, until all is emulsified into a smooth mayonnaise. Stir in the cheese, cayenne, salt and pepper, and a little extra lemon if desired.
2. Toss the lettuce and croutons with the dressing, and divide onto 8 plates, arranging croutons on top. If desired, shave curls of Parmigiano over each salad, using a vegetable peeler. Dressing may be made up to 1 week in advance.

Crunch This!

The weirder the bread, the better the crouton. Guests will "ooh" and "aah" when you announce that your squash bisque boasts a garnish of Irish soda bread croutons. Cornbread makes spectacular croutons, as do rye bread and pumpernickel. Toss with a few drops of oil, spread on a sheet pan, and bake at 325 degrees for about twenty minutes, until crisp.

Croutons: Crunchy Nuggets of Frugality

Nothing beats croutons as a way to turn any stale bread into a valued household essential. Forget about store-bought products loaded with artificial ingredients. Virtually any loaf bread can be diced, seasoned, and toasted to make crunchy bits of leftover magic, perfect for sprucing up soups and salads, or just for snacking.

Store croutons in airtight containers for up to two weeks in the cabinet, or freeze them for long-term storage. Excellent breads to use include cornbread, crusty country breads, pumpernickel, or just plain white bread. Once breads become a little stale, they're easier to cut, and quicker to toast into croutons. Here's how:

Use a sharp serrated knife to cleanly cut even-sized cubes from any bread, about ¼- to ½-inch bits. Toss gently with olive oil or vegetable oil (1½ teaspoons per cup of diced bread) and herbs or seasonings (if desired—good options include grated Italian Parmesan cheese; dried herbs such as oregano, basil, or thyme; chopped or granulated garlic; and salt and pepper). Spread croutons in a single layer onto a baking sheet. Bake at 325 degrees for about twenty minutes, or until croutons are crisp all the way through and starting to brown at the corners. Cool to room temperature before use.

Washing and Drying Greens Properly

Greens need a thorough wash and dry before they go into your mouth. Pesticide residue isn't part of a healthy diet and even organic sandy grit ruins a salad. Proper washing means washing twice. Fill a sink or basin with cold fresh water, submerge greens and gently toss them around with your hands. Lift the greens out of the water, drip them dry, and discard the old water, making sure to wipe accumulated grit from the bottom of the sink or basin. Refill the sink and repeat with a thorough second wash.

Drying greens is especially important when used in salads. Dressings adhere to dry leaves, but run right off wet ones. If possible, use a lettuce spinner. This device contains a basket on a spindle, which centrifuges wet greens and collects the water below. Spinners are standard equipment in fine restaurant kitchens, which is why salads are often much more special when dining out— they really take on the dressing's flavor. In the absence of a spinner, fold a clean kitchen towel around the wet greens like a sling. Swing the greens around at high enough speed to extract as much water as you can.

Bean There . . . Working with Dried Beans

A pantry full of multicolored dried beans is beautiful and comforting. There, lying in wait for years if necessary, are satisfying, nutritious stores of food perfect for any season. They're a culinary security blanket at only pennies per serving.

Beans are an excellent source of protein and, combined with proper grains or "farinaceous" edibles, complete all the essential amino acids your body needs. They're also low in fat.

Years after buying them and socking them away in the cabinet, they may still be perfectly good to eat, but don't assume they last forever. Beans actually do grow stale after a time. Signs of this are extremely little water absorption when soaking them, or very long cooking times required to make them tender. Mostly, this is due to the gradual loss of the beans' minuscule water content as they age. Fresh dried beans cook much faster than older ones, and have an earthy flavor, not a dirty one.

To soak . . . or not to soak? That is the question. It is up to you whether 'tis wiser to suffer the long cooking time required of unsoaked beans in order to keep them whole and shapely, or to submerge them for convenience, cutting their required boil by as much as an hour. Some chefs soak beans as a matter of course, submerging them in enough water to cover them by two inches overnight, and discarding that soaking water before cooking. While the beans cook more quickly than nonsoakers, certain types tend to fall apart, or burst their skins during cooking this way (lima beans are the most egregious example).

Whether or not you soak your beans, it is always important to wash them thoroughly and check them visually for impurities. Small stones are tumbled with beans to remove shells and burnish the beans' surface. Occasionally, tiny remnants of these stones remain in the finished, bagged product, and must be removed by the chef's hand, lest a diner chomp down on one and crack a tooth. That can really ruin a meal.

Finally, cooked beans are very perishable. Cook and refrigerate them as quickly as possible. They keep in the refrigerator for about one week, but it's a good idea to give them the nose test any time. When spoiled, they give off an odor that's as close to spoilt meat as most vegetarians will ever encounter. One way of ensuring longer shelf life for cooked beans is to cook them in salted water, which acts as a natural preservative. Just remember that the salt concentrates in the beans as water evaporates, so more water should be added along the way if the beans require a long cook. Figure one teaspoon of salt to one pound of beans cooked in two and a half quarts of water.

Three Bean Salad

V

When taken as part of a lunch buffet with some form of grain salad (such as Wild Rice Salad, page 22, or Tabbouleh, page 23) bean dishes like this complete the amino acids necessary in our diet, forming complete proteins. And it's simply delicious!

Serves 6

16-ounce can green beans
16-ounce can yellow wax beans
16-ounce can red kidney beans
1 onion
1/2 cup sugar

2/3 cup vinegar
1/3 cup vegetable oil
1/2 teaspoon salt
1/8 teaspoon pepper

Drain the beans. Slice the onion thinly, then cut the slices into quarters. Whisk together the sugar, vinegar, oil, salt, and pepper. Combine the beans, onions, and dressing, mixing well. Chill at least 4 hours, or overnight, stirring occasionally. If desired, salad can be drained before serving.

Polynesian Banana Salad

Excellent with spicy food and rice, this rich, sweet salad can be part of a meal, snack, or dessert.

Serves 4

4 bananas
1 cup coconut cream
2 tablespoons curry powder
1 cup soft raisins
4 teaspoons shredded coconut

Slice the bananas about 1/2-inch thick, on a slight diagonal bias. Whisk together the coconut cream and curry powder. Add the bananas and raisins; toss gently to coat. Transfer to a serving dish, and sprinkle with shredded coconut.

Insalata Caprese
(Tomato-Mozzarella Salad)

Since the essence of this salad is its purity of flavors, only the highest quality of ingredients should be used. If you are unable to find fresh basil or good fresh kneaded mozzarella, make something else.

Serves 4

4 large, ripe red tomatoes
*2 loaves fresh mozzarella (**or** mozzarella di Bufala)*
8 top sprigs of fresh basil
2 tablespoons very high quality extra-virgin olive oil
Coarse (kosher) salt and freshly ground black pepper

1. Slice each tomato into 4 thick slices, discarding the polar ends. Cut each mozzarella into 6 even slices. Shingle alternating tomato and mozzarella slices onto 4 plates, starting and ending with tomato slices.
2. Garnish with 2 sprigs basil each, and drizzle olive oil over all. Sprinkle with salt and a few grinds of black pepper. Serve immediately.

It Comes in Colors

Sophistication is rising among consumers. As in coffee, there's more connoisseurship, but even those who seek higher quality extra-virgin (XV) oils are often judging by color alone. There is some merit to color distinctions when choosing fine oils, since younger, early harvest olives produce greener, gutsier, spicy oils preferred by many. But color can be deceptive, and assertive oils are not right for all applications. "Greener is better" is not always true. Later harvests have a more buttery, smoother flavor.

Shuffle Off to Buffalo Mozzarella

All mozzarella cheese is not created equal. In fact, two kinds of mozzarella cheese appear in U.S. markets: fresh mozzarella and shrink-wrapped mozz. Both are delicious, but they're not interchangeable. Most Americans are familiar with the shrink-wrapped variety, which is sold in one-pound blocks, labeled either "whole milk" or "part skim." This processed cheese is sometimes sold preshredded in bags, and has become a pillar of Italian-American cuisine. The other type, called "fresh" or "kneaded" mozzarella, has a milkier, less salty flavor; a whiter color; and a softer, springier texture.

Fresh mozzarella is milder in flavor, making it perfect for salads, pastas, and other sauced and dressed dishes. It is essential to the southern Italian tomato, basil, and cheese salad known as Caprese, drizzled with very fine olive oil and cracked black pepper. Unlike packaged mozzarella, it does not become very stringy when cooked, but keeps a satisfying resilience to its bite. It is kept submerged in the milky water in which it was made, or wrapped in plastic film just before sale. Smoked, it acquires an even "meatier" texture and adds complexity to dishes. Smoked fresh mozzarella is increasingly available in cheese sections of supermarkets. In Italy, there is another mozzarella that is almost worshipped:

Mozzarella *di Bufala* comes from the countryside surrounding Naples in southern Italy, and possesses a fresh, tangy, milky flavor. Unlike other fresh mozzarellas made from cow's milk, this regional delight is made from the milk of water buffalo. Retreating Nazis destroyed the buffalo herd that had lived in the region since the second century A.D., but the resourceful Italians imported new buffalo from India after the war. If you see this cheese, buy it. It is shipped daily from Rome, packed in eight-ounce kneaded balls suspended in their own whey. It's a perfect cheese for a Caprese salad, or simply to slice and serve all by itself.

Grilled Vegetable Antipasto

If a gas stove or grill is unavailable, the broiler element of an electric or gas oven will also work for roasting peppers. Arrange them two inches from the heating element, and follow same procedure as the stovetop method.

Serves 8

1 medium eggplant, cut into
 16 wedges, lightly salted
2 yellow squash, quartered lengthwise
2 zucchini, quartered lengthwise
4 plum tomatoes, halved lengthwise
2 each green and red bell peppers,
 roasted
2 tablespoons olive oil
Salt and pepper
Pinch of crushed red pepper (optional)
8 portobello mushrooms, stems
 removed
2 heads radicchio, core intact,
 quartered

Dressing:

½ cup extra-virgin olive oil
1 tablespoon balsamic vinegar
Pinch of sugar (optional)
2 shallots, finely chopped
4 sprigs fresh thyme, leaves picked
 and chopped
Salt and pepper
8 sprigs parsley

1. Heat grill (or a stovetop grill pan) to medium-hot. In a large mixing bowl, toss eggplant, squash, zucchini, and tomatoes with 1 tablespoon olive oil, crushed red pepper, salt, and pepper. Use a pastry brush or your hands to brush remaining oil on tops of mushrooms and radicchio; season well.
2. Cook vegetables on the grill, without turning, until they are slightly more than halfway done. Eggplant and mushrooms will take longest, while the radicchio will take only a few moments. Cook the tomatoes skin-side down only. Turn the other vegetables to finish, then arrange on a serving platter.
3. Whisk together the extra-virgin olive oil, vinegar, sugar, shallots, and chopped thyme. Season to taste, and drizzle over cooked vegetables while they're still warm. Marinate 20 minutes before serving, garnished with parsley sprigs.

Roasting Peppers [V]

The sweet vegetal flavor and silky texture of roasted pepper fillets breathe freshness into all they touch. There's a floral, garden-y aroma they convey that can't be duplicated. The process of roasting and peeling peppers over a gas stove or grill is simple:

1. Place bell peppers (any color or shape) directly onto the burner grate over a high flame. Allow the flames to lick the skin of the peppers, making them blister and turn black. Rotate the peppers using metal tongs or forks.

2. Once peppers are blackened all around, transfer them to an airtight container, sealed plastic bag, or plastic-wrap-covered bowl. Allow them to steam for ten minutes.

3. Slip skins off from peppers with your fingers. Remove and discard stems and seeds, but try to keep the pieces of pepper as whole as possible. If desired, you may rinse the pepper fillets under cool water, but this washes away some of the flavorful natural juices. Enjoy.

Stovetop Grills

Cast-iron or alloy pans with a ridged cooking surface allow cooks to create a grilled taste and appearance in the kitchen. These "grill pans" are very popular in professional kitchens, where space considerations and ventilation issues prevent flame grilling. A twelve-inch diameter cast-iron grill pan is an inexpensive (about $20) item that can revolutionize your cooking. It allows quick low-fat cooking year-round.

To grill on a grill pan without food sticking, heat it very hot, and season it with a few drops of oil. Also toss any vegetables or other foods you grill with a few drops of oil. The key to stick-free grilling here is to leave cooking foods undisturbed for the first few minutes of cooking, allowing them time to form a crust. Then, using a thin spatula and a pair of tongs or a roasting fork, gently loosen items and turn them.

Mushrooms, polenta, garden vegetables, and potatoes make wonderful antipasti (appetizers), simply tossed with a few drops of olive oil and salt and pepper, and seared on a stovetop grill. Drizzle them with fine balsamic vinegar for a taste of Mediterranean Italy anytime.

Wild Rice Salad with Mushrooms and Almonds   V

Pair grains like wild rice with beans and legumes for complete proteins, essential to the vegetarian diet, and a curiously good culinary combination!

Serves 8

8 ounces uncooked wild rice
1 cup whole almonds
1 tablespoon extra-virgin olive oil
*8 ounces Shiitake **or** other exotic mushrooms, sliced*
Salt and pepper to taste
¼ cup yellow raisins, soaked in 1 cup warm water for 30 minutes
    up to overnight
2 scallions, chopped
Juice of 1 lemon (about ¼ cup)
1 teaspoon ground cumin, toasted in a dry pan until fragrant

1. Boil the wild rice in lightly salted water until tender, and most grains have burst open (about 35 minutes); drain. Lightly toast almonds in a dry skillet over medium heat until most have small browned spots and they attain an oily sheen; spread on a plate to cool to room temperature. Heat oil in a medium skillet over high heat for 1 minute, then cook the mushrooms until tender, about 5 minutes; season with salt and pepper.
2. In a mixing bowl, combine rice, almonds, mushrooms (with their cooking oil), raisins, and scallions. Dress with lemon and cumin, and season with salt and pepper. Toss well to coat. Serve chilled or at room temperature.

Tabbouleh

Middle Eastern bulgur wheat absorbs water quickly, giving it a pliable and chewy texture unlike anything else in the world. This is an everyday dish in Egypt. Perfect with stuffed grape leaves.

Serves 6

1 cup cracked (bulgur) wheat
1 small cucumber, chopped
3 scallions, finely chopped
2 ripe tomatoes, seeded and chopped
2 tablespoons chopped chives
1 cup chopped Italian parsley
½ cup extra-virgin olive oil
Juice of 2 lemons (about ½ cup)
Salt and pepper

1. Soak the wheat in 1 quart of water for 15 minutes (***or*** overnight). Drain and squeeze out excess moisture by tying up in a cheesecloth or clean kitchen towel.
2. Combine with cucumber, scallions, tomatoes, chives, and parsley in a mixing bowl. Dress with olive oil, lemon, salt, and pepper.
3. Set aside to marinate for 2 to 3 hours before serving.

Olive Oil

Spain is the largest exporter of high quality olive oil, but the United States imports mostly Italian oil. Most (over half) of Italian production comes from the regions of Puglia, Calabria, and Sicily, but in the United States, the only region most people know is Tuscany, which accounts for only a tiny fraction of Italy's extra-virgin exports.

Tofu Salad

Soy foods are a vegetarian's best way to get complete, natural proteins. Keeping delicious, snackable marinated tofu, like the kind below, on hand for sandwiches, salads, and wraps will ensure that you get these nutrients in a satisfying way. Marinated tofu will remain fresh in the fridge for four to five days. One of the best ways to store the cubes is in a zip lock bag with all the air squeezed out of it (keeps the cubes from getting a dry patch).

Serves 6

5 tofu cakes, cut into 1-inch cubes

Marinade:

2 tablespoons water
Black pepper
2 teaspoons sugar
*¼ cup dry sherry **or** Chinese cooking wine*
¼ cup soy sauce
¼ cup white wine vinegar
1 clove garlic, chopped
Pinch of anise seed, toasted and ground
1 tablespoon sesame oil
1 tablespoon vegetable oil

Salad:

1 carrot, julienne
¼ pound snow peas, julienne
1 cup finely chopped cabbage
*5 cremini **or** white mushrooms, sliced*
4 scallions, julienne

Dressing:

½ teaspoon salt
2 teaspoons sesame oil
2 teaspoons tamari soy sauce
Juice of ½ lemon
Black pepper to taste
1 tablespoon sugar

1. Spread tofu into a single layer in a baking dish or sheet pan. Whisk together the ingredients for the marinade, and pour it over the tofu. Marinate for 3 hours or overnight in the refrigerator, turning occasionally.
2. Combine salad ingredients, toss with dressing, and place in the refrigerator to marinate 1 hour. Add tofu, and toss gently to combine just before serving.

Do You Tofu?: Tofu and Other Soy Foods

Since soybeans contain all nine of the protein-building essential amino acids our bodies can't produce themselves, foods made from them constitute an important part of the vegetarian diet. Even if you decide to include soy-based foods in your daily diet, you don't ever have to eat a soybean if you don't want to.

One of the best soy foods is bean curd (tofu). It comes in white blocks, or "cakes," which look like feta cheese. By itself, it has about as much flavor as a gum-soled shoe. That blandness, combined with its porous nature, makes it perfect for marinating and seasoning. It absorbs savory and sweet marinades equally well, develops a wonderful crust when seared in a pan, and gains flavor and character from any dish it marries with.

Tofu is made from a "milk" of ground soybeans and water, which is heated, then separated into curds by the addition of a coagulant (usually a mineral extracted from sea water or mined gypsum). The curds are skimmed from the liquid and pressed into blocks to cool.

Tofu can be pressed to give it a different texture and make it more absorbent, puréed into a smooth cream, frozen for storage and a "meatier" mouth feel, and prepared in any number of other ways. I particularly like it marinated overnight in an Asian vinaigrette, and stuffed in a barley-corn wrap, or served over a spinach salad. One of the most common uses is to add texture and nutrition to a stir-fry. Various firmnesses accommodate the needs of specific dishes, with firmer types used for stir-fries and salads; softer ones for desserts, dressings, and sauces; and newly available "silken tofu," a super-smooth version with a custardlike consistency perfect for shakes, smoothies, and delicate dishes.

Tofu's cousin, tempeh, is a cake of pressed aged soybeans and grains. It has a more resilient texture than tofu, and a nuttier, more assertive flavor. Tempeh comes in shrink-wrapped loaves that are easily cut into myriad shapes and slices. It's often viewed as a meat substitute due to its high protein content, chewy texture, and savory taste.

Sweet and clean-tasting, soy milk is much lighter and more refreshing than dairy milk by virtue of being naturally low in fat. Like dairy milk, it's usually fortified with vitamins A and D, but soymilk is also fortified with vitamin B_{12}, especially important for vegetarians. Chocolate- and coffee-flavored soymilk is commonplace in supermarkets now.

Cooked black soybeans come in cans for making chili, dips, salads, and salsas. Fresh, dried, or frozen soybeans can be used for casseroles, pâtés, and more. Vegan couch potatoes love snacking on salted, roasted soy nuts by the handful. In fact, you could chew soybeans all day long!

Choosing Balsamic Vinegar

Sweet and woodsy, the best balsamic vinegars balance their acidity with complex flavors of herbs and country air. This mahogany condiment from the north-central Italian region of Emilia Romagna is the signature specialty of the ancient city of Modena. At its best, it's a luxurious flavor that elevates simple good foods to high cuisine. At its worst, it's a sugary two-dimensional rip-off in a fancy, dark bottle.

Prices for balsamic vinegars range from $2.99 for a twelve-ounce bottle of sweet-n-sour swill to $7 to $14 for serviceable rendition to $25 plus for sublime. Most of the time, you get what you pay for. I recommend that most people have two bottles of Balsamic in their pantry: one bottle of midlevel vinegar for everyday use in dressings, marinades, and sauces, and another bottle of the good stuff for special occasions.

Most of the distinction between good and great balsamic vinegars has to do with the length of time they're aged. They grow sweeter and more complex through the years. Four years of aging in wood barrels yields a delightful condiment. Eight years makes a very special vinegar, and anything over twelve years merits the trumpets of Gabriel. Avoid the very cheapest versions, which are aged for only a few months, if at all, and sometimes sweetened artificially through the addition of sugar.

Make sure to look at labels for how long it was aged, and to make sure that it comes from Modena, Italy. Some manufacturers have begun using very deceptive labels bearing the slogan, "Eight Years Gold," while the fine print indicates that the vinegar in that bottle was aged only one year. Giuseppe Giusti makes a favorite of mine.

Sweet White Salad with Shaved Asiago

Serves 4

4 ounces (about 2 heads) frisee **or** fine curly endive
4 heads Belgium endive, cut into 1-inch pieces
1 cup julienne of jicama
1 small sweet onion, sliced into paper-thin rings
Juice of ½ lemon (about 2 tablespoons)
1 tablespoon extra-virgin olive oil
1 teaspoon orange juice concentrate
Salt and pepper to taste
Wedge of Asiago cheese, Parmigiano Reggiano, **or** other
   good "grana" cheese

1. Wash and dry the frisee; combine with Belgium endive, jicama, and onions. Whisk together the lemon juice, olive oil, orange juice concentrate, salt, and pepper; toss with salad to coat.
2. Arrange salad onto 4 plates, piling it as high as possible. Using a swivel peeler, gently shave 4 or 5 curls of Asiago cheese over each salad, and serve immediately.

What Are Grana Cheeses, and Do They Come in a Green Shaker Can?

Grana cheeses are the hard, aged "grating" cheeses, and the short answer is: No. They don't come in a green shaker can. Grana, literally, means "grainy," and describes these crumbly cheeses very well. They'll sprinkle into flakes or fine powder on a grater. The undeniable king of the grana cheeses is Parmigiano Reggiano. This Parmesan cheese has a nutty, savory flavor and, sometimes, delicate crystalline specks in it that impart a dynamic texture.

Barley and Corn Salad

Whole grains like barley provide many of the B vitamins vegetarians need to fight off diseases, and are higher in protein, vitamin E, zinc, phosphorus, and other phytonutrients than refined grains.

Serves 8

1 cup barley
1 pound frozen sweet corn kernels
1 carrot, chopped finely
2 ribs celery, chopped finely
1 medium red onion, chopped finely
1 tablespoon red wine vinegar or cider vinegar
2 tablespoons extra-virgin olive oil
½ cup chopped fresh herbs, such as parsley, chives, basil, oregano, mint and/or cilantro
Salt and freshly ground black pepper to taste

1. Boil the barley in 2 quarts of lightly salted water until it is very tender, about 30 minutes. Drain and spread on a platter to cool. Heat a dry cast-iron pan or skillet over a high flame for 1 minute. Add the corn and cook without stirring until some kernels attain a slight char, and the corn has a smoky aroma, about 5 minutes.
2. Combine the barley, corn, carrot, celery, and onion in a mixing bowl. Add all remaining ingredients and toss well to coat.

Common Vegetable Cuts

Julienne are thin matchsticks, ⅛" × ⅛" × 1½"
Batons are larger sticks, ¼" × ¼" × 2"
Dice are cubes of ¼" × ¼" × ¼" (small dice are called "brunoise," and larger dice are usually just called cubes)
Chopped items are cut roughly into small pieces, using a knife or food processor
Slices are ⅛-inch thick unless otherwise specified

Jicama and Other Latino Vegetables

Despite looking like a tan, papery-skinned turnip, jicama, a Mexican tuber ranging from baseball-sized to as big as a bowling ball, is sweet, crisp, and juicy. Its crunchy white flesh is refreshing eaten raw, and goes extraordinarily well with citrus juices. It is one of a number of Mexican vegetables that have made their way into U.S. markets in the last decade. Others include:

- **Yautia** (manioc) and **Yuca**, starchy roots that are eaten cooked, or ground for flour and used for savory pastries and baking
- **Aloe**, a succulent leaf high in vitamin E, often used for medicinal purposes
- **Prickly Pears**, fruit of a desert cactus, which has become much favored in (would you believe?!) Southern Italy
- **Plantains**, both green (savory) and yellow (sweet). While these starchy relatives of the banana are immature and mature versions of the same fruit, they have completely different characters and uses. Green plantains are used more like potatoes—fried or boiled and mashed with seasonings. Sweet yellow plantains are often a dessert item, or added to stews for a sweet counterpoint.

All of these vegetables can be found in markets in Latino neighborhoods, and are increasingly found at gourmet supermarkets. They can be ordered for delivery anywhere via the Internet. See the Resources Appendix for details on where to find Latino produce.

Mixed Baby Greens
with Balsamic Vinaigrette

A nice, basic house salad.

Serves 6–8

8 ounces baby mixed greens (mesclun)
1 bunch chives, cut into 2-inch pieces
1 tablespoon good quality balsamic vinegar
2 tablespoons good quality extra-virgin olive oil
1 tablespoon finely chopped shallots
Salt and freshly ground pepper to taste

Wash greens and spin dry; combine with chives. Whisk together the vinegar, oil, and shallots. Season to taste.

What Is Mesclun?

Since the 1980s, restaurant menus have offered salads of mesclun as first courses and side plates. Mesclun is a southern French term meaning "mixture," and is used there to refer to field greens collected and combined for salad. Here, it has come to mean any mixture of salad greens, but usually contains baby greens such as red and green oak leaf lettuce, young arugula, frilly lolla rossa, frisee, mizuna, and assorted other greens. Sometimes, fresh herbs and edible flowers are included in the mix.

The tender, delicate greens in mesclun make delightful salads, dressed very lightly with simple dressings such as vinaigrettes. They usually sit nice and high on the plate, add color and texture to a simple dish, and create a wonderful bed for a more substantial item such as a quiche or sandwich. Though usually priced by the pound at something like $7 or $8, mesclun is actually pretty inexpensive. Just try to fill one of those market produce bags with a pound of the stuff, and you'll see it bursting at the seams before you get halfway there.

Warm Spinach Salad with Potatoes, Red Onions, and Kalamata Olives V

Use this recipe as a master recipe—a starting point from which to make myriad variations of your own, perhaps with the help of our chart.

Serves 4

1 pound fresh curly-leaf spinach, washed, stems removed

¼ cup extra-virgin olive oil

1 pound small red potatoes, cut into ½-inch slices, boiled 10 minutes, and drained

1 medium red onion, halved, thinly sliced

20 Kalamata or other black olives, pitted

1 tablespoon balsamic vinegar

Salt and pepper to taste

1. Place spinach in a large mixing bowl. Heat olive oil in a large skillet over high heat for 1 minute; add potatoes and onions. Cook over high heat until lightly browned, about 5 minutes. Remove from heat; add olives, vinegar, salt, and pepper.

2. Pour potato mixture over spinach, and invert skillet over bowl to hold in heat. Allow to steam 1 minute, then divide onto 4 plates, arranging potatoes, onions, and olives on top. Serve warm.

Create Your Own Warm Salad

On chilly autumn and winter nights, warm salads are an elegant and delicious way to start a meal. Using the same method as described in the Warm Spinach Salad with Potatoes, Red Onions, and Kalamata Olives, try your own variations, substituting items from the following chart. In place of the spinach, choose a green from **Column A.** Instead of the potatoes, choose a vegetable from **Column B,** and replace the olives with an ingredient from **Column C.**

Column A	Column B	Column C
Frisee (Curly Endive)	Grilled Eggplant	Diced Smoked Mozzarella
Dandelion Greens	Summer Squash	Chopped Tomatoes
Chicory	Zucchini	Orange Segments
Assorted Asian Greens	Wild Mushrooms	Sun Dried Tomatoes
Beet Greens	Roasted Peppers	Caper Berries

Toasting Spices for Flavor and Aroma

You'd become bland, too, if you just sat on the shelf for months! You'd be glad if someone lit a fire under your seed casing. Spices lose their potency from the moment they go into the jar. The best way to bring out the most flavor and aroma in them is to "wake them up" with a light toasting. Usually, this simply enhances the power of the spice, so you get more flavor from less spice. Sometimes, as in the case of cumin and anise, it gives the spice a roundness and new dimension that the spice never would have had without toasting.

For best flavor, buy spices in the most whole form you can find, whether it's seeds, like cumin, coriander, and anise; nuts, like nutmeg; or bark, like cinnamon sticks. I keep a small electric coffee grinder for grinding spices. Natural oils in spices are what give them flavor. These oils evaporate and dissipate with exposure to air. They remain much more intact inside the whole seeds, nuts, roots, or bark, and are unlocked by toasting and grinding. Even powdered spices can benefit greatly from a light toasting. The method is simple:

Sprinkle the spice into a small dry skillet, and heat it over a medium flame until the spice's aroma comes forth. If you're using a powdered spice, that's all you need to do. Go ahead and use the spice from there. For whole spices, you may choose to grind them after toasting. Usually, you don't seek to brown the spices at all, and you never want to turn any part of them black. But certain dishes call for lightly browned spices, which attain a greater degree of flavor complexity.

Lentil Salad

V

One of the oldest foods known to man, lentils have been found among the remains of prehistoric communities and are mentioned in the earliest books of the Bible. They cook more quickly than other beans, and never require soaking. Small, green lentils from Le Puy in France retain their shape and color better than the more common brown lentils most often sold here, and are worth seeking out in health food and gourmet stores.

Serves 8

1 pound dried lentils
2 medium onions, finely chopped
3 scallions, chopped
1 green pepper, finely chopped
1 tablespoon toasted cumin powder
Pinch of cayenne pepper
Juice of 1 lemon (about ¼ cup)
2 tablespoons extra-virgin olive oil
Salt and freshly ground black pepper

Wash lentils and pick through to take out any stones. Boil in 2 quarts of lightly salted water until tender but not broken up. Spread on a pan to cool. Combine with onions, scallions, and green pepper. Dress with remaining ingredients, and serve with a bed of dressed baby greens.

Choosing and Working with Avocados

Avocados provide healthy fats and impart a luxurious richness to foods. Of the many varieties grown, there are two types commonly available in American markets. The Florida avocado is large (about the size of a grapefruit or bigger), and has a lower oil content and sweeter, fruitier flavor. It is often less expensive than the California-grown avocado, known as a Hass avocado. The Hass is about the size of an average pear and has a smoother, silkier texture.

Check Hass avocados for ripeness by sight and touch. Their skin goes from forest green to charcoal black as they ripen. A ripe Hass avocado should yield to gentle pressure from the palm of your hand. They feel a little like modeling clay through their skin. Another telltale sign is that the small stem nub will fall out easily from a ripe avocado. Florida avocados remain green when ripe, so touch is the only indicator of ripeness. Since all avocados are harvested unripe, you will rarely find a ready-to-eat one in the market. They ripen quickly at room temperature, and can be rushed by storing them in a closed paper bag.

Removing the skin can be done two ways: Peeling or scooping. Peeling is almost always the method of choice for Florida avocados, since their size makes scooping a sloppy procedure. To peel, cut the avocado halves in half again, lengthwise. Starting at the stem end, pry the skin back while pushing gently from the back of the arched fruit. Once peeled, avocados should be served immediately, or brushed with lemon juice to prevent them from turning brown. For Hass avocados, halves can simply be scooped from their skin using a large serving spoon. Keep the edge of the spoon angled slightly toward the skin, and scrape along from the bottom polar end to the stem end. This method is much faster than peeling, and is perfect for chopped or mashed preparations like guacamole, where perfect appearance isn't necessary.

California Garden Salad with Avocado and Sprouts [V]

The fruity taste of large, green Florida avocados gives this salad a lighter, more summery flavor, though the Hass is the more authentic California item.

Serves 4

2 heads Boston or Bibb lettuce
2 ripe tomatoes, cored, cut into 8 wedges each
1 ripe avocado
1 cup alfalfa sprouts

Dressing:
1 tablespoon fresh-squeezed lemon juice
3 tablespoons extra-virgin olive oil
*1 tablespoon finely chopped shallot **or** chive*
½ teaspoon salt
¼ teaspoon freshly ground black pepper

1. Make the dressing: Combine the lemon juice, olive oil, shallot, salt, and pepper in a small bowl, mixing well.
2. Arrange lettuce leaves, stem-end in, onto 4 plates, making flower-petal pattern. Inner leaves will be too small, so reserve them for another use.
3. Toss tomatoes in 1 tablespoon dressing; place 4 onto each salad. Peel avocado, cut into 8 wedges, and toss with 1 tablespoon dressing. Place 2 wedges on each salad. Divide sprouts into 4 bunches, and place a bunch in the center of each salad. Drizzle salads with remaining dressing, or serve on the side.

Marinated Beet Salad

The natural sweetness and delicate texture of fresh beets seem to have been forgotten by many Americans, who have relegated this noble root vegetable to a curiosity in many places. This simple salad highlights these distinctive characteristics.

Serves 6

*1 pound fresh beets, stem end
  trimmed*
1 tablespoon red wine vinegar
*6 large romaine lettuce leaves,
  washed*

Dressing:

*1 tablespoon rice wine vinegar **or**
  white wine vinegar*
2 tablespoons extra-virgin olive oil
¼ teaspoon dried oregano leaves
¼ teaspoon dried basil leaves
½ teaspoon freshly chopped parsley
1 teaspoon finely chopped shallots
Salt and pepper to taste

1. Boil beets in a small saucepan with red wine vinegar and enough water to cover. Cook until tender, about 30 minutes. Chill, then peel and cut into ¼-inch slices.
2. In a bowl, combine rice wine vinegar, olive oil, oregano, basil, parsley, and shallots. Season with salt and pepper. Add beets, and marinate 10–15 minutes. Place lettuce leaves on 6 plates, trimming stem end to fit inside rim. Arrange beets in an overlapping pattern atop lettuce leaves, and drizzle with remaining marinade.

Note: Beets can be cooked and marinated up to 2 days in advance.

How to Peel Cooked Beets with a Towel

To remove the skins of cooked beets or potatoes cleanly and easily, simply wrap them in a clean, dry kitchen towel or paper towel, and rub the thin outer skin right off. This is best done while they are still warm from cooking. Be warned that beets will color your towel red, but most of that color will wash out.

Peeling this way removes only the thinnest peel, and thus is less wasteful than a swivel peeler or paring knife.

Basic Egg Salad

Read the tip below about making perfect hard-boiled eggs. With it, you could (dare I say it?) rule the world!

Yields about $^2/_3$ cup

1 tablespoon cream cheese
$^1/_4$ cup salad dressing or mayonnaise
1 tablespoon finely minced onion
4 hard-boiled eggs, chopped (or 6 hard-boiled eggs chopped with 4 of the yolks removed for a lighter, healthier option)
1 tablespoon sweet pickle relish, slightly drained, or 1 tablespoon chopped sweet pickles
Salt and pepper to taste

Soften the cream cheese and combine well with the salad dressing and onion. Combine dressing with the chopped egg and relish. Add salt and pepper. Chill before serving.

The Secret to Making Perfect Hard-Boiled Eggs

The perfect hard-boiled egg has a delicate white and a fully cooked yolk, without even a hint of the unattractive gray shadow that affects improperly cooked egg. The perfect hard-boiled egg is also easy to peel. To achieve this, put the eggs in enough cold water to cover them by one inch and boil for one minute only. Then remove from heat, cover the pan, and let it sit undisturbed for exactly fifteen minutes. Then, transfer the eggs to a bath of ice water for fifteen to twenty minutes. They should then peel easily.

Warm Potato Salad with Balsamic Vinegar and Onions

This substantial main-course salad is highly adaptable. Serve it atop fresh spinach leaves in the springtime for a hearty lunch, or beside scrambled eggs for a winter breakfast.

Serves 8

2 tablespoons extra-virgin olive oil
2 medium onions, thinly sliced
1 tablespoon fresh thyme leaves (about 3 sprigs) **or** *1 teaspoon dried*
½ teaspoon sugar (optional)
1 tablespoon balsamic vinegar
1 pound small white "boiling" potatoes (a.k.a. "creamer" potatoes), halved, boiled until very tender, and drained
Salt and pepper to taste
Pinch of fresh chopped Italian parsley

1. Heat olive oil over medium heat in a medium skillet for 1 minute; add onions, thyme, and sugar. Cook slowly, stirring regularly with a wooden spoon, until onions are very soft and browned to the color of caramel, about 10 minutes.
2. Stir in balsamic vinegar; remove from heat. Toss gently with warm cooked potatoes, and season with salt and pepper. Allow to rest 10 minutes before serving, garnished with chopped parsley.

Testing Potatoes for Doneness

To check a potato for doneness, poke the tip of a knife into the thickest part, then lift the knife up, handle first. If the potato falls off, it's done. If it hangs on, then it needs more time.

Proper Breeding

Would you want a poodle for a guard dog? Didn't think so. You probably wouldn't want a knockout spicy Sicilian olive oil to perfume a delicate plate of white asparagus either. Different varieties of olives used are a major factor in the character of the oils producers make. Spain, the largest olive oil producing country, uses fruity-tasting olives like the *Arbequina* and *Cornicabra*, while Italy favors types like *Frantoio, Picholine, Ogiarola,* and *Cetrala*. Some of these names will surely become household words like chardonnay, merlot, and cabernet as the taste for finer olive oil matures in this country. Regional distinctions will also bring certain brands cache or upturned noses, as national distinctions like Italian, Spanish, Greek, Turkish, and others do today.

Already, many consumers know the fresh, fruity, peppery character of Tuscan olive oil by name. Others can identify Sicilian. Many consumers are discovering the more delicate qualities of Spanish oils produced in regions like Catalonia and Toledo. All are good. Depending on the olive type or region, you could say that this region or that is stronger, sweet, peppery . . . it's in the eye of the taster. In Spain and Italy, the regional distinctions in olive oil character are well known by everyday cooks. Those countries are now trying to increase that awareness here.

European Union authorities have singled out certain regional products for special distinction on the continent. In Italy, those designations are referred to as Protected Designation of Origin (PDO), and cover cheeses, hams, cured meats, agricultural products, and olive oils. The items are selected based on their close identification with their region of origin, and their uniqueness. Twenty regional Italian olive oils qualify for PDO status, including the well-known Toscano, Umbria, Terra di Bari, and Valli Trapanesi regions. Criteria are established for each region regarding acidity levels, olive types, and zone of olive origin. Since massive amounts of inferior olive oil arrive in the United States daily, bearing a "bottled in Tuscany" or "packed in Italy" label when the oil was produced in Romania, Turkey, Cyprus, or some other country, it's important to know the distinctions to look for that certify real origins.

Olive Oil—Beyond Italy

Who buys Greek olive oil? It used to be an ethnic question. People in the Greek neighborhood bought Greek olive oil. It wasn't even in some top stores. It was very snobbish. That's silly. Any place can be proud of carrying XVs from Greece and Spain. Personally, I use Greek at home. It really tastes olive-y—really, really good, and so reasonable you can fry in it; bottles at $5 to $7 are still common.

Curried New Potato Salad

Simple to make, but with a complex taste, this is a great, attractive buffet item for a picnic lunch.

Serves 8

2 pounds red-skinned new potatoes, cut into bite-size chunks
3 hard-boiled eggs, cut into bite-size chunks
1 recipe Madras Curry Dressing (page 7)
1 tablespoon chopped cilantro

Boil potatoes in lightly salted water until very tender, about 15 minutes; cool. Combine with eggs and curry dressing; toss to coat. Serve chilled, garnished with cilantro leaves.

Beef Fries?

McDonald's finally came clean this year, confessing that, yes, beef flavorings are included in the company's French fries. The news came as a severe shock to millions of vegetarians who've guiltlessly (or so they thought) snacked on the spud sticks for years, since Mickey D's announced in 1990 that it would no longer *fry* in beef tallow. The announcement also vindicated thousands of outraged protesters, maligned for years as mere conspiracy theorists, who've broadcast their suspicions that there was "something funny about those fries."

The case is a lesson for vegetarians that true vegetarianism requires constant vigilance. Vegan travelers in India, for example, should be aware that most foods are cooked with butter there. Airline passengers who request vegetarian meals should ask whether there is also a vegan option, if that's really what they want. And if a waiter says there's "no meat" in a dish, especially a soup, it's wise to ask if it was made with a meat-based stock. Some European cuisines rely on the use of gelatin in many desserts (Bavarians, charlottes, and *panna cottas*, for example) and may even use it in a "vegetable terrine" appetizer or dish. It always pays to ask, especially when traveling.

Hors d'Oeuvres

Artichoke Dip

Serves 8

2 cans (15 ounces each) quartered
   artichoke hearts, drained and
   rinsed.
1 red pepper, chopped finely
1 green pepper, chopped finely

3 cloves garlic, minced
2 cups mayonnaise
White pepper
1 pound grated Parmesan cheese

Preheat the oven to 325 degrees. Mix all ingredients except ¼ of the Parmesan cheese. Spread into a 9" × 9" baking dish or 1½-quart casserole dish, sprinkle remaining Parmesan over the top, and bake 45 minutes until golden brown. Serve with crackers or bread.

Potato Pakoras (Fritters)

Serves 8

1¼ cups sifted chickpea flour
2 teaspoons vegetable oil
1½ teaspoons ground cumin
½ teaspoon cayenne **or** paprika
¼ teaspoon turmeric
2½ teaspoons salt

Approximately ½ cup cold water
1 large **or** 2 medium baking
   potatoes (about 8 ounces),
   peeled, then sliced into ⅛-inch
   pieces
Oil for frying

1. In a food processor or blender, pulse flour, oil, cumin, cayenne, turmeric, and salt 3 or 4 times until fluffy. With blade spinning, gradually add water, processing for 2 to 3 minutes until smooth. Adjust consistency by adding water until the mixture is slightly thicker than the consistency of heavy cream. Cover and set aside for 10 minutes.
2. Heat fry oil to 350 degrees. Dip potato slices into batter one by one, and slip them into the fry oil in batches of 6 or 7. Fry 4–5 minutes each side, until golden brown and cooked through. Serve immediately with chutney for dipping.

Baba Ghanouj

Serves 4

2 cloves garlic, peeled
1 whole eggplant, roasted 1 hour
   in a 400 degree oven, cooled,
   pulp scooped out
1 tablespoon tahini
1½ teaspoons kosher salt
2–3 teaspoons toasted cumin
   powder (see "Toasting Cumin
   Seeds for Your Baba")

Juice of 2 lemons
¼ cup extra-virgin olive oil, plus
   a little extra for garnish
Freshly ground black pepper
Paprika and chopped parsley
   for garnish (optional)
Pita bread for dipping

1. In a food processor, chop the garlic until it sticks to the walls of the processor bowl. Add eggplant pulp, tahini, salt, cumin, and half of the lemon juice. Process until smooth, gradually drizzling in the olive oil. Season to taste with black pepper, additional salt, and lemon if necessary.

2. Spread onto plates, and garnish with a drizzle of extra-virgin olive oil, a few drops of lemon, a dusting of paprika, and some chopped parsley. Serve with wedges of warm pita bread.

Toasting Cumin Seeds for Your Baba

Toast whole cumin seeds in a dry pan until they give off a slight smoke, and brown slightly, about two minutes over medium heat. Pulverize them in a coffee grinder. This will make your Baba Ghanouj unforgettable. If you are using powdered cumin, just give it a quick toast in a dry pan, until it becomes highly fragrant, about one minute.

Crudités with Three Dips   V

Veggies with dip is an essential at virtually any type of party—from the big football game to a family holiday bash to a classy affair.

Serves 8

About 6 cups of assorted vegetables, cut into bite-size pieces, such as carrot sticks, celery sticks, various colored bell peppers, zucchini and yellow squash, radishes, blanched broccoli florets, cauliflower florets, and green beans, fennel, cooked beets, etc.

Assorted black and green olives
Rosemary or thyme sprigs for garnish
Three dressings or dips, such as the ones following

Arrange vegetables attractively on a serving platter or in a basket, placing different colors beside one another. Garnish with olives and herb sprigs. Serve with dips or drizzled with any dressing.

It's Easy Being Green!

Quickly parboiling green vegetables, or "blanching" them, locks in nutrition, flavor, and especially bright color. The key to successful blanching is to bring the vegetables immediately up to a boil, cook them only enough to tenderize them, and to stop the cooking by plunging them immediately into ice-cold water, a step known as "shocking" the vegetables. Salt plays an important role in keeping green vegetables green, and it is recommended in both the blanching and shocking waters.

The most important strategy, though, is to put only small batches of vegetables into a large amount of rapidly boiling water, ensuring that the water never stops boiling as they are added. If too much is added at once, the water cools, and the vegetables will fade. One pound of green beans, for example, should be cooked in four small batches, in four quarts of boiling, salted water. Each batch (about a handful) should boil rapidly from the moment it's put in the pot, until it is removed and shocked in ice water. Remove each batch from the shock water before adding the next.

Curry Dip

Yields 2½ cups

1 teaspoon olive oil
½ cup finely chopped onion
½ medium jalapeño pepper, finely
   chopped (about 1 teaspoon)
2 teaspoons finely chopped red bell
   pepper
1 teaspoon Madras curry powder
1 teaspoon ground cumin
½ teaspoon ground coriander

½ teaspoon ground turmeric
Pinch of cayenne pepper
¼ teaspoon salt
1 tablespoon very fresh, soft raisins
   (**or** any raisins, soaked overnight
   in ½ cup water, drained)
1½ cups soy mayo
1 tablespoon chopped fresh cilantro
A few drops fresh lemon juice

1. Put the oil in a small skillet over medium heat. Add onions, jalapeño, and red pepper; cook stirring occasionally until onion is translucent, about 5 minutes. Add curry powder, cumin, coriander, turmeric, cayenne, and salt. Cook a minute more, until spices are very fragrant. Add raisins and about 1 tablespoon of water. Remove from heat.
2. Transfer to a food processor. Chop on high speed for 30 seconds; scrape down sides of bowl with a rubber spatula. Add soy mayo and cilantro; process 30 seconds more, until smooth and even. Adjust seasonings with lemon, salt, and pepper.

What Is "Curry Powder"?

What we know as "curry powder" is actually a blend of spices, invented by the British to resemble one of the famous masalas (spice blends) of India. In addition to ground coriander, cumin, mustard seed, turmeric, and other spices, good Madras curry (such as Sun Brand) contains ground, dried curry (or "kari") leaves, which are a typical spice of southern and southwestern India. Most authentic Indian recipes call not for curry powder, but a combination of spices (a masala) specifically designed for that dish.

Watercress Dip

Yields 1½ cups

1 bunch watercress, stems trimmed by 1 inch, roughly chopped
1 cup soy mayo
¼ teaspoon salt
¼ teaspoon black pepper

In a food processor, purée watercress until very fine, about 1 minute.
Add mayonnaise; pulse to combine. Season with salt and pepper.

Red Garlic Mayonnaise (Rouille)

Yields 1½ cups

2 cloves garlic, chopped very fine
*1 cup mayonnaise **or** soy mayo*
1 small red pepper, roasted (see directions on page 21), peeled,
  and puréed
Salt to taste
½ lemon
Pinch of cayenne

Whisk together garlic, mayonnaise, and roasted pepper purée. Season
with a pinch of salt, a squeeze of lemon, and cayenne.

Eggplant Caviar

Serves 4

1 large eggplant	*1 tablespoon tomato paste*
2 tablespoons olive oil	*Salt and pepper to taste*
1 large onion, finely chopped	*Crackers or French bread*
3 cloves garlic, finely chopped	

1. Heat oven to 400 degrees. Place eggplant in a baking dish and roast on middle rack of the oven until very well done, about 1 hour; cool. Cut the eggplant in half and scoop out the soft pulp with a serving spoon. Place on a cutting board and chop thoroughly, until it has the consistency of oatmeal.
2. Heat the olive oil in a large skillet over medium heat for 1 minute. Add onions; cook until they are very soft, but not brown, about 10 minutes; add garlic and cook 1 minute more. Stir in tomato paste; cook 1 minute.
3. Add chopped eggplant and cook until mixture is thickened. An indentation should remain when a spoon is depressed into the mixture. Season to taste. Serve with crackers or sliced French bread.

Facts about Eggplant's Bitterness

When sliced eggplant is sprinkled with salt it sheds some of its inherent bitterness along with the salty droplets that form along its surface. Eggplants vary widely in flavor and intensity, and some delicate bitter edge helps define this beautiful vegetable's character. Therefore, many people choose not to take the step of salting an eggplant and rinsing the extracted juices at all. Those who do leave the eggplant for ten to twenty minutes, then rinse the eggplant and use it according to their recipe. Long, slender, violet-hued Japanese eggplants contain none of the bitterness of America's large black variety. Pear-sized Italian-style eggplants are similar to our regular ones, but white-skinned varieties are milder. I've been told that eggplants with a dimple in the flower end (polar opposite to the stem) have fewer seeds and are less bitter, but I've never done a comparison.

Fried Green Tomato Bruschetta

Canapés on grilled bread, called "bruschetta," surprise many visitors to restaurants in Italy, when they appear as complimentary hors d'oeuvres.

Serves 4

4 medium green tomatoes, sliced ½-inch thick
Flour, eggs, and bread crumbs for dredging
Oil for frying (preferably olive oil)
1 tablespoon balsamic vinegar
¼ cup chopped fresh basil leaves (plus a few whole leaves
*   for garnish)*
12 green olives with pimento, halved lengthwise
¼ cup extra-virgin olive oil
1 loaf crusty country bread, sliced 1-inch thick

1. Dredge tomato slices in flour, egg, and bread crumbs, shaking off excess after each dip, and fry them at low heat (about 325 degrees) until golden and mostly tender (a little underdone is good). Place the still-hot tomatoes flat on a cutting board and dice them into ½-inch pieces.
2. In a large mixing bowl, gently toss the diced tomatoes with the vinegar, basil, and olives. Set aside.
3. Brush the bread slices with extra-virgin oil, and grill or oven-toast (400 degrees) them until lightly browned. This can also be done under the broiler. Top each of 6 slices with tomato mixture, cut each in half, and serve garnished with a small basil sprig.

Guacamole

Serves 8

2 cloves garlic, chopped
¼ cup chopped red onion
1 small jalapeño pepper, finely chopped
4 ripe Hass avocados, halved, pitted, and scooped from the skin
2 tablespoons lime juice
½ teaspoon salt
Freshly ground black pepper to taste
¼ cup chopped cilantro
1 plum tomato, seeded and chopped (optional)

In a mortar and pestle, or in a mixing bowl with a fork, mash together the garlic, onion, and jalapeño. Add the avocado and mash until it forms a chunky paste. Add lime juice, salt, pepper, and cilantro, and stir to combine. Garnish with chopped tomato if desired. Serve with tortilla chips, or as an accompaniment to spicy food.

Pitting an Avocado

For both types of avocado, start by cutting through the skin, down to the pit, and scoring the fruit lengthwise. Gripping both halves, give a quick twist to separate one half from the pit, leaving the other half holding that large nut. If you plan to use only half of the avocado, it's best to leave the pit in the unused portion, since it prevents the fruit from turning brown overnight. To remove the pit, hack into the middle of it with the blade of your knife, gripping the fruit in the palm of your other hand; twist the knife clockwise to loosen the pit. It should fall right out of a ripe avocado.

Hummus

Yields 2 cups

1 cup dried garbanzos (chick
peas), soaked overnight if
*desired, **or** 1 (16-ounce) can*
2 cloves garlic, peeled
3 tablespoons tahini
½ teaspoon kosher salt
2–3 teaspoons toasted cumin
powder (see "Hummus Tip,"
below)

Juice of 1 lemon, divided in half
¼ cup extra-virgin olive oil, plus a
little extra for garnish
Freshly ground black pepper
Paprika and chopped parsley for
garnish (optional)
Pita bread for dipping

1. If using dried chick peas, cook them in lightly salted water until very, very tender (See "Bean There . . . Working with Dried Beans," page 16). If using canned chick peas, drain and rinse them. In a food processor, chop the garlic until it sticks to the sides of the bowl. Add chick peas, tahini, salt, cumin, and half of the lemon juice. Process until smooth, gradually drizzling in the olive oil. Add up to ¼ cup cold water to achieve a softer hummus if desired. Season to taste with black pepper, and additional salt and lemon to taste.

2. Spread onto plates and garnish with a drizzle of extra-virgin olive oil, a few drops of lemon, a dusting of paprika, and some chopped parsley. Serve with wedges of warm pita bread.

Hummus Tip

Toast whole cumin seeds in a dry pan until they give off a slight smoke, and brown slightly, about two minutes over medium heat. Pulverize them in a coffee grinder. This will make your hummus unforgettable. If you are using powdered cumin, just give it a quick toast in a dry pan, until it becomes highly fragrant, about one minute.

Kosher Salt: The Chefs' Seasoning

Chefs know that judicious use of salt is essential to bring certain flavors to life. Almost all professional chefs, except those creating dishes for people with specific medical conditions, use some amount of salt in their cooking. In finer restaurants, the salt of choice in the kitchen is seldom the fine powdered table salt most home cooks are familiar with. Instead, they use either complex-tasting crystal sea salt or coarse, flaky white salt known as "kosher" salt. It is so-named because it is the type used for certain processes involved in the Jewish dietary laws of "kashrus." It is available at most supermarkets.

The advantage of the large crystalline flakes characteristic of kosher salt is in ease of control. Properly seasoned food should taste full-flavored, but not salty (except in the case of certain foods like pretzels, where it's desired). While seasoning is a must for full flavor, the degree of seasoning required is a matter of taste—up to the cook's palate. Kosher salt has less "saltiness" by volume than ordinary table salt. That means a pinch of kosher salt is milder than an equal pinch of table salt, giving the cook a chance to taste and season gradually.

Some people have told me they "don't cook with salt." I conclude that their food is either unbearably bland, or seasoned with copious amounts of other condiments containing lots of salt. One friend, for example, uses soy sauce (a lot of salt) on almost everything, believing that somehow this is "healthier." It's not. It just makes everything taste like soy sauce. Unless you've been diagnosed with hypertension (high blood pressure) or heart disease, or have been recommended a low-sodium diet by your doctor for some other reason, there's no reason to fear a little salt here and there.

Manchego-Potato Tacos
with Pickled Jalapeños

Serves 8

*1 cup leftover mashed potatoes, **or** instant mashed potatoes,*
*   made firm*
8 soft corn tortillas
*¼ pound Spanish Manchego cheese **or** sharp cheddar, cut into*
*   16 small sticks*
16 slices pickled jalapeño pepper (available in Mexican
*   sections and ethnic specialty stores)*
4 tablespoons unsalted butter

1. Spoon 1 tablespoon of mashed potato into the center of each tortilla. Flatten out the potatoes, leaving a 1-inch border. Lay 2 pieces of Manchego and 2 pieces pickled jalapeño onto each tortilla, and fold closed into a half-moon shape.
2. In a skillet over medium heat, melt half of the butter. Gently lay 4 of the tacos into the pan, and cook until nicely browned, about 3 to 4 minutes on each side. Drain on paper towels. Repeat with remaining tacos. Snip tacos in half before serving with salsa.

Softening Store-Bought Tortillas

Right from the package, corn tortillas are cardboardy and mealy, and flour tortillas are tough like leather. Both should be exposed to either dry or moist heat for a minute before serving. This is done either by steaming them for a minute, one at a time, in a standard steamer basket, or by placing them directly onto the burner of a gas stove, allowing the flames to lightly brown the tortillas on both sides. You'll notice a definite "puff" in most tortillas when properly softened. Another alternative is to toast briefly in a toaster oven.

Mini Lentil-Scallion Pancakes with Cumin Cream

These delectable crunchy cakes may be easier to make into round shapes with more egg and flour, but they'll be softer—you decide.

Serves 8

1 cup brown lentils, boiled until
   soft but not broken
3 scallions, chopped fine
1 tablespoon curry powder, toasted
   in a dry pan until fragrant
Pinch of cayenne
1 teaspoon salt
¼ cup chopped cilantro **or** parsley
1 egg, beaten

1 tablespoon milk **or** water
1 tablespoon all-purpose flour
3 tablespoons olive oil for frying
1 cup sour cream
2 teaspoons cumin seeds, toasted
   in a dry pan, then ground
   (**or** 2 teaspoons ground cumin,
   toasted in a dry pan until
   fragrant)

1. Gently combine lentils, scallions, curry, cayenne, salt, and cilantro (or parsley) in a mixing bowl. Mix in the beaten egg and milk (or water) with your hands, and dust with enough flour to form a cohesive batter.
2. Heat oil in a large nonstick skillet until hot, but not smoky. A bit of the batter should sizzle when placed in the oil. Drop teaspoonfuls of batter into the pan; flatten them out and shape them into round cakes with the back of the spoon. Some lentils may fall away, but the cakes will stick together once they're cooked. Leave at least 1 inch of space between cakes. Fry 2–3 minutes per side, until lightly browned and crisp. Drain on paper towels.
3. Whisk together the sour cream and cumin. Arrange the lentil cakes on a serving platter, and top each with a dollop of cumin cream.

Mini Goat Cheese Pizzas

Serves 8

1 package frozen puff pastry dough (17 ounces—2 sheets), thawed
½ cup marinara sauce
1 package (4 ounces) fresh goat cheese
*1 tablespoon chopped fresh thyme **or** parsley*

1. Heat oven to 400 degrees. Using a 1-inch diameter cookie cutter, or the top of a small bottle, cut 24 disks of puff pastry; line onto an ungreased baking sheet. Stack another, matching pan atop the disks, and bake until golden brown, about 15 minutes. The second pan will keep the disks from rising too high.
2. Make a slight indentation on each disk with the tip of a small knife. Spoon in a bit of marinara sauce, crumble on a pinch of goat cheese, and sprinkle with chopped thyme. To serve, warm again in the oven for 1 minute, until the goat cheese attains a slight shimmer; serve hot.

Crumbling Goat Cheese

Fresh cheese made from goats' milk, called "chèvre" in France, has a tangy flavor and smooth, creamy texture, even though it's lower in fat than most other cheeses. Cold from the refrigerator, it crumbles between the fingers, or by flaking it away with the tines of a fork, into attractive snowy-white nuggets. Chèvre is usually sold in three- to four-ounce logs. Push the tines of a fork down into the open end of a log, and pry down, twisting to produce attractive crumbs perfect for sprinkling on salads, garnishing soups, or piling on small rounds of French bread.

Vegetable Gado-Gado

This appetizer of vegetables with a spicy peanut sauce is Indonesian in origin.

Serves 8

*16 each: 2-bite carrot sticks, broccoli florets, trimmed green beans,
    batons of yellow bell pepper and/or yellow summer squash, and
    assorted other vegetables*
½ cup smooth peanut butter
¼ cup honey
¼ teaspoon salt
⅛ teaspoon cayenne pepper
1 tablespoon lime juice
¾ cup (6 ounces) coconut milk

1. Blanch all the vegetables quickly in lightly salted boiling water; plunge immediately into ice-cold water to stop the cooking process. Drain and arrange in an attractive pattern on a serving platter.
2. Combine peanut butter, honey, salt, cayenne, and lemon juice in a food processor or mixing bowl; pulse or whisk together until smooth. Gradually work in coconut milk, until a saucy consistency is reached. Adjust consistency further, if desired, with hot water. Serve as a dipping sauce with blanched vegetables.

Stuffed Mushrooms

Serves 6

1 pound mushrooms (caps approximately 1½ inches across)
3 tablespoons butter
½ cup onion, finely chopped
¾ cup bread crumbs
½ teaspoon salt
Freshly ground black pepper to taste
1 teaspoon dried thyme
¼ cup half-and-half
¼ cup grated Parmesan cheese
2 tablespoons fresh parsley, chopped

1. Turn on oven broiler. Clean the mushrooms and gently pull the stem from each cap, setting the caps aside. Chop the mushroom stems and set aside. Heat butter in a skillet over medium heat. Add onion and cook for 2 minutes, until translucent. Add mushroom stems, and cook 2–3 minutes more. Stir in bread crumbs, salt, pepper, and thyme; cook 1 minute more. Remove from heat and stir in cream and grated cheese.
2. Using a small spoon, fill each mushroom cap with the mushroom mixture. Place the filled mushrooms on a baking sheet and put under the preheated oven broiler for 5 to 7 minutes, until the tops are browned and the caps have softened and become juicy. Sprinkle the tops with chopped parsley and serve hot or warm.

True Grit

Dried wild mushrooms are an excellent way to bring passionate flavors from forests to your dining table. Soak them for a few hours or overnight in room temperature water, then use them as you would fresh mushrooms. The soaking liquid acquires a wonderful flavor—use it in soups or stocks. Pour the water into a clear container, and discard any sediment.

Sweet Fennel with Lemon
and Shaved Parmigiano

My friend Skip Lombardi shared this simple but delicious snack with me. It typifies the essence of his beloved Italian cuisine: Use the best ingredients without overcomplicating them.

Serves 4

2 bulbs fresh fennel
½ fresh lemon
1 wedge (at least 4 inches long) Parmigiano Reggiano cheese **or** Asiago cheese

1 tablespoon very high quality extra-virgin olive oil
Pinch of salt

1. Trim the stems and hairlike fronds from the fennel tops. Break the bulbs apart, layer by layer, using your hands to make long, bite-size pieces. Discard the core. Arrange the pieces pyramid-shape onto a small, attractive serving plate.
2. Squeeze the lemon over the fennel. Using a peeler, shave curls of cheese over the fennel, allowing them to fall where they may; make about 10 curls. Drizzle the olive oil over the plate, and sprinkle with salt. Serve at room temperature.

Even-Seasoning Secret

To avoid salty patches in some parts of your food and bland, unseasoned patches on other parts, take a cue from pro chefs: Season from a great height. Most chefs pinch salt between their thumb and forefinger and sprinkle it down onto food from a great height, more than a foot above the item being seasoned. It tends to shower broadly over the food this way, covering evenly.

Sweet Potato and Rosemary Pizza

Simple four- or five-ingredient pizzas like this one perfume every street corner in some parts of Rome. I based this variation on a savory potato and rosemary pie I fell in love with near the Pantheon, one of Rome's ancient architectural wonders.

Serves 6

*1 can store-bought pizza crust, **or** pizza dough of your choice*
1½ tablespoons extra-virgin olive oil
1 large sweet potato, peeled
*2 sprigs fresh rosemary, **or** 1 teaspoon dried rosemary leaves*
Salt and freshly ground black pepper

1. Preheat oven to 400 degrees. Spread dough to ¼-inch thickness onto a doubled-up, lightly greased sheet pan. Brush on a light coating of olive oil.
2. Shred the sweet potato into a ¼-inch-thick layer over the pizza crust using the large-holed side of a box grater. Distribute rosemary leaves evenly on top of potato. Sprinkle remaining olive oil over the pizza, and season it with salt and pepper. Bake 20–25 minutes, until potato is cooked through, and begins to brown.

What Is a Doubled-up Greased Sheet Pan?

To buffer baking foods from the direct heat of oven elements, chefs often stack two identical baking sheets (known in the industry as "sheet pans") together, creating an air pocket that protects victuals from burning onto the food-contact surfaces. Commercially manufactured pans, such as "Bakers' Secret" pans, incorporate this concept into their insulated bakeware.

Tomato and Black Olive Bruschetta

Serves 8

4 slices Italian country bread, **or** other crusty rustic bread, about ½-inch thick

½ cup extra-virgin olive oil

2 cloves garlic, finely chopped

3 ripe tomatoes, roughly chopped

½ teaspoon salt

¼ teaspoon freshly ground black pepper

½ cup black olives (about 24), such as Gaeta, Kalamata, **or** black oil-cured, pitted (see "Pitting Olives," page 295)

¼ cup roughly chopped Italian parsley

Juice of 1 lemon

1. Heat a stovetop grill, barbecue grill, or broiler. Cut the bread slices in half. Combine the olive oil and garlic; brush the bread liberally with some of this garlic oil, using a pastry brush or your hands. Grill or broil until well toasted on both sides.
2. Toss chopped tomatoes with 1 tablespoon of garlic oil (make sure to get some pieces of garlic in there), salt, pepper, olives, and parsley. Season to taste with lemon juice. Top each piece of grilled bread with a small mound of tomato-olive mixture. Arrange neatly on a serving platter.

Which Olives to Buy?

Avoid buying canned supermarket grade factory-pitted olives. They have usually been overprocessed, and retain little or no true olive flavor. It is best to select olives from the delicatessen department, or buy a good, imported olive in a glass jar, and pit them by hand. It's very easy.

Spicy White Bean—Citrus Dip

Tangy, spicy, unique, and easy to throw together, this stupendous dip, taught to me by Stuart Tarabour and Dona Abramson of the Bright Food Shop in New York City, is perfect for tortilla chips, fried plantains, raw vegetables, or as a spread in a burrito.

Serves 12

2 cans (15 ounces each) white navy beans, drained and rinsed
¼ cup sour cream
1 tablespoon orange juice concentrate
1 teaspoon chipotle purée (see "Chipotle" Tip) **or** *hot pepper sauce*
1 teaspoon lime juice
Zest of 1 orange, grated
½ teaspoon salt
½ cup diced white onions
1 tablespoon chopped cilantro

Purée the beans, sour cream, orange juice concentrate, chipotle, lime juice, orange zest, and salt in a food processor until smooth. Add onions and cilantro; mix with a rubber spatula until combined.

Chipotle

Chipotle is a smoked jalapeño pepper. They are sold in small six-ounce cans, and are very useful for imparting a smoky flavor and medium heat to dishes. Purée them with the sauce in which they're packed, using a blender or food processor. They are available from the ethnic food section of your grocer (Mexican), or from gourmet, specialty, and Mexican food shops.

¡Hola! I Must Be Going: Mexican Specialty Foods

Most people know tamales are *hot* well before they ever know what a tamale is. (It's a steamed cake made of stone-ground cornmeal, usually stuffed with some kind of filling and wrapped in a corn husk. It's mostly hot sauce that makes 'em hot.) In the United States, trying to find the special flour and hominy corn used for tamales used to be like looking for Gorgonzola cheese in China. Not so any more.

The "New American" cuisine movement over the last twenty years has highlighted the regional cuisines of America, including the now-beloved Southwest cuisine. Mexican influence on that cookery brought chilies, different corn varieties, Yucatan spices, and dessert vegetables into most markets. Canned and dried products, tortillas, and even fresh Mexican import vegetables like jicama and prickly pear cactus regularly appear in specialty food shops.

Key items for your Mexican-inspired pantry include pickled jalapeño peppers, chipotle (smoked chilies) in *adobo* (tomato-based sauce), nopales (pronounced "noh-*pah*-lays"; slices of delicious cactus perfect in salads, stews, and wraps), and Mexican chocolate disks (the best hot chocolate you'll ever taste—it's made with cinnamon bark and ground almonds!). If your local specialty store is lacking, get them by mail order or over the Internet (see the Resources Appendix).

Wild Mushroom Ragout in Puff Pastry Shells

Most supermarkets carry small frozen puff pastry hors d'oeuvre shells in the freezer section. They are great for quick homemade bites like these, which have a touch of refinement that store-bought frozen foods can't.

Serves 8

24 pieces frozen puff pastry hors d'oeuvre shells
1 tablespoon unsalted butter
2 cups (about ½ pound) assorted wild mushrooms, such as morels, chanterelles, oysters, shiitakes, and/or domestic and cremini mushrooms
½ teaspoon salt
2 sprigs fresh rosemary, leaves picked and chopped
*¼ cup vegetable stock **or** water*
1 teaspoon cornstarch dissolved in 1 tablespoon cold water
Freshly ground black pepper to taste
Squeeze of lemon

1. Bake puff pastry shells according to package directions. In a medium skillet over medium heat, melt the butter. Add the mushrooms and cook without stirring for 5 minutes, until a nice brown coating has developed. Add salt and rosemary; cook 3 minutes more. Add the stock and cornstarch; stir until thickened and bubbling. Remove from heat; adjust seasoning with black pepper, a few drops of lemon, and salt to taste.
2. Spoon ½ teaspoon of mushroom ragout into each shell. Serve piping hot.

Fungus among Us

The term "wild mushrooms" has come to mean not just foraged fungus, but also a host of "exotic" mushrooms that are cultivated on mushroom farms just like the familiar white button mushrooms. While not as intensely flavorful as their truly wild cousins, they are much cleaner, more uniform, and of higher consistent freshness.

Cultivated exotics include delicate silver-gray, fan-shaped *oyster mushrooms*; long, thin-stemmed, tiny-capped snow white *enoki mushrooms*; and dark brown, firm, flat-topped *shiitake mushrooms*. Other widely available mushroom varieties closely related to white button mushrooms include mahogany-topped *cremini mushrooms* and their titanic brothers, *portobello mushrooms*.

True wild mushrooms—such as woodsy, honeycomb-textured *morels*; rich, savory, velvet-fleshed *porcini mushrooms* (a.k.a. *"ceps"*); and elegant, golden, buttery *chanterelles*—cost about four times the price of cultivated exotics, and are available only in the spring and fall seasons. These amazing flavors are worth seeking out in season, and best used in simple preparations like risottos and omelets. Wonderful dried wild mushrooms are also now common. They're so good, people sometimes mistake them for fresh.

Dried wild mushrooms are an excellent way to bring passionate flavors from forests and meadows to your dining table. To use them, soak them for a few hours or overnight in room temperature water, then use them as you would fresh mushrooms. The soaking liquid acquires a wonderful flavor, and should never be discarded. Use it in soups or add it to stocks. Pour the water into a clear container, and discard any sediment that sits at the container's bottom.

Salsa Fresca (Pico de Gallo)

Serves 8

4 medium tomatoes, seeded and diced fine (about 1½ cups)
1 small white onion, finely chopped
1 jalapeño pepper, seeded and finely chopped
1 tablespoon puréed chipotle in adobo (optional)
½ teaspoon salt
2 teaspoons lime juice
¼ cup chopped cilantro

In a blender or food processor, purée one-third of the tomatoes. Combine with remaining tomatoes, onions, jalapeños, chipotle, salt, lime juice, and cilantro. Best if used within 2 days. Serve with chips, with a cheese omelet, or as a sauce with other Mexican foods.

———————

Spiced Pecans

Yields 3 cups

1 ounce (2 tablespoons) unsalted butter
1 pound whole, shelled pecans
2 tablespoons light soy sauce
1 tablespoon hoisin sauce
A few drops of hot pepper sauce

1. Heat oven to 325 degrees. Melt butter in a large skillet. Add nuts; cook, tossing occasionally, until nuts are well coated. Add soy sauce, hoisin sauce, and hot pepper sauce; cook 1 minute more. Stir to coat thoroughly.
2. Spread nuts into a single layer on a baking sheet. Bake until all liquid is absorbed and nuts begin to brown. Remove from oven. Cool before serving.

Vegetable Stock

Other veggies, such as fennel, ginger, parsnips, herbs, and so on, may be substituted for any of the ingredients. This is a very changeable recipe, open to personalization.

Yields about 4 cups

1 onion, sliced
1 leek, white part only, cleaned thoroughly and sliced
1 carrot, peeled and sliced
2 stalks celery, roughly chopped
1 turnip, peeled and sliced
5 cloves garlic, peeled and sliced

6 cups cold water
Small bunch of parsley stems
10 black peppercorns
8 sprigs fresh thyme
1 bay leaf
Salt and pepper (optional)

Combine all ingredients in a large stock pot. Simmer 1 hour; strain. Season with salt and pepper, if desired; cool. Keeps refrigerated for 1 week. Freezes well.

Taking Stock

Adventurous cooks who get into diverse cuisines look to broths that provide an appropriate palette on which to build their dishes. By adding one or two ingredients to the basic Vegetable Stock recipe, you can make many stocks with the one recipe. For Chinese stock, add one thinly sliced two-inch piece of fresh ginger, and two sliced garlic cloves (additional to the original five the recipe calls for). For Vietnamese stock, add one star anise and one chopped stalk of lemongrass (or ¼ cup dried). When making stocks for Mexican foods, add one *ancho* chili pod and one cinnamon stick. For Middle Eastern dishes, a stock with zest of one lemon adds another dimension.

Red Bean and Pasta Soup

This is a hearty winter soup to warm up chilly nights.

Serves 8

1 medium onion, chopped
3 cloves garlic, sliced
3 tablespoons olive oil
1 teaspoon oregano
2 bay leaves
1 (8-ounce) can tomato sauce
2 teaspoons salt
1 tablespoon soy sauce
1 (16-ounce) package red beans, soaked overnight in 1 quart cold
   water and drained
10 sprigs Italian parsley, including stems
*6 cups vegetable stock **or** water*
2 cups cooked pasta (any small shape, such as orzo or ditalini)

1. In a pot large enough to hold all ingredients, cook onions and garlic with olive oil over medium heat for 5 minutes, until onions are translucent. Add oregano, bay leaves, tomato sauce, salt, and soy sauce. Bring to a simmer and add beans, parsley, and stock (or water).
2. Bring to a boil, then reduce to a low simmer and cook for 90 minutes, until beans are tender enough to mash between two fingers. In a blender, purée ⅓ of the beans very well; add them back to the soup. Add cooked pasta, and bring back to a boil for 1 minute more before serving garnished with a dollop of sour cream if desired.

Cream of Asparagus Soup

Asparagus presents a challenge to the frugal chef: what to do with the sizable trimmings from the bottom stalks of this expensive vegetable. Here's the answer:

Serves 6

2 tablespoons olive oil
1 medium onion, chopped
4 cloves garlic, finely chopped
1 bunch of fresh asparagus, or trimmings from several bunches equal to 1 pound, roughly chopped
1 teaspoon salt
1 teaspoon dried basil

¼ cup white wine or sherry (optional)
3 cups vegetable stock or water
1 package (10 ounces) frozen green peas
2 cups cream or half-and-half
Freshly ground black pepper to taste (about ¼ teaspoon)

1. In a large, heavy-bottomed pot over medium heat, heat olive oil for 1 minute. Add onion, garlic, asparagus, and salt; cook 15 minutes, until onions are translucent but not browned. Add wine or sherry; cook 1 minute, until alcohol evaporates; add the stock. Simmer 20 minutes, until asparagus is very tender. Remove from heat; stir in frozen peas.
2. Purée in a blender or food processor until smooth; transfer back to pot, and heat, just to a simmer. Add cream; season with salt, black pepper, and basil. May be served hot or cold.

Green Peas for Color

The oldest trick in the book: Since asparagus, favas, and some other green veggies fade when cooked in a soup, chefs sometimes add a cup of frozen peas to the hot soup just before puréeing it. It revives the soup's color and adds a touch of sweetness.

Tomato Soup

Serves 6

2 tablespoons olive oil
1 medium onion, chopped
2 cloves garlic, finely chopped
4 pounds ripe tomatoes, peeled, seeded, and roughly chopped
1 teaspoon salt
Freshly ground black pepper to taste (about ¼ teaspoon)

In a large soup pot over medium heat, heat olive oil for 1 minute. Add onion and garlic; cook 5–10 minutes, until onions are translucent but not browned. Stir in tomatoes; simmer 25–30 minutes, until tomatoes are submerged in their own juices. Purée in a blender or food processor until smooth. Season with salt and black pepper. May be served hot or cold. Add cream, if desired, for cream of tomato soup.

Smooth Moves: Blender vs. Food Processor

They seem interchangeable sometimes, but they're not. Blenders and food processors are different tools with different strengths. For ultra-smooth purées, a blender is the first choice. For rougher purées, or chopping jobs with drier ingredients, use a processor.

Wild Mushroom Soup with Thyme

I usually put the shallots and mushrooms though a commercial mixer's grinder attachment, but I've found that hand-chopping the shallots and pulsing the mushrooms quickly in small batches in the food processor works just as well. The final purée should definitely be done in a blender, since it guarantees a smoothness that the food processor can't accomplish.

Serves 8

1 pound white mushrooms

½ pound shiitake mushrooms, stems removed

1 teaspoon olive oil

4 sprigs fresh thyme, **or**
    ½ teaspoon dried

4–5 shallots, peeled and chopped very fine

¼ cup dry white wine

2 cups vegetable stock **or** water

2 teaspoons butter

½ pound assorted wild mushrooms such as chanterelle, shiitake, oyster, cremini, black trumpet, etc., sliced into bite-size pieces **or** an equal amount of sliced white mushrooms

3 cups cold milk

Salt and freshly ground black pepper

1 tablespoon chives, finely chopped

1. Pulse the white mushrooms in about 4 small batches in a food processor to finely chop them, stopping before they clump. Roughly hand-chop the shiitakes, and pulse them the same way.
2. Heat the oil in a 2½-cup saucepan over medium-high flame, toss in the thyme and allow to sizzle for a moment, then add the shallots and sauté for 3 minutes until translucent. Add the chopped mushrooms. Sprinkle in a pinch of salt and cook 5–7 minutes, until mushrooms are soft.
3. Add white wine and cook 2 minutes, then add the stock. Simmer for 10 minutes.
4. Meanwhile, sauté the sliced mushrooms in the butter, in small batches over high heat, seasoning them with salt and pepper as they cook. Set aside.
5. Put ⅓ of soup in blender, with 1 cup cold milk, and purée until very smooth. Repeat with remaining soup, then season to taste. Be careful to vent the blender to avoid dangerous splashing. Serve with a spoonful of sautéed mushrooms in each bowl and a sprinkling of chives.

Mushroom Vegetable Stock

Yields about 6 cups

*1 ounce dried mushrooms, such as porcini or Chinese black
    mushrooms*
1 tablespoon olive oil
1 onion, sliced
1 carrot, peeled and sliced
2 stalks celery, roughly chopped
*1 package (8–10 ounces) white mushrooms, washed and roughly
    chopped*
3 cloves garlic, peeled and sliced
4 cups cold water
Small bunch of parsley stems
10 black peppercorns
8 sprigs fresh thyme
1 bay leaf
2 teaspoons salt

Soak the mushrooms in 4 cups water for 1 hour. Heat the oil in a
stock pot; add onion, carrot, and celery. Cook over medium heat until
onions begin to brown, about 15 minutes. Add the dried mushrooms,
their soaking liquid, the fresh white mushrooms, garlic, water, parsley
stems, peppercorns, thyme, bay leaf, and salt. Bring to a boil, then
lower flame. Simmer 45 minutes; strain. Keeps refrigerated for 1 week.
Freezes well.

Carrot Purée with Nutmeg

Tasting and feeling like a cream soup, this soup will surprise your guests who won't believe there's no cream in this sweet, delicious soup. For best smoothness, use a blender to purée, not a food processor.

Serves 6

2 tablespoons oil
1 medium onion, chopped
2 tablespoons white wine
4 cups carrots, peeled, halved lengthwise, and sliced thin
*2 cups vegetable stock **or** broth (canned is okay)*
1 teaspoon salt
Ground white pepper to taste
Pinch of nutmeg
1¼ cups milk
*2 teaspoons freshly chopped chives **or** parsley*

1. Heat oil in large saucepan over medium-high heat. Add onion, sauté for 5 minutes, add wine, and carrots. Cook for 1 minute, until wine evaporates.
2. Add stock, salt, pepper, and nutmeg. Bring to a boil, then reduce to simmer for 20 minutes.
3. Ladle into a blender, add 1 cup milk, and blend until very smooth. Adjust consistency with more milk if necessary. Be careful when puréeing the hot liquid, starting the blender on the slowest speed, and/or doing the job in 2 batches. Serve garnished with a sprinkling of chives or parsley.

Smoky Black-Eyed Pea Soup with Sweet Potatoes and Mustard Greens [V]

Black-eyed peas offer some of the delicious earthiness of green peas, but also a savory touch. Use any dark leafy greens you'd like, fresh or frozen, in place of the mustard greens. Julienne kale or collard greens are excellent choices, and are equally antioxidant-rich.

Serves 10–12

1 tablespoon olive oil
1 medium onion, chopped
2 ribs celery, chopped
1 carrot, peeled, chopped
2 teaspoons salt
1 teaspoon dried thyme
2 teaspoons dried oregano
1 teaspoon ground cumin
1 dried chipotle chili, halved
2 bay leaves

*1 pound dried black-eyed peas **or** navy beans, washed and picked through for stones*
*2 quarts vegetable stock **or** water*
1 large sweet potato, peeled, diced into 1-inch cubes
1 package (10 ounces) frozen mustard greens, chopped
1 can (22 ounces) diced tomatoes
*Croutons of cornbread **or** other bread for garnish*
Chopped cilantro for garnish

1. In a large, heavy-bottomed Dutch oven over medium heat, heat the oil for 1 minute. Add celery, carrot, onion, and salt; cook 5 minutes, until onions are translucent. Add thyme, oregano, cumin, chipotle chili, and bay leaves; cook 2 minutes more. Add black-eyed peas and vegetable stock. Bring to a boil, then simmer 2 hours until beans are very tender, adding water or stock if necessary.

2. Add the sweet potatoes and cook 20 minutes more. Stir in chopped mustard greens and diced tomatoes. Cook 10 minutes more, until the potatoes and greens are tender. Adjust seasoning with salt and pepper, and consistency with additional vegetable stock or water. The soup should be brothy. Serve garnished with cornbread croutons and a sprinkling of chopped cilantro.

Pumpkin Soup with Caraway Seeds

Butternut squash or even acorn squash substitute very well for pumpkin in this soup. Each imparts its own character, making this three recipes in one. Chipotle and/or Spanish paprika (both in gourmet stores) impart subtle smokiness for an additional dimension.

Serves 8–10

2 tablespoons unsalted butter **or** olive oil
1 medium onion, chopped
½ dried chipotle chili **or** ½ teaspoon smoked Spanish paprika
1 large carrot, peeled and sliced thin
2 cups peeled, cubed pumpkin
¼ teaspoon whole caraway seeds
1½ cups vegetable stock **or** broth (canned is okay)
3 cups cold milk

1. Melt the butter in a heavy-bottomed soup pot over medium heat. Add the onion, carrot, pumpkin, and caraway seeds, and sauté, stirring occasionally, 8–10 minutes, until pumpkin becomes tender and begins to brown (some may stick to pan).
2. Add stock (or broth) and simmer for 20 minutes. Remove from heat and stir in 2 cups milk.
3. Purée in batches in a blender until smooth, adjusting consistency with remaining milk. Season with salt and pepper to taste. Sprinkle the chipotle chili or Spanish paprika on top.

Using Smoked Chilies or Spices to Add Smoky Flavor

For a smoky flavor, nonvegetarian recipes often call for smoked pork bones or bacon. Vegetarians can achieve a similar result by adding smoked chilies, such as chipotles (smoked jalapeños) to those dishes.

Chilled Curry Potato-Fennel Soup

While this soup is delicious hot or cold, I particularly love the way it refreshes in the summer, with enough substance to stand on its own as a main course.

Serves 10–12

1 large Idaho russet potato, peeled
1 large Spanish onion, peeled
1 head sweet fennel, tassel-like fronds removed and set aside
1 red bell pepper
1 (1-inch) piece of fresh ginger root, peeled and finely chopped
1 tablespoon olive oil
2 cloves garlic, peeled and finely chopped

2 teaspoons good-quality Madras curry powder
3 cups vegetable stock
1 jalapeño pepper, seeded and finely chopped (optional)
1 quart buttermilk
1 cup half-and-half
Salt and white pepper to taste
1 tablespoon chopped Italian parsley

1. Chop the potato, onion, fennel, and red bell pepper coarsely. In a large soup pot over medium-high heat, heat the oil for 1 minute. Add the chopped vegetables, ginger, and garlic. Cook until onions are translucent, about 5 minutes; stir in curry powder and cook 5 minutes more. Add vegetable stock; raise heat to high and bring to a full boil. Reduce to a simmer; cook until potatoes are falling-apart tender, about 15 minutes.
2. Chill and purée the soup in a blender or food processor. Add the chopped jalapeño, buttermilk, and half-and-half. Season to taste with salt and white pepper. Serve garnished with chopped parsley and/or sprigs from the reserved fennel fronds.

Smooth Cauliflower Soup with Coriander

Another no-cream "cream soup." This soup is equally delicious hot or chilled.

Serves 4–6

*2 tablespoons unsalted butter **or** olive oil*
1 onion
*2 tablespoons white wine **or** dry sherry*
1 medium head (about 2 pounds) cauliflower, cut into bite-size
*   pieces*
2 cups vegetable stock
1 teaspoon salt
Ground white pepper
1 teaspoon ground coriander
¾ cup cold milk
*Chopped chives **or** parsley*

1. In a large saucepan or soup pot, over medium-high heat, melt butter. Add onion; cook until it is translucent, but not brown, about 5 minutes. Add wine and cauliflower; cook for 1 minute to steam out the alcohol. Add the stock, salt, pepper, and coriander; bring up to a rolling boil.

2. Simmer until cauliflower is very tender, about 15 minutes. Transfer to a blender. Add half of the milk and purée until very smooth, scraping down the sides of the blender vase with a rubber spatula. Be very careful during this step, since hot liquids will splash out of blender if it is not started gradually (you may wish to purée in two batches, for safety). Transfer soup back to saucepan, and thin with additional milk if necessary. Season; garnish with chopped herbs just before serving.

Gazpacho

V

Nothing could be simpler than buzzing together a refreshing summer soup in minutes in a blender. Serve with a few drops of garlic-infused olive oil drizzled on top and a crust of country bread on the side.

Serves 6

8 tomatoes, seeded
1 large cucumber, peeled
2 green bell peppers, seeded
1 slice bread, torn into postage-stamp-size pieces
1 clove garlic, sliced
2 tablespoons extra-virgin olive oil
1½ teaspoons red wine vinegar
1 teaspoon salt
1 to 2 cups tomato juice
Hot pepper sauce (optional)

Roughly chop the tomatoes, cucumber, and peppers. Combine with bread, garlic, olive oil, vinegar, and salt in a food processor or blender. Purée at high speed until consistency is soupy, but still slightly chunky. Stir in tomato juice to desired consistency, and season with hot pepper sauce to taste.

Yellow Split Pea Soup with Cactus and Hominy   V

This Southwestern soup is more like a stew. I was taught how to make it by fusion chef Dona Abramson. The Mexican specialty ingredients are increasingly available in ethnic sections of mainstream markets, and certainly in specialty and gourmet shops.

Serves 12

1 tablespoon olive oil
1 medium onion, chopped
2 ribs celery, chopped
1 carrot, peeled and chopped
1 tablespoon dried marjoram **or** oregano leaves
1 teaspoon ground toasted cumin
½ teaspoon ground coriander
1 bay leaf
1 pound dried yellow split peas
2 quarts vegetable stock **or** water
2 ancho **or** guajille chili pods, oven-toasted for 2 minutes at

350 degrees, seeded, boiled for 5 minutes in a cup of water, and puréed in a blender
1 tablespoon vegetable oil
1 can (30 ounces) hominy corn kernels, drained and rinsed
1 small can (15 ounces) cactus (a.k.a. nonpalitos), drained and rinsed
Salt and pepper to taste
Chopped cilantro for garnish
Croutons (optional)

1. In a large soup pot over medium heat, heat olive oil for 1 minute. Add onion, celery, and carrot; cook for 5 minutes, until onions turn translucent. Add marjoram, cumin, coriander, and bay leaf. Cook 1 minute more. Add split peas and stock. Raise heat to high and bring to a full boil; reduce heat to a simmer. Add puréed chili and cook 45 minutes, until peas are very tender and starting to fall apart.
2. Add hominy and cactus; bring back to a boil. Cook 1 minute more; season to taste with salt and pepper, and remove from heat. Serve garnished with chopped cilantro and croutons.

Vichyssoise (Potato and Leek Soup) [V]

Elegant, classic French soups like this make the right first course for a formal occasion. Serve chilled or warm, and make sure to use the prettiest leek pieces, cut very precisely, for the garnish. People will notice.

Serves 12

1 tablespoon olive oil
1 medium onion, chopped
*1 pound (about 3 or 4) potatoes, any variety, peeled and cut into
    1-inch chunks*
*2 bunches leeks, chopped, thoroughly washed twice; 1 cup of the
    best parts set aside for garnish*
1 teaspoon dried sage leaves
1 bay leaf
¼ cup white wine
*2 quarts vegetable stock **or** water*
Salt and white pepper to taste

1. In a large soup pot over medium heat, heat olive oil for 1 minute. Add onion, potatoes, and all but 1 cup of the chopped leeks; cook 10 minutes, until onions turn translucent. Add sage, bay leaf, and wine. Cook 1 minute more. Add stock. Bring to a full boil; reduce heat to a simmer and cook for 45 minutes, until potatoes are very tender and starting to fall apart.
2. Carefully purée the soup in a blender in small batches. Season to taste with salt and white pepper. Steam, boil, or sauté the remaining cup of leeks, and serve the soup garnished with a spoonful of leeks in the center.

Minestrone with Basil Pesto

Rich and hearty, this Italian vegetable soup has humble origins as a peasant dish, but is elevated to fine dining with a beautiful pesto garnish.

Serves 10–12

2 stalks celery
1 large carrot
1 potato
1 medium zucchini
1 medium yellow "summer" squash
1 large Spanish onion
1 tablespoon olive oil
2 leeks, chopped, thoroughly
   washed twice
3 cloves garlic, finely chopped
1 teaspoon salt
3 teaspoons chopped fresh
   oregano **or** 1 teaspoon dried
   oregano leaves
3 teaspoons chopped fresh thyme
   or 1 teaspoon dried thyme
   leaves

1 bay leaf
2 quarts vegetable stock **or** water
1 can (30 ounces) diced tomatoes
2 cups cooked pasta (any small
   shape, such as ditalini)
1 can (14 ounces) red kidney **or**
   white cannellini beans
Salt and white pepper to taste
1/2 recipe Basil Pesto (see recipe
   following), **or** store-bought
   pesto
Grated Parmesan cheese
   (optional)

1. Cut celery, carrot, potato, zucchini, yellow squash, and onion into medium (1/4-inch) dice. In a large soup pot or Dutch oven over medium-high heat, heat the olive oil for 1 minute. Add all diced vegetables, leeks, garlic, salt, oregano, thyme, and bay leaf. Cook 10–15 minutes, until onions turn translucent. Add stock and tomatoes. Bring to a full boil; reduce heat to a simmer and cook 45 minutes, until potatoes are cooked through and tender.

2. Add cooked pasta and beans. Bring back to a boil for 1 minute; season to taste with salt and white pepper. Serve in bowls, topped with a teaspoon of basil pesto. Pass grated Parmesan cheese at the table, if desired.

Basil Pesto

This is an exquisite sauce for pasta, vegetables, grilled items, and soup garnish.

Serves 8

5 cloves garlic, peeled
½ cup toasted pine nuts
1 large bunch basil, stems and veins removed, washed thoroughly
1½ cups extra-virgin olive oil
⅓ cup grated Parmesan cheese
Coarse salt and freshly ground black pepper

1. Pulse garlic in food processor until finely chopped. Add nuts and pulse a few times to give them a rough chop. Scrape the bowl to loosen anything stuck to the sides.
2. Pile in all of the basil. Drizzle half of the oil over the leaves, and pulse until basil is medium chopped, about the size of fresh thyme leaves. Remove from food processor to a mixing bowl.
3. Using a plastic spatula or a wooden spoon, fold in the Parmesan cheese, season with salt and pepper, and thin to sauce consistency with the remaining olive oil. Will keep in the refrigerator for 1 week, or in the freezer for up to 2 months. When using frozen pesto, do not thaw, but break off what you need from a frozen state.

Lentil Soup with Cumin

This is the fastest bean soup you can make, ready in about an hour, without any soaking of beans. It gets better as it sits overnight, when the flavors marry, so make enough for two or more meals.

Serves 8

1 large carrot, peeled
1 stalk celery
1 medium onion
1 potato, peeled
2 cloves garlic
1 tablespoon olive oil
½ teaspoon whole cumin seeds, toasted in a dry pan for 1 minute,
   until fragrant
1 cup lentils
8 cups vegetable stock
Salt and pepper (optional)

1. Chop carrot, celery, onion, and potato into bite-size pieces; cut garlic into very small slices.
2. Heat the oil over medium flame in a pot large enough to hold everything, and add the cut vegetables, garlic, and cumin, plus 2 teaspoons of salt. Cook for 5 minutes, then add the lentils and vegetable stock. Raise heat to bring to a boil, then reduce flame to medium-low.
3. Simmer 1 hour, season with salt and pepper; serve with a dollop of Tofu Sour Cream (page 87) if desired.

Soaking Beans—What It Means

Some chefs submerge beans in water overnight before cooking them. The beans swell with water and cook in much less time. I find that soaked beans tend to break up more than unsoaked ones, so I usually cook my beans from a dry state, unless using someone else's recipe.

Tuscan White Bean Soup

One of the trendiest soups of the 1990s, this Northern Italian classic survived that decade with its integrity unscathed. It's just as hearty, wintry, and delicious as it was in our grandfathers' generation. Tuscans place a hunk of rustic bread at the bottom of the bowl before adding the soup. The crust of bread soaks up soup and becomes a velvety "reward" waiting to be found.

Serves 8

1 tablespoon olive oil
1 medium onion, chopped
1 large leek, white part only, finely chopped
3 cloves garlic, finely chopped
*3 teaspoon fresh rosemary leaves, **or** 1 teaspoon dried*

1 bay leaf
*3 quarts vegetable stock **or** water*
2 cups large white (Great Northern) beans (soaked overnight if desired)
Salt and white pepper to taste
1 tablespoon extra-virgin olive oil

1. In a large soup pot over medium heat, heat olive oil for 1 minute. Add onion, leeks, and garlic; cook 10 minutes, until onions turn translucent, stirring frequently. Add rosemary and bay leaf; cook 5 minutes more. Add stock and beans. Bring to a full boil; reduce heat to a simmer, and cook 90 minutes, until beans are very tender and starting to fall apart (cooking time will vary depending on age of beans and whether or not they were soaked—assume 30 minutes less for soaked beans).
2. Carefully purée ⅔ of the soup in a blender; add back to rest of soup. Season to taste with salt and white pepper. Serve with a few drops of fine extra-virgin olive oil sprinkled on top.

Flavored Oils

To infuse oil with flavor and complexity, stuff herbs, spices, and garlic cloves into a bottle of it, and steep for at least three days, up to two weeks or more. Fine olive oil becomes a transcendent condiment when perfumed by rosemary, thyme, savory, garlic, peppercorns, dried mushrooms, or truffles. Or you can buy infused oils at gourmet stores.

Cuban Black Bean Soup with Coriander Tofu Sour Cream   V

Cubans flavor this soup with a smoked pork bone. The same smoky effect comes from chipotle, a smoked jalapeño chili, or smoked Spanish paprika, available in specialty stores, via the Internet, or from one of the sources in the Appendix.

Serves 10–12

1 tablespoon olive oil

1 medium onion, chopped

1 large leek, white part only, finely chopped

4 cloves garlic, finely chopped

1 teaspoon cumin seeds, toasted lightly then ground, **or** *1½ teaspoons ground cumin, heated in a dry pan until fragrant*

1 bay leaf

1 teaspoon smoked Spanish paprika **or** *half of a seeded chipotle chili (optional)*

2 cups black beans (soaked overnight, if desired)

3 quarts vegetable stock **or** *water*

½ bunch fresh cilantro (optional)

Salt and pepper to taste

1 recipe Tofu Sour Cream (page 87) **or** *store-bought equivalent*

2 teaspoons ground coriander

1 tablespoon chopped cilantro, for garnish

1. In a large soup pot over medium heat, heat olive oil for 1 minute. Add onion, chopped leeks, and garlic; cook 5 minutes, until onions turn translucent, stirring frequently. Add cumin, bay leaf, and paprika or chipotle if using. Cook 5 minutes more. Add beans and stock. Bring to a full boil; reduce heat to a simmer, and cook 90 minutes, adding cilantro halfway through, until beans are very tender and starting to fall apart (cooking time will vary depending on age of beans and whether or not they were soaked—assume 30 minutes less for soaked beans). Carefully purée ⅔ of the soup in a blender; add back to rest of soup. Season to taste with salt and white pepper.

2. Whisk together the tofu sour cream and coriander until well combined. Serve the soup topped with a teaspoon of the sour cream and a sprinkling of chopped cilantro.

Corn and Potato Chowder

Corn and dairy form a complete protein, making this a very nourishing dish for vegetarians.

Serves 12

8 ears sweet corn, shucked
1 tablespoon olive oil
2 large onions, chopped
2 stalks celery, chopped
1 pound red potatoes, cut into
   1-inch chunks
3 sprigs fresh thyme **or** 1 teaspoon
   dried thyme leaves
1 bay leaf
3 teaspoons salt

1 smoked chili (optional)
4 ounces (1 stick) unsalted butter
3 quarts vegetable stock **or** water
4 teaspoons cornstarch, dissolved in
   ¼ cup water
1 quart cream **or** milk
White pepper and additional salt to
   taste
2 tablespoons chopped fresh chives

1. Cut corn kernels from the cob using a slicing motion with a kitchen knife. Reserve the cobs, and set kernels aside. In a large soup pot over medium-high heat, heat olive oil for 1 minute. Add the corn cobs, onions, celery, potatoes, thyme, bay leaf, salt, and chili if using. Cook until onions are translucent, about 5 minutes. Add the butter and cook gently, allowing the vegetables to stew in the butter, for about 5 more minutes.

2. Add the vegetable stock. Raise flame to high and bring to a full boil. Lower to a simmer and cook 10 minutes more. Remove the corn cobs; add cornstarch mixture and simmer 5 minutes more. Stir in the cream, and adjust seasoning with salt and white pepper to taste. Serve sprinkled with chives.

Brothy vs. Thick Chowders

While generations of canned soups have conditioned us to believe that chowder is, by definition, a thick, pasty soup, some of the most delicious handmade versions of these chunky soups feature a thin, though rich, broth.

Mushroom, Barley, and Collard Greens Soup [V]

This should be called "Health Soup" for its concentration of cancer-fighting antioxidants, folate-rich greens, nourishing whole grains, and complete protein-forming combinations. Who knew medicine for the body and soul could taste so good?!!

Serves 12

2 tablespoons olive oil
2 pounds mushrooms (any variety)
1 large onion, chopped
1 carrot, peeled and chopped
2 stalks celery, chopped
4 cloves garlic, roughly chopped
2 bay leaves
2 tablespoons fresh **or** 2
    teaspoons dried marjoram **or**
    oregano leaves
1 ½ teaspoons fresh **or** ½
    teaspoon dried rosemary leaves

2 teaspoons salt
½ teaspoon fresh ground black
    pepper
2 cups pearl barley, rinsed
3 quarts vegetable stock **or** water
1 bunch fresh collard greens,
    cooked until tender in boiling
    water and chopped, **or**
    2 packages
    (10 ounces each) frozen
    chopped collards

1. Heat the oil in a large soup pot over medium-high heat for 1 minute. Add mushrooms, onions, carrot, celery, garlic, bay leaves, marjoram, rosemary, salt, and pepper. Cook until vegetables have softened significantly and are stewing in their natural broth, about 15 minutes. Stir in barley and stock. Bring the soup up to a full boil, then reduce to a medium simmer and cook until barley is tender, about 40 minutes.
2. Add the collards; cook about 10 minutes more. Season to taste.

Tofu Sour Cream

[V]

This delicious spread not only provides a vegan alternative to fat-rich sour cream, but also provides essential protein for vegetarians. It is important to include soy foods as a daily part of a vegetarian diet.

Yields about 1½ cups

1½ cups firm silken tofu, broken up
1 tablespoon extra-virgin olive oil
1 tablespoon vegetable oil

2 teaspoons fresh lemon juice
2 teaspoons apple cider vinegar
½ teaspoon sugar
½ teaspoon salt

Combine all ingredients in a blender or food processor. Process or blend until smooth. Chill. Keeps for up to 10 days.

Feed Bag (An Emergency Vegetarian Travel Kit)

Flip through the pages of your average vegetarian monthly lifestyle magazine and you'll find page after page of advertisements for new vegetarian convenience foods. Now, while many of these power bars, snack chips, and instant soup-cups aren't an important part of your daily diet, they can come in mighty handy when traveling. I recommend that the roaming vegetarian assemble a small bag with a few of these lightweight, vitamin-enriched items just in case the flight attendant tells you there's no vegetarian meal for you, or the waiter says even the salads are washed in meat.

Don't take much—just enough for an emergency meal—and make sure it's lightweight. Forget about beverages (a pint is a pound the whole world 'round)—thankfully Coca-Cola is still porkless. One or two nutritional food bars, a bag of whole-grain crackers, an instant soup cup, and a small bag of soy nuts or cereal may weigh only a few ounces, but are worth their weight in gold when you're hungry. Avoid anything even remotely perishable, like fruits, vegetable sticks, or nonhermetically sealed cheeses unless you plan to eat them that day. Discovering that your emergency travel kit has spoiled is slightly more irritating than chewing on aluminum foil.

Pinto Bean Soup with Salsa Fresca

A restaurant secret to elevating simple soups to finer cuisine is to place an attractive garnish right in the middle of the portion just before serving. In this case, we use a refreshing Salsa Fresca to brighten this Mexican soup.

Serves 6

1½ cups dried pinto beans
7 cups water
¼ cup olive oil
2 medium yellow onions, diced
1 teaspoon salt
½ teaspoon freshly ground black
   pepper

4 cloves garlic, crushed
¼ teaspoon dried thyme
6 cups vegetable stock **or** water
1 cup Salsa Fresca (page 64)
Tofu Sour Cream (page 87)

1. Rinse the beans well and place in a saucepan with the water, bring to a boil, lower to a simmer, and cook until very tender, about 1½ hours.

2. In a large soup pot, heat the oil over a medium flame. Add the onions, salt, and pepper; cook until the onions brown slightly, about 10 minutes. Add the garlic and thyme; cook 2 minutes more. Add the beans, along with their cooking liquid and the stock or water. Bring to a boil; reduce heat and simmer uncovered, stirring occasionally, until the beans start to break apart, about 30 minutes.

3. Purée the beans in a blender until smooth (work carefully in small batches, so as not to splash hot liquid—a blender works best for this). Adjust seasoning. Ladle the soup into warmed shallow soup plates, topping each with a spoonful of salsa and, if desired, a dollop of Tofu Sour Cream.

Acorn Squash Soup with Anise and Carrots

When the weather turns chilly, fall and winter squashes like Acorn squash start showing up in the markets—just in time to make this smooth, soothing velvety soup. Remove the seeds from the squash. Salt and toast them for twenty minutes in a medium-temperature oven for a crunchy soup garnish.

Serves 6

1 tablespoon olive oil
2 medium onions, chopped
1 teaspoon salt
*1 medium Acorn squash (about
    2 pounds), peeled, cut into
    1-inch chunks*
*2 carrots, peeled and cut into
    1-inch chunks*

*1 teaspoon anise seeds, toasted
    in
    a dry pan for 2 minutes, until
    fragrant*
*¼ cup Cognac **or** brandy*
1 pint vegetable stock
1–2 cups skim milk
Fresh parsley, chopped

1. Heat the olive oil in a heavy medium saucepot over a medium flame. Add the onions and salt; cook until translucent and slightly browned, about 10 minutes. Lower the flame. Add the squash, carrots, and anise seeds; cook slowly, stirring the browned bits from the bottom of the pan frequently with a wooden spoon. These browned natural sugars will give the soup its caramelized complexity.
2. When the squash is soft and nicely browned, add the Cognac; cook for 2 minutes to steam off the alcohol. Add the stock; simmer 15 minutes.
3. In a blender, purée the soup with as much skim milk as necessary for a thick but soupy consistency. Season to taste. Serve garnished with toasted squash seeds and a sprinkling of chopped parsley.

Miso Soup

The delicious cloudy broth you've been served in Japanese restaurants, with diced tofu and seaweed, is made with a fermented soybean and grain paste called miso.

Serves 4

*5 cups vegetable **or** mushroom stock*
1 piece kombu (kelp, a dried seaweed), about 5 inches square
1 teaspoon soy sauce
3 tablespoons light (yellow) miso, such as shiro mugi miso
2 scallions, chopped
2 ounces firm tofu, diced into small cubes
4 teaspoons wakame seaweed (instant)

1. Bring stock and kombu to a boil in a soup pot. Cover; remove from heat and let stand 5 minutes. Strain; stir in soy sauce.
2. In a mixing bowl, mix about ¼ cup of the warm stock into the miso paste with a wire whisk until the miso is dissolved. Pour this mixture back into the remaining stock. Place scallions, diced tofu, and *wakame* into four bowls. Gently ladle soup into the bowls.

Root Vegetables

White Potato Pie

Serves 8 as side dish, or as lunch with a green salad and cold cuts

*7 cups diced thin-skinned white
   potatoes
1 stick butter **or** margarine, chopped
1 medium onion, chopped
½ cup chopped parsley
2 teaspoons salt*

*1 package frozen pie dough (not
   sweet) **or** 1 recipe Basic Pie
   Dough (following)
1 egg, beaten, mixed with
   1 tablespoon cold water (egg wash)
1 cup cream*

1. Heat oven to 350 degrees. Combine potatoes, butter, onion, parsley, and salt. Roll half of the pie dough ¼-inch thin, and settle it into a 10-inch pie pan. Brush the rim of the crust with egg wash. Arrange the potato mixture in the crust so that it mounds slightly. Roll the top crust ¼-inch thin, and place it onto the pie. Trim edges and crimp the pie firmly shut, using either fingers or the tines of a fork. Cut a circular vent in the center of the pie.
2. Bake 90 minutes. Bring cream to a boil, and add it through the vent (it may not all fit—that's okay). Bake 30 minutes more.
3. Make sure potatoes are very soft. Allow to cool about 15 minutes.

Basic Pie Dough

Yields enough dough for 1 pie

*2 cups flour (pastry flour is best,
   but you can use all-purpose)
½ teaspoon salt*

*6 ounces (1½ sticks) unsalted butter,
   cold, cut into pea-size pieces
½ cup very cold water*

1. Sift flour and salt together over a bowl containing the diced butter. Using your hands, break up the butter into the flour until the flour assumes the color of the butter. There should still be some nuggets of unmixed butter.
2. Sprinkle in most of the water, and work quickly with your hands until dough clumps together. Add extra water if the dough feels too dry to roll. Do not overmix. Separate dough into two balls, wrap separately, and refrigerate for at least 30 minutes.

Roasted Yukon Gold Potatoes   Ⓥ

Here's a mess-free way of making Roasted Yukon Gold Potatoes, which works as well on the barbecue grill as in the oven. It calls for wrapping the seasoned, cut potatoes in a foil pouch before cooking.

Serves 4

1 medium onion, roughly chopped
2 tablespoons olive oil
¼ cup chopped parsley
3 or 4 cloves garlic, minced
1½ pounds Yukon Gold potatoes, washed, sliced ½-inch thick
1 teaspoon salt
Pepper

1. Heat oven to 425 degrees. Put onion, olive oil, parsley, and garlic in blender or food processor, and purée until smooth. Toss with potatoes and salt, then wrap in a ready-made foil oven bag, or a sheet of foil crimped to seal. Potatoes should be no more than 2 layers deep.
2. Bake on a sheet pan, in center rack for 45 minutes, until potatoes are tender when poked with a fork. Season with pepper.

Turnip and Potato Gratin

Serves 8

2 garlic cloves, finely chopped
2 tablespoons unsalted butter
2½ pounds all-purpose potatoes, peeled and cut into ½-inch cubes
*2 pounds turnips **or** rutabagas, peeled and cut into ½-inch cubes*
4 cups heavy cream
Salt and freshly ground black pepper

1. Preheat the oven to 350 degrees. Grease the bottom and sides of a 9-inch square baking dish with the butter and spoon the garlic all over.
2. Mix the potatoes and turnips and arrange them in the pan. Bring the cream to a boil on the stove and season with salt and pepper (about 2 teaspoons salt and 1 teaspoon pepper), then pour it over the vegetables, and cover the pan with foil.
3. Bake 30 minutes, then uncover and cook another 20–25 minutes. The potatoes and turnips should be very tender and the sauce should be bubbling and browned on top when done.

Penny for Your Thawed?

Did you know that nutritional content is often higher in frozen vegetables than in fresh? Vitamins begin to dissipate in certain vegetables, such as corn and peas, within minutes of picking. By a few hours, they may have lost up to half of their nutrient value. Freezing quickly after harvest is sometimes the best way to lock in flavor and food value. Also, since the frozen vegetable companies have huge buying power, they often get the best part of the crop.

Parsnip Purée

In New England, farmers leave some parsnips in the ground at the end of the fall harvest season. Through the winter, starches turn to sugars in these parsnips deep below the frozen earth. When the ground thaws in the spring, the farmers dig these supersweet roots and send them to market, bringing a rare treat to lucky cooks-in-the-know.

Serves 6

2 pounds parsnips
½ cup milk
8 tablespoons unsalted butter
Salt

1. Peel the parsnips and boil in salted water. Cook until very tender, about 10 to 15 minutes. Drain in a colander. While the parsnips are draining, heat the milk in a small pot.
2. Combine the parsnips and milk in a food processor or blender. With the motor going, gradually add the butter, making sure it is well mixed, and the purée is very smooth. Season lightly with salt.

Yuca con Mojo
(Yuca with Garlic and Lime) $\boxed{\text{V}}$

Earthy-tasting yuca (a.k.a. cassava) has a potatolike texture, but a nutty, somewhat mushroomlike fragrance and taste. A woody spine in the center can be removed after cooking. To peel the waxy brown skin, cut the root into cross sections and pare using a cook's knife. Frozen yuca is also available, and is fine for this dish.

Serves 8

1½ pounds peeled yuca, cut into 1½-inch chunks
½ teaspoon salt
2½ tablespoons fresh-squeezed lime juice
¼ cup extra-virgin olive oil
3 large cloves garlic, finely chopped
*1 tablespoon chopped fresh herb, such as cilantro **or** parsley (optional)*

1. Simmer the yuca about 25 minutes in enough water to cover it, along with the salt and ½ teaspoon of the lime juice, in a covered pot. It should be fork tender, but not mushy. Drain; remove woody center core. Transfer to a plate, and cover to keep warm.
2. In a small skillet, heat the oil. Remove pan from heat, and add the garlic. Stir in remaining lime juice and herbs. Pour this sauce over the yuca, and serve immediately.

Storing Potatoes and Other Root Vegetables

Tubers and roots contain lots of starch, which turns to sugar in the cold. Many people enjoy the resulting sweeter flavor, and keep these foods for long periods in unheated "root cellars," or refrigerator drawers. Whatever your taste preference, store root vegetables in a dark place, away from heat sources. They should not be stored in plastic bags, as they are living things and need to breathe.

Roasted Beets

Roasting brings natural juices to the surface of these magenta roots and caramelizes them into a sweet, intensely flavored crust.

Serves 8

2 pounds beets (about 8, tangerine-size), peeled, cut into 1-inch wedges
1 tablespoon olive oil
¼ teaspoon ground cinnamon
¼ teaspoon salt
Chopped Italian parsley (optional)

Heat oven to 350 degrees. Toss beets with olive oil, cinnamon, and salt. Spread into a single layer on a baking sheet (preferably non-stick). Roast on the middle rack of the oven until tender, about 1 hour, turning once, after 30 minutes. If desired, serve sprinkled with chopped parsley.

Cooking Beets—Preserving Nutrition

The flavorful, nutrient-rich juices in beets are water-soluble. To lock in the sweetness, color, and food value of these wonderful vegetables, consider cooking them in their skins. When boiling them, put a few drops of red wine vinegar in the water, which also helps seal in beet juices. Beets can also be baked whole, like potatoes, then peeled and sliced.

French Fries

The key to crispy, golden French fries is cooking the rinsed, high-starch potatoes twice—once at a moderate temperature to cook them through, then a second time at a higher temperature to crisp them.

Serves 8

*2 pounds (about 5) high-starch potatoes, such as Burbank Russets
    (a.k.a. Idaho Baking Potatoes)* **or** *Yukon Golds, peeled*
Peanut oil for frying
Salt

1. Cut potatoes into 2½-inch-long strips, ½-inch wide and thick; soak in enough cold water to cover them for 30 minutes. Drain and dry with absorbent towels.
2. Heat oil to 350 degrees. Fry potatoes in small batches until they are soft and tender enough to mash between your fingers, about 2 minutes (make sure to allow time between each batch for the oil to come back up to temperature—a fry thermometer is essential); drain on paper towels. The potatoes may be fried again once cooled (about 5 minutes), or set aside to be refried later.
3. Heat the oil to 365 degrees. Fry again in small batches, stirring lightly with a tool, so they don't stick together. When golden brown (about 2 to 3 minutes), remove from oil, shake off any excess, and drain on paper towels. Sprinkle immediately with salt, and serve in a napkin-lined basket.

Frying vs. Sauté

Frying means cooking at moderate temperature (usually 340 to 360 degrees) in a large amount of oil, such as a pan filled two inches deep, or a pot filled with oil for deep-frying. Sauté is a cooking method using small amounts of oil, usually measured in teaspoons or tablespoons, and very high heat—nearly at the oil's smoking point.

Carrot Timbales

Serves 4

1 tablespoon unsalted butter
2 cups peeled, sliced carrots,
    cooked soft, chopped in a food
    processor
¼ cup chopped shallots
2 tablespoons Port wine
    (optional)
½ teaspoon salt

Pinch of freshly grated nutmeg
Black pepper to taste
1 cup cream **or** half-and-half
3 large eggs
¼ cup grated Parmesan cheese
Chopped tarragon **or** parsley to
    garnish

1. Heat oven to 375 degrees. Butter four 6-ounce ramekins or custard cups.
   In a small skillet over medium heat, melt 1 tablespoon of butter; add the
   carrots and cook until soft, about 3 minutes. Add the shallots to the carrots, along with the Port, salt, nutmeg, and pepper. Heat the cream until
   steaming but not boiling. Whisk the eggs into the vegetable mixture, then
   gradually whisk in the cream.
2. Divide the mixture into prepared cups, and line them up in a shallow
   casserole or roasting pan. Add enough hot tap water to come two-thirds
   up the sides of the custard cups. Cover pan with foil, and bake in center
   of oven until almost set, 25–30 minutes. Open oven door, loosen but do
   not remove foil, and bake for 10 minutes more. Allow to rest at room
   temperature for 10 minutes before loosening with a knife, inverting, and
   unmolding. Garnish with chopped tarragon or parsley.

Substitutions

Other vegetables may be substituted for carrots in the Carrot Timbales recipe,
including cauliflower, broccoli, zucchini, or fresh sweet corn.

Honey-Orange Beets

If you are able to find fresh beets with the greens still attached, wash them thoroughly, dress them with lemon and olive oil, and use them as a bed for this dish, creating a warm-salad main course.

Serves 4

6 medium-sized fresh beets
1 teaspoon grated orange zest
2 tablespoons orange juice
2 teaspoon butter

1 teaspoon honey
¼ teaspoon ground ginger
Salt and freshly ground pepper
*   to taste*

Boil beets in enough water to cover for 40 minutes, or until tender. Drain beets and let cool slightly. Slip off skins and slice. In a saucepan, heat the orange zest, orange juice, butter, honey, and ginger over low heat until the butter melts. Add the beets and toss to coat. Season with salt and pepper.

Rutabaga Oven Fries

Though not really fried, these golden batons look and feel like French fries, and are great for dipping in ketchup or aïoli (garlic mayonnaise).

Serves 4

1 large rutabaga ("wax turnip"),
*   thickly peeled*
*1 tablespoon olive **or** vegetable oil*
Kosher salt

1 tablespoon finely chopped thyme,
*   rosemary, **or** parsley*
Freshly ground black pepper

Heat oven to 400 degrees. Slice rutabaga into 2½" × ½" sticks (batons); soak in cold water for 30 minutes. Dry thoroughly with towels. Toss gently with oil and a light sprinkling of salt. Spread fries into a single layer on a sheet pan and bake, turning occasionally, until lightly browned and tender, about 30 to 40 minutes. Remove from oven and toss with thyme, salt, and fresh ground pepper.

Herb-Mixed Turnips

Rutabagas and turnips have a naturally buttery flavor, especially when young and fresh in the autumn. This makes the pairing with herbs and crisp breadcrumbs natural.

Serves 4

1½ pounds turnips and rutabagas, peeled
2 tablespoons butter
1 tablespoon chopped parsley
2 teaspoons chopped chervil **or** *tarragon*
2 tablespoons chopped chives
1 clove garlic, finely chopped
Kosher salt and black pepper
½ cup fresh breadcrumbs browned in 1 tablespoon olive
  oil **or** *butter*

Cook the turnips and rutabagas separately in salted water until they're al dente (tender, but firm—approximately 10 minutes for turnips, 20 minutes for rutabagas); drain. In a large skillet over medium heat, melt the butter. Add the turnips and rutabagas, and cook over medium-high flame until golden brown. Add herbs, garlic, salt, and pepper, and toss to coat. Serve topped with breadcrumbs.

Curried Parsnips

The herby sweetness of parsnips lends itself well to curries. Try this one over brown rice with a little lentil dal for a delicious dinner that's a complete protein dish to boot!

Serves 4

1½ *pounds parsnips, peeled, cut into bite-size pieces*
2 *tablespoons butter* **or** *oil*
1 *red onion, thinly sliced*
2 *Bosc pears* **or** *Golden Delicious apples, cored, thinly sliced*
1 *teaspoon Madras curry powder, toasted in a dry pan until fragrant*
½ *teaspoon ground coriander, toasted in a dry pan until fragrant*
Kosher salt and black pepper
¼ *cup yogurt*
¼ *cup mango chutney (such as Major Grey's)*
2 *tablespoons chopped cilantro*

Boil the parsnips until halfway done, about 5 minutes; drain. Melt the butter in a large, heavy-bottomed skillet. Add the onion, pears, curry, and coriander and cook over medium flame, stirring regularly until onions are soft, about 10 minutes. Add the parsnips, season well, and cook 5 minutes more, until the parsnips brown lightly. Remove from heat before stirring in the yogurt, chutney, and cilantro.

Heavy Metal

Burnt onions? It may be the pan you're using. Thin, flimsy stainless steel pans don't conduct heat well, resulting in hot spots where foods burn and cold spots where they don't cook at all. Better pans have a thick core of highly conductive aluminum or even copper bonded to their bottoms. The best are made completely of conductive metal, except for a stainless steel "jacket," which is neutral (nonreactive) and won't give food an "off" flavor.

Celery Root, Artichoke, and Potato Gratin

Rich and savory, this is the perfect cold weather supper, with a watercress-endive salad and a glass of Zinfandel.

Serves 8

4 tablespoons butter **or** olive oil

3 cloves garlic, chopped

4 large artichokes, trimmed, choke removed, cut into eighths

1 large celery root (about 1 pound) trimmed and cut into 1-inch cubes

8 ounces potatoes, peeled and cut into 1-inch cubes

1 ½ teaspoons kosher salt

Freshly ground black pepper

4 cups heavy cream

½ cup parsley

1. Heat oven to 400 degrees. Butter an 11" × 13" casserole or gratin dish and sprinkle the chopped garlic evenly around, rubbing some onto the sides of the pan. Blanch the artichoke for about 10 minutes in rapidly boiling salted water, adding the celery root for the last 3 minutes. Drain well, combine with potatoes, and add to casserole. Season thoroughly with salt and pepper; add cream and parsley.

2. Place the casserole onto a sheet pan to catch any overflow. Cover with aluminum foil and bake for 1 hour, until cream is bubbling and potatoes are tender. Uncover and cook 15–20 minutes more, until sauce is thick and starting to brown on top. Allow the casserole to rest at room temperature for at least 10 minutes before serving.

Cleaning and Trimming Artichokes

To get to the "heart," or bottom, of an artichoke, use a very sharp knife to cut off most of the leaves and trim around the solid core attached to the stem. This part forms a concave well in the center that is filled with fibrous, inedible material ("choke"), which can be scooped with a spoon. Cleaning artichokes is especially easy after they have been cooked in water with lots of lemon juice in it.

Celery Root Mash

Serves 6

2 pounds celery root (sometimes
   called "celeriac" or "apio")
1 pound white potatoes
½ cup milk

8 tablespoons unsalted butter
1 tablespoon snipped chives
   (optional)
Salt

1. Peel and dice the celery root and potatoes roughly into 1-inch pieces. Boil in lightly salted boiling water until very tender, about 20 minutes. Drain in a colander, then return to the pot and heat for 30 seconds to steam out any residual water. Heat the milk and butter in a small pot.
2. Using a stiff wire whisk or potato masher, crush the vegetables until they are a soft mash. Gradually mash in the milk-butter mixture, making sure it is well mixed before adding more; fold in the chives if desired. Season lightly with salt.

Gingered Mashed Sweet Potatoes

This may become a staple on your Thanksgiving table.

Serves 5 or 6

4 medium sweet potatoes **or** yams (about 1½ pounds)
¼ cup milk
2 tablespoons butter
1 tablespoon mashed candied ginger **or** 1 tablespoon brown sugar plus
   ½ teaspoon ground ginger

Peel and quarter the sweet potatoes, and cook in boiling salted water until tender, about 20 minutes. Drain and return to the pan. In a small saucepan or in the microwave, heat the milk and butter; add to the potatoes, along with the candied ginger; mash by hand or with an electric mixer. Texture will be thicker than mashed white potatoes.

Parsnip and Carrot Bake

Serves 4

1 pound carrots, peeled, cut roughly into 2½" × ½" batons
8 ounces parsnips, peeled, cut roughly into 2½" × ½" batons
¾ cup vegetable stock
2 tablespoons butter, chopped
½ teaspoon salt
Chopped fresh chervil **or** *tarragon*
Freshly ground black pepper

Heat oven to 375 degrees. Place carrots, parsnips, stock, butter, and salt into a shallow baking dish. Cover with aluminum foil and bake until the vegetables are soft, about 45 minutes. Uncover and bake until vegetables brown lightly, 10–15 minutes more. Sprinkle with chervil and black pepper before serving.

Common Fresh Herbs

Most supermarkets now carry a variety of fresh herbs including thyme, chives, rosemary, sage, and oregano. But even if they don't, you can almost always find fresh Italian (flat-leaf) parsley, the best kind for cooking. Dill and cilantro are now quite common, and I recently saw fresh flash-frozen herbs in the freezer section of a store.

Carrot and Mushroom Terrine

Serves 8

¼ cup butter, plus 1 tablespoon
2 cloves garlic, chopped
1 pound mushrooms, chopped
1 cup roughly chopped shallots
4½ cups grated carrots
5 eggs
1 cup breadcrumbs
1 cup grated pecorino Romano **or** Parmesan cheese
Salt and pepper to taste
½ teaspoon oregano
½ teaspoon rosemary

1. Heat oven to 350 degrees. Butter a 2-quart terrine or loaf pan. Melt
   ¼ cup of butter in a heavy-bottomed skillet. Add the mushrooms,
   garlic, and shallots; cook until shallots soften, about 10 minutes.
2. In a mixing bowl, combine the shallot mixture with the carrots, eggs,
   half of the breadcrumbs, the cheese, salt and pepper to taste,
   oregano, and rosemary. Pour mixture into terrine and sprinkle with
   remaining breadcrumbs and dot with remaining butter; cover with foil.
   Bake 30 minutes, then uncover and bake 5 minutes more, until
   browned. Let stand 10 minutes before serving.

Crisp Potato Pancakes

These scrumptious, simple "latkes" make wonderful snacking, and can be made as miniature hors d'oeuvres. It's traditional to serve them with either sour cream or applesauce.

Serves 4

1 large egg
*3 large baking potatoes (such as Idaho Russet Burbank **or** other high-starch variety), peeled*
1 medium onion

1 teaspoon salt
1 tablespoon flour
*Clarified butter (ghee) **or** olive oil for frying*

1. Beat the egg in a large bowl. Using the large-hole side of a box grater, shred the potatoes in long motions, forming the lengthiest shreds possible. Quickly grate in the onion. Add the salt and sprinkle in the flour; toss with your hands to combine well.
2. Heat the clarified butter until it shimmers but does not smoke (a piece of potato should sizzle upon entry). Form 8 pancakes from the batter, and pan-fry them in batches of 3 or 4, squeezing out excess water before gently sliding them into the pan. Cook slowly, without moving them for the first 5 minutes; then loosen with a spatula. Turn after about 8 minutes, when the top appears 1/3 cooked. Finish cooking on other side, about 4 minutes more. Drain on paper towels.

Frying Mediums—Why Butter Works for Crisping Potato Cakes

For browning and crispness, clarified butter achieves the best results. This may be because residual proteins in the butter caramelize on foods, or it may simply be the high temperatures that clarified butter can reach without burning. When sautéing, I often start off with a neutral oil, such as peanut oil, and add a nugget of whole butter to get a better brown.

Rosemary New Potatoes

Fresh rosemary perfumes the cooking oil in this Italian classic, imparting its robust herbal flavor to the browning potatoes. "New" connotes young, small potatoes.

Serves 4

1 pound golf-ball-size red-skinned new potatoes
2 tablespoons extra-virgin olive oil
3 sprigs fresh rosemary
Kosher salt and freshly ground black pepper

1. Heat oven to 375 degrees. Slice the potatoes into ½-inch thick rounds, and boil them in lightly salted water until crisp-tender, about 7 minutes. Drain well, and dry very well with a towel.
2. Heat the olive oil in a large, heavy, oven-safe skillet until it shimmers, but does not smoke. Add the rosemary sprigs (they should sizzle), and then slip in the potatoes. Cook without disturbing for 5 minutes. Once potatoes have browned lightly on the first side, turn them over, and put the pan in the oven. Cook 10 minutes. Transfer potatoes to a serving platter, season with salt and pepper, and garnish with additional rosemary sprigs.

What Does "Lightly Salted Water" Really Mean?

Lightly salted water tastes like tears. Thoroughly salted water tastes like seawater. For foods that absorb a lot of water as they cook, like beans or pasta, lightly salted is the way to go, since your aim is to draw out the natural flavors of the food, not to make them "salty." For foods that don't absorb water, such as green vegetables, the point is to use salt's properties of sealing in nutrients, color, and flavor. For that reason, you would salt the water more assertively. Excess salt can easily be washed from those vegetables. Make no mistake, though: Salt is an important part of coaxing the best flavors from your good ingredients.

Roasted Garlic Mashed Potatoes

The amount of garlic in this recipe may seem huge, but the garlic mellows and sweetens as it roasts. All your guests will taste is heavenly, heady, light potatoes "to die for."

Serves 6

3 heads garlic
2 pounds potatoes (preferably thin-
    skinned creamers, red bliss, **or**
    round white Eastern potatoes),
    peeled

8 tablespoons butter
½ cup milk **or** cream
1½ teaspoons salt
White pepper (optional)

1. Heat oven to 350 degrees. Wrap all three garlic heads into a pouch, fashioned from aluminum foil, and place in the center of the oven. Roast until garlic is very soft and yields to gentle finger pressure, about 1 hour and 15 minutes. Roughly cut potatoes into large chunks, and boil in enough lightly salted water to cover until very tender, about 25–30 minutes depending on type and size of potato pieces. Cut the garlic bulbs in half laterally. Using your hands, squeeze out the roasted garlic, and push it through a sieve. Heat the butter and milk together in a small pan until the butter melts. Drain the potatoes well, then return them to the pot, put them on the stove, and cook over moderate heat for 30 seconds to 1 minute to steam off any excess moisture.

2. For smoothest mashed potatoes, force the potatoes through a ricer (see "For Supersmooth Spuds," page 111). Otherwise, mash them with a potato masher or stiff wire whisk. Add the roasted garlic purée, salt, pepper, and the cream mixture to the potatoes, and mix just enough to incorporate. Serve immediately, or keep warm for later service in a double boiler.

Twice Baked Potatoes

This is an elegant way to serve flavored potatoes. Prepare them up to two days ahead, and then bake them whenever you wish, easy as pie.

Serves 4–6

4 large potatoes
2 tablespoons unsalted butter
*2 tablespoons chopped onion **or** shallot*
⅓ cup sour cream
Salt and pepper to taste
*½ cup shredded Gruyère **or** Swiss cheese*
1 egg, beaten, divided
About ¼ cup milk

1. Bake the potatoes and allow to cool until they can be handled. Meanwhile, melt the butter in a small skillet and cook the onion until softened, about 3 minutes. Halve the potatoes lengthwise and scoop out the flesh, being careful to leave a ¼- to ½-inch shell.
2. In a large bowl, combine the potato, sour cream, onions and butter, salt and pepper, and half of the beaten egg. Mash them together thoroughly, then beat by hand or with an electric mixer, adding as much milk as necessary for a smooth consistency, slightly firmer than mashed potatoes. Stir in the cheese.
3. Heat oven to 350 degrees. Mound the mixture in the potato shells (for extra beauty, pipe the mixture in through a pastry bag with a wide star tip). Whisk the remaining egg with a teaspoon of water, and brush the tops of the stuffed potatoes with this mixture. Bake them for 30 minutes, until nicely browned on top and hot all the way through.

Mashed Potato No-No's—
What Makes 'Em Gluey, Watery, or Lumpy

Here are some troubleshooting tips for common mashed potato problems:

- Lumpy mashed potatoes can be avoided by fully cooking the potatoes, so they mash very easily with a potato masher or stiff wire whip.
- Leaving the potatoes in their cooking water after they're done may result in watery, washed-out tasting mashed potatoes. Most chefs drain them well after cooking, put them back in the pot, and place the pot over a low burner to cause excess water to steam off.
- Too much mashing, or using the wrong (i.e., very starchy, like an Idaho russet) type of potato can result in gummy, gluey consistency.

For Supersmooth Spuds

Pro chefs often force cooked potatoes through a device known as a "ricer" to break up any lumps and avoid over-mashing, which could result in gluey or gummy mashed potatoes. The ricer looks much like an oversized garlic press, with a plunger and a grate with small holes. You'll find them at better kitchen supply stores or from one of the equipment suppliers in our Resources Appendix.

Old-Fashioned Glazed Carrots

For added finesse to this lovely classical dish, cut the carrots on a 45-degree bias, rotating them a quarter-turn after each cut, to make an angular shape chefs refer to as "oblique."

Serves 8

1 pound carrots, peeled, cut into 1-inch chunks
2 tablespoons unsalted butter
½ cup water
1½ teaspoons sugar
¼ teaspoon salt

Combine all ingredients in a heavy-bottomed skillet or pan large enough to accommodate a crowded single layer. Over medium-high heat, simmer about 5 minutes, then toss or flip the carrots. Continue cooking until the liquid is mostly evaporated, and what remains is a glaze adhering to the carrots. Be careful not to go too far, or the glaze will break and become oily.

Chapter Five

Grains, Beans, and Legumes

Red Beans and Yellow Rice

Serves 8

Dominican Red Beans:

1 medium onion, chopped
3 cloves garlic, sliced
3 tablespoons olive oil
1 teaspoon oregano
2 bay leaves
*1 (8-ounce) can Goya brand
   Spanish-style tomato sauce*
*2 teaspoons adobo con pimienta
   (seasoned salt with white
   pepper)*
*1 packet Goya brand sazón
   (optional)*
*1 (16-ounce) package red beans
   soaked overnight in 1 quart cold
   water, drained*
*½ small bunch fresh cilantro,
   including stems, roughly chopped
   (optional)*

1. Sauté onions and garlic with olive oil over medium heat for 5 minutes in a pot large enough to hold all ingredients. Add oregano, bay leaves, tomato sauce, *adobo*, and *sazón*. Bring to a simmer and add beans and cilantro, adding enough water to cover them (about 3 cups).
2. Bring to a boil, then reduce to a low simmer, and cook 90 minutes, until beans are tender enough to mash between 2 fingers.

Yellow Rice:

3 tablespoons oil
*2 tablespoons achiote (annatto
   seeds)*
1 medium onion, chopped
1 tablespoon adobo con pimienta
*4 cups long-grain rice, such as
   Canilla or Goya brand*

1. Heat *achiote* in oil, in a large pot with a tight-fitting lid, over a medium-high flame until seeds sizzle and give up their color. Oil should be a dark orange hue. Remove from heat and carefully remove seeds with a slotted spoon or skimmer.
2. Add onion and *adobo* to *achiote* oil and sauté over medium heat for 5 minutes, until translucent. Add rice, and stir until it is well coated with oil. Add 6 cups water, and raise flame to high.
3. Bring to boil, and then reduce to simmer, cover tightly, and cook 20 minutes, until all water is absorbed. Remove from heat and let stand, covered, 5 minutes. Fluff with a fork

Rice and Beans World Tour

Steaming plates of rice and beans conjure up images of mom's home cooking. Like sleeping late or downing a milkshake, the aromatic Latino staple satisfies in a tangible way. Aromatic vapors waft noseward carrying hints of oregano, garlic, and perhaps tomato or smoked chili.

Cheap chow, nutritious and filling rice and beans soothe the soul for pennies a plate. They can be made in advance, and are actually better the second day. And there's a virtual rainbow coalition of options. Skin color clues you in to whose recipe it is. Black beans are Cuba's favorite, while the Dominican Republic serves predominantly red beans. Mexicans choose pintos for *frijoles refritos* (refried beans) and Italian influence in South America led Peru and Ecuador to favor white beans. Puerto Rico is home of *gandules* (pigeon peas) and *habachuelas rosatas* (pink beans). In the Spanish-speaking world, rice and bean recipes are as important as their language.

Mexico has different components in its rice-and-beans-based cuisine than the Caribbean islands do. Vegetarians should ask what's in the recipe when ordering beans and rice in ethnic restaurants. Calling them *"frijoles"* instead of the Caribbean-Spanish *"habachuelas,"* south-of-the-border chefs make their beans richer with the addition of pork drippings or lard to offset spicy, chili-infused regional specialties. But many places make their beans vegetarian. Scooping up rice and beans in corn or flour flat breads (*tortillas*), the staples often become part of the Mexican versions of sandwiches: *tacos, burritos,* and *tortas*. Leftover vegetables atop *arroz y frijoles* in a store-bought flour tortilla is a wrap.

Although Mexicans use many types of beans, including black (*veracruzanos*) and white beans (*aluvias*), the most common are pinto beans (*pintas*). The famous dish *frijoles refritos* is often translated as "refried beans," but actually means "very fried beans," since the brothy, precooked beans are fried until almost dry. Mexicans habitually add the prefix "*re*" to words for emphasis. Before frying, these beans are cooked much the same way as on the islands: simmered slow and low.

Rice can be as simple as fluffy white grains, or as elaborate as vegetable-scented Mexican rice. Caribbean cooks tint rice yellow with seeds of the annatto tree (*achiote*), and flavor it with olives, peppers, and onions. No self-respecting Latino cook would use par-boiled ("converted") rice. Long-grain whites, like those sold by Goya, Canilla, and Adolphus are fine. Rice can be reheated easily in the oven or microwave. Beans are generally better the second day, after the flavors marry. Quickly cooled after cooking, they freeze well or keep in the refrigerator for about one week.

Red Beans and Rice Pie with Oregano and Tomatoes

This warm, herb-laced pie is made in two simple stages. First, the pie shell is pre-baked. Then it is filled with already-cooked ingredients, and baked a second time, allowing the flavors to marry. Rice and beans have long been recognized by nutritionists as providing the building blocks for proteins required for good health.

Serves 6

1 medium onion, chopped
1 tablespoon olive oil
½ bunch fresh oregano, roughly
   chopped, **or** 1 tablespoon dried
1 (15.5-ounce) can red kidney beans,
   drained and rinsed
Salt and pepper to taste
1 egg, beaten
1 cup brown rice, cooked
1 16-ounce can stewed tomatoes, drained

Pie Dough:

1 cup pastry **or** all-purpose flour
¼ teaspoon salt
6 tablespoons unsalted butter, cold,
   cut into small pieces
About 3 tablespoons water, ice-cold
1 bag dried beans (any kind) for
   prebaking the crust

1. Make the pie dough in advance: Mix together the flour, salt, and butter with your hands until butter is mostly, but not completely incorporated. Add the water, a little at a time, mixing until the dough comes together. Knead briefly, just to smooth out. Some small nuggets of butter may still be seen in the dough, which will make the crust flaky. Wrap the dough in plastic and refrigerate for no less than 30 minutes.
2. Roll the dough thin (¼-inch), on a floured surface, mold into a buttered 9-inch pie pan, and trim the edges. Cover with wax paper, then fill with dried, uncooked beans, and bake 25–30 minutes in a 350-degree oven until golden. This precooking is called "blind baking" the pie shell. Allow to cool before removing the baking beans. Throw these beans away, or use for another pie crust.
3. Meanwhile, sauté onion in olive oil until translucent, add the oregano, and cook for 1 minute longer. Toss in the red beans, season with salt and pepper, and remove from heat. Separately, stir beaten egg into cooked brown rice.
4. Spread half of rice-egg mixture into bottom of pie shell. Distribute beans evenly over the rice, and layer on 1 can of stewed tomatoes. Cover with remaining rice. Bake for 30 minutes at 350 degrees.

Puerto Rican Gandules (Pigeon Peas) ⊻

Pigeon peas are the beloved bean of Puerto Rico, where they are served over oily long-grain white rice.

Serves 6

1½ cups pigeon peas, soaked overnight, rinsed and drained
1 tablespoon olive oil
1 small Spanish onion, chopped
⅓ green pepper, chopped
2 cloves garlic, minced
2 bay leaves
1½ teaspoons salt
¼ teaspoon fresh ground black pepper
¼ cup chopped fresh thyme **or** *1 tablespoon dried*
1 medium tomato, seeded, chopped

1. Simmer beans in 4 cups water for 1 hour, until tender. Meanwhile, heat the olive oil in a 10-inch skillet, then add onion, green pepper, garlic, bay leaves, salt and pepper, and thyme, and sauté until onion is translucent (about 5 minutes). Add chopped tomato and cook 2 minutes more.
2. Add the vegetables to the beans and cook 45 minutes more, until beans are very soft. Serve with white or yellow rice.

Soaking Beans

Dried beans, when submerged for several hours or overnight, absorb much water, and swell to as much as 150 percent of their original size. They'll cook much more quickly than starting from dried, and the results may be more even, especially if the beans are old. Never cook them in the soaking water. Soaking is seldom truly necessary, and I usually cook them right from the bag (after washing them, of course).

Quinoa Salad with Tomatoes and Cilantro Ⅴ

Quinoa, an ancient grain, which has made a comeback in the last few years due to much attention from high-profile chefs, has a very attractive light golden hue, a springy, crunchy texture, and the kernels have an appealing, ringletlike shape. It cooks quickly.

Serves 6

1 cup quinoa, boiled for 15 minutes, drained
1 cup Red and Yellow Plum Tomato Chutney (page 179)
¼ teaspoon kosher salt
1 tablespoon extra-virgin olive oil (herb-infused olive oil is great here. Try rosemary flavored.)

Combine the cooked quinoa and tomato chutney. Season to taste. Dress with olive oil, and serve with extra olive oil at the table.

Spinning Straw into Gold: Risotto Cakes "Restaurantize" Leftovers

Chefs have tricks that turn the mundane into the memorable. One of them is salvaging leftovers by transforming them into individual garnishes like risotto cakes. Spread leftover risotto in a one-inch layer in whatever flat pan it will fit. Refrigerate for a day or two; then use a cookie cutter or knife to make shapes. Dip them top and bottom in coarse cornmeal, and panfry the cakes until golden. The outside will be crispy and brown, while the inside will retain the saucy consistency for which risotto is famous.

Minted Sweet Peas

Serves 4

2 cups shelled fresh peas (about 2 pounds unshelled)
½ teaspoon sugar
2 tablespoons margarine
Salt and pepper to taste
3 tablespoons chopped fresh mint leaves

Simmer the peas and sugar until bright green and tender, about 5 minutes; drain. Toss peas with butter, salt, pepper, and mint.

Fresh Seasonal Shell Beans

Fresh beans are one of the harbingers of spring. When you see fava beans, cranberry beans, and sweet green peas in the pod at the greenmarket, the balmy days of summer can't be far off. There's something therapeutic about the process of cracking open these bean pods and scooping out the beans. And there's a sweet smell and taste to fresh beans that can't be duplicated with dried. Favas have a thick skin around each bean, which slips off easily once the beans have been quick-boiled for a minute. Other shell beans you may find fresh include limas and pintos. And green peas are a must in season.

Shelling peas is one of the great pleasures of springtime cooking. Snap open a pod and run your fingers through its smooth, waxy lining to release the fruit. Pea pods are aromatic and, as you shell, your fingers will pick up the scent of a garden. You may find the aroma so intoxicating that you'll be tempted to crunch on the sweet-smelling pod itself. Do. Yes, it's more or less rabbit food, with no nutritional value and virtually impossible to digest, but it tastes good. A trick my grandfather taught me was to bend a piece of pod inside out until it snaps, then peel back the tough outer skin like you would the backing of a self-adhesive sticker, revealing the moist inner flesh. Enjoy!

Sushi Rice

Contrary to popular belief, the term "sushi" does not connote raw fish. Instead, it refers to the vinegar-seasoned short-grain rice central to the Japanese diet. Sushi forms the base for delicious appetizers and dinners, which need not involve any fish at all. The best rice for sushi is short-grain Japanese-style rice. If unavailable, other short-grain varieties, such as Italian arborio or carnaroli are acceptable.

Yields 4½ cups

2 cups Japanese-style short-grain rice
1 one-inch square kelp (optional)
3 tablespoons sake (optional)
¼ cup rice vinegar

1 tablespoon sugar
½ teaspoon salt

1. In a bowl or pot, under cold running water, rinse the rice very well, agitating it with your hands until all the starch has been washed off and the wash water runs clear; drain. Place the drained rice in a pot with a tight-fitting lid, along with the kelp and 2¼ cups water. Cover pot, and bring to a boil; lower to a simmer. Cook until all water is absorbed, about 8 minutes. Remove from heat, and let stand, covered, for at least 10 minutes.
2. Combine the sake, vinegar, sugar, and salt. Transfer the rice to a large bowl; sprinkle with vinegar mixture and gently fold to combine. Spread rice onto a large sheet pan or platter to cool and dry, fanning and gently turning it occasionally. Keep covered and slightly warm for use in making sushi preparations.

Sushi-Rolling Mats

Ten-inch square bamboo mats for rolling sushi help to maintain even pressure when folding seasoned rice into sheets of dry-roasted seaweed called nori. This is how sushi rolls, or "maki," are made. While not essential (I've rolled sushi without a mat many times), these tools are inexpensive and helpful in making your sushi more attractive. They're often sold in sushi-making "kits," along with wooden paddles for handling rice, and other accoutrements, at supermarkets' Japanese foods areas.

Common Sushi-Related Ingredients

Wasabi: ground Japanese horseradish root; spicy enough to tickle your nose with a peacock feather. It's usually ground into a green paste. Rarely sold fresh in the United States, it's available as an instant powder or, increasingly, prepared paste sold in tubes.

Nori: roasted seaweed sheets. With an herbal, vegetal scent, these black or black-green sheets are at once crispy and pliable. Nori is used to wrap short-grained, vinegared rice for sushi. Cone-shaped wraps are called hand rolls, while cylinders are "maki." Extra-thin julienne of nori are also available for those who prefer to skip the rolling, and simply garnish their rice with flavorful, nutritious weeds of the briny deep.

Rice Vinegar: less acidic than American wine vinegar. It has a clean taste and is as clear as water. In combination with sugar, it's used to flavor the rice for sushi. If you can't find it, use another mild vinegar, such as cider vinegar.

Pickled Ginger: thin slivers of fresh ginger root in a sweet cure; often tinted pink. It's traditional to chew a piece of pickled ginger in between bites of sushi to refresh the palate.

Sake: Japanese rice wine. It is excellent in marinades, and useful for brightening up sleepy flavors.

Shoyu: milder Japanese soy sauce. It is often used with sushi.

Mirin: sweet rice wine. It is used for flavoring marinades and sometimes for sushi rice.

Sushi Rice: short-grain Japanese-style rice. With high starch content, this rice sticks to itself when cooked, allowing it to be shaped into handrolls, maki, and sushi portions.

Make Your Own Pickled Ginger

Pink, sweet, refreshing, and mildly spicy, pickled ginger pops up on every plate of sushi. If you can't find commercially made stuff, don't fret. Slice ginger as thin as you can (it's especially easy with a mandolin), simmer it with a pinch of saccharin or Sweet-N-Low, water, and a dash of grenadine, grape juice, or beet juice for color. Chill for a half hour before serving.

Avocado Kappa Maki Sushi Rolls

These crunchy, simple rolls feature protein-rich tofu. They're equally delicious made with brown sushi rice, a heart-healthy option.

Yields 6 rolls

1 recipe Sushi Rice (page 120), 4½ cups total
7 sheets of nori
1 cup fine julienne of cucumber (I use a mandolin to make these strips extra fine)

1 ripe Hass avocado, cut into thin strips, sprinkled with lemon juice and salt
*½ recipe marinated tofu (from Tofu Salad, page 24), store-bought marinated tofu, **or** flavored tempeh, cut into small strips*
2 teaspoons wasabi

Place one sheet of nori on a sushi-rolling mat (see "Sushi-Rolling Mats," page 120), long edge toward you. Spread about ¾ cup rice onto the nori, leaving a 1-inch strip free at the far end. Use your hands, moistened with water, to smooth the rice into an even layer. At the part closest to you, spread a thin line of wasabi. Arrange a sixth of the cucumber, a sixth of the avocado, and a sixth of the tofu into a strip near the wasabi-laced edge. Using the mat as a helper, roll the assembly jelly-roll style away from yourself. Keep pressure even and firm, and keep the mat clear of the roll. Repeat the procedure with remaining nori and fillings. Allow to stand for 5 minutes before slicing each roll into 6 pieces. Serve with wasabi and pickled ginger.

All-Purpose Asian Dipping Sauce

For crisp fried snacks like spring rolls, tempura, and chips to hot dim-sum dumplings or chilled vegetables, an easy dipping sauce can be whipped up in a minute by combining equal amounts of soy sauce and rice vinegar, and sprinkling in a few drops of Asian sesame oil. For extra flavor, add chopped or julienne fresh ginger and/or a few sesame seeds.

Chickpeas in Potato-Onion Curry

Thirty-minute main dishes like this are a lifesaver when you come home hungry and nothing's ready. Put on a pot of basmati rice before you start this dish, and you'll be dining before you know it.

Serves 4

2 cups onions, cut into 1-inch pieces
3 tablespoons oil, divided
1½ cups cubed (1 inch) potatoes
1 can (14 ounces) coconut milk
1 can (15 ounces) chickpeas (garbanzos), drained and rinsed
5–6 cloves garlic, peeled
1 teaspoon kosher salt
1½ teaspoon ground coriander
½ teaspoon ground turmeric
1 teaspoon chili powder
1 teaspoon ground cumin
Juice of ½ a lemon

1. In a skillet over high heat, cook the onions in 1 tablespoon oil until lightly browned, about 5 minutes. Add the potatoes and coconut milk; cover and cook until potatoes are tender, about 20 minutes; add the chickpeas. In a food processor, combine the garlic, salt, coriander, turmeric, chili powder, and cumin; process until it becomes a paste, scraping down sides as needed.
2. Heat remaining oil in a small skillet, and fry the garlic mixture for 1 minute, allowing it to become fragrant and slightly browned. Add the garlic mixture to the chickpea pot. Simmer for 2 to 3 minutes; season to taste with lemon and additional salt. Serve with basmati rice and/or Indian breads.

Indian Chapati Pan Bread

The fastest, easiest bread I ever made, this recipe takes under an hour for sixteen breads. It's the traditional partner to Indian curries, which are eaten by scooping up morsels into the bread, to be eaten from the hand. If you work with a partner, one of you can be cooking the chapatis while the other one rolls, saving up to a quarter of preparation time.

Yields 16 chapati

1 cup chapati flour (Indian whole wheat flour)
⅓ cup warm water (generous)
1 teaspoon oil

1. In a mixing bowl, make a well in the center of the flour. Pour the warm water and oil into this depression; fold ingredients together with a fork until a dough forms. Knead the dough in the bowl for 10 minutes. It should be smooth and elastic.
2. Divide the dough into 4 pieces. Roll 1 of the pieces against the table with your hands to form a cylinder; cut the cylinder into 4 nuggets. Cover remaining dough with a damp cloth while you work. Form each nugget into a ball the size of a marble, and roll it on a floured surface with a rolling pin into thin disks (¹⁄₁₆-inch—a little thicker than a CD). Repeat with remaining dough. They can be stacked.
3. Heat an iron skillet over a medium flame for 5 minutes, until hot enough for a drop of water to sizzle on it. Dust off the excess flour from a chapati and place it flat into the dry pan. Leave it until bubbles and air pockets are visible on the top; flip it to cook the other side. Some brown spots are fine. Repeat with remaining dough. Stack the cooked chapatis on a plate, and cover with a dry towel to keep warm.

Avocado-Beet Wraps with Succotash [V]

Serves 4

4 flour tortillas (10-inch diameter or larger)
2 tablespoons vegan mayonnaise **or** vegan sour cream
2 cups Succotash Salad (page 11)
1 large **or** 2 small beets (about 8 ounces), boiled until tender,
    peeled (see "How to Peel Cooked Beets with a Towel," page 36)
1 ripe Florida avocado, peeled and cut into 1-inch wedges
Kosher salt

1. Soften and lightly brown the tortillas by placing them directly over the burner of a gas stove, and flipping them until the surface blisters slightly (alternately, steam, broil, or toast them for a minute until soft). Spread ½ tablespoon of mayonnaise into a line across the center of each tortilla. Spoon ½ cup of succotash onto each tortilla. Halve the beets, and cut the halves into ½-inch slices. Divide the beets and avocado slices evenly onto the tortillas, placing them on the side of the succotash line closest to you.
2. Place 1 of the tortillas on a work surface directly in front of yourself. Fold the near edge of the tortilla over the fillings, and roll it, jellyroll fashion, away from yourself, keeping even pressure to ensure a tight roll. Place seam-side-down on a plate; repeat with remaining tortillas.

Kasha Varnashkas

This is my mother's recipe, more or less, for a classic Jewish dish I loved as a child. While Jewish cooking is pretty meat-o-centric, there are a few really good vegetarian dishes like this one.

Serves 8

2 cups coarse **or** medium granulation kasha (toasted buckwheat)

2 eggs (**or** 3 egg whites)

4 cups stock **or** water, hot

3 tablespoons butter **or** margarine

1 tablespoon olive oil

1 medium onion, roughly chopped

1 package (10 ounces) mushrooms, sliced

1 pound bow-tie shaped pasta (farfalle) **or** egg noodles, cooked medium-soft

1 can (10.5 ounces) condensed cream of mushroom soup

Salt and pepper to taste

1. Heat a large skillet over high heat. Combine kasha and eggs, and mix with a wooden spoon until well coated. Pour the kasha mixture into the hot pan, and cook, stirring and breaking up lumps, until the egg has dried onto the kasha, and grains are separate. Add the hot stock and the butter carefully (it may spatter). Lower flame to low heat, cover tightly, and cook 7–10 minutes, until all liquid is absorbed.

2. In a separate pan, heat the olive oil. Sauté the onions and mushrooms together until soft, about 5 minutes. In a mixing bowl, combine the cooked kasha, onions, mushrooms, cooked pasta, and cream of mushroom soup; mix well. Salt and pepper to taste. Transfer to a casserole and bake 20 minutes at 350 degrees until hot and slightly crusty on top.

Vegan Chili

This hearty warm-up goes especially well with Spicy Southwestern Corn-bread (page 315) and a tall glass of lemonade.

Serves 8

¼ cup olive oil
2 cups chopped onions
1 cup chopped carrots
*2 cups chopped assorted bell pep-
pers*
2 teaspoons salt
1 tablespoon chopped garlic
*2 chopped, seeded jalapeño pep-
pers*
*1 tablespoon ground ancho chili
pepper (see "¡Hola! I Must Be
Going: Mexican Specialty Foods,"
page 61) **or** ½ teaspoon
crushed red pepper flakes*
1 chipotle in adobo, chopped
*1 tablespoon toasted cumin seeds,
ground (see "Toasting Spices,"*

*page 32) **or** 4 teaspoons
ground cumin, toasted briefly
in a dry pan*
*1 (28-ounce) can plum tomatoes,
roughly chopped, juice included*
*3 (16-ounce) cans beans: 1 each
red kidney, cannellini, and
black beans, rinsed and
drained, **or** an equal amount
of home-cooked beans (start
with about 1½ cups dried
beans)*
1 cup of tomato juice
Finely chopped red onions
Chopped fresh cilantro

1. Heat the oil in a heavy-bottomed Dutch oven or soup pot. Add the onions, carrots, bell peppers, and salt; cook 15 minutes over medium heat, until the onions are soft. Add the garlic, jalapeños, *ancho*, chipotle, and cumin; cook 5 minutes more.
2. Stir in tomatoes, beans, and tomato juice. Simmer about 45 minutes. Serve garnished with red onions and cilantro.

Wheat and Corn Wraps with Tofu Ⅴ

Neater to eat and easier to carry than sandwiches, wraps like these are catching on all over. Substitute almost any grain you like for the wheat berries used here.

Serves 4

½ cup wheat berries, spelt, faro **or** *other whole grain, boiled until tender, usually about 30 minutes*

2 ears corn, kernels sheared from the cob and boiled 1 minute, **or** *1 package (10 ounces) frozen sweet corn, thawed.*

Juice of 1 lemon

1 tablespoon extra-virgin olive oil

½ teaspoon ground cumin

Salt and pepper to taste

2 tablespoons salad dressing

4 medium flour tortillas (10–12-inches)

½ recipe marinated tofu from Tofu Salad (page 24), **or** *1 cup store-bought flavored tofu*

1. In a bowl, toss the cooked grain, corn, lemon juice, olive oil, salt, and pepper until combined.
2. Spread the dressing in a line across the equator of each tortilla. Spoon in the grain salad; arrange the tofu alongside the grain.
3. Roll, jellyroll style, away from yourself. Tuck in ends.

The Frozen Veggie Whack

Frozen vegetables are not only a great convenience, but surprisingly nutritious. In many cases, they retain more of their natural nutrients than fresh vegetables in the produce section, due to the rapid loss of nutrient value at room temperature once a vegetable is picked. One problem though, is that frozen vegetables are sometimes a pain in the neck to work with because they freeze into a solid rock. One easy (and emotionally therapeutic) solution to petrified veggies is to slam the sealed packet against the floor, refrigerator door, local congressman's head, or any other flat, hard surface to unstick the vegetables from one another.

Fried Rice with Green Peas and Egg

An all-purpose fried rice that can be adapted to your taste—try it with sliced mushrooms, snow peas, water chestnuts, or your own favorite garnishes.

Serves 4

3 eggs, beaten
*2 tablespoons peanut **or** other oil*
2 tablespoons chopped ginger
2 tablespoons chopped garlic
½ cup chopped scallions
4 cups cooked white rice
1 package (10 ounces) frozen green peas
1 small carrot, peeled, diced, and blanched (optional)
1 tablespoon soy sauce (optional)
Sesame seeds, for garnish (optional)

1. Heat a 10-inch nonstick skillet with a few drops of oil over medium heat; add the eggs. Cook without stirring until completely cooked through, about 3 minutes. Slide the cooked egg sheet onto a cutting board; let it cool for 5 minutes. Roll the egg into a cylinder, and crosscut to form long julienne.
2. Heat the oil in a large skillet or wok. Add the ginger, garlic, and scallions, and cook for 1 minute; they should sizzle. Add the rice. Over high heat, chop and stir the rice to break up any lumps; cook until very hot, and some rice forms crunchy bits, about 5 minutes. Add the peas, and the carrots if using. Cook until peas are hot, then stir in the egg julienne, and soy sauce if desired. Serve garnished with additional chopped scallions and/or sesame seeds.

Tuscan White Bean Ragout

Eaten on its own, or as a base for a larger item, such as Polenta with Butter and Cheese (page 142), Wild Rice Vegetable Pancakes (page 132), or Grilled Marinated Portobello Mushrooms (page 227), this hearty stew packs flavor and nutrition.

Serves 8

*1 pound great Northern (large white) beans, cooked very soft (see "Bean There . . . Working with Dried Beans," page 16); retain cooking liquid (**or** one 28-ounce can of large white beans)*

2 tablespoons olive oil

2 tablespoons chopped garlic (about 5 cloves)

2 medium onions, diced

*2 teaspoons chopped fresh rosemary, **or** one teaspoon dried rosemary leaves*

*1 dried New Mexico chili, **or** ¼ teaspoon crushed red pepper flakes*

*1 head escarole (about 6 cups washed leaves), **or** an equal amount of spinach, torn into large pieces*

6 ripe plum tomatoes, seeded and diced (about 1½ cups)

2 ounces unsalted butter

¼ cup roughly chopped Italian parsley

½ cup grated Parmigiano Reggiano cheese (optional)

Kosher salt and freshly ground black pepper

A few drops top quality extra-virgin olive oil (flavored, if desired—see "Flavored Oils," page 83)

1. Strain the cooking liquid from the beans and reserve (you should have about 2 cups of liquid—add water if necessary to reach this amount). Heat the olive oil in a large skillet or Dutch oven over medium heat; add the garlic and cook until it turns white and fragrant, only about 30 seconds. Stir in the onions, rosemary, and chili. Cook gently until the onions are very soft, about 10 minutes, stirring occasionally. Add the beans, and enough bean-cooking liquid to make the mixture brothy; simmer 5 minutes.

2. Stir in the escarole; simmer until it is all wilted. Add the tomatoes, butter, parsley, and cheese if using. Remove from the heat, and stir until the butter is melted in, adding additional bean liquid as necessary to keep it brothy. Season well with salt and pepper. Serve warm, drizzled with extra-virgin olive oil.

Note: This stew can be prepared through step 1, and refrigerated for up to 3 days. The flavors will mingle, and the dish will be even better.

Raj's Chickpeas in Tomato Sauce

This quick, delicious healthful dish can be thrown together in minutes using ingredients from the pantry. It was taught to me by renowned concert pianist Raj Bhimani, a lifelong vegetarian gourmet.

Serves 6

*2 tablespoons peanut **or** safflower oil*
1 tablespoon cumin seeds
1 tablespoon chopped fresh ginger
¼ teaspoon crushed red pepper flakes
1 large onion, halved and sliced into half-moons
1 medium can (15–20 ounces) tomatoes, either crushed or diced
Salt and black pepper
2 cans (15 ounces each) chickpeas (garbanzos), drained and rinsed
Chopped cilantro (optional)

1. Heat the oil in a large saucepan over medium heat. Add the cumin seeds and cook until they are fragrant, about 1 minute. Stir in the ginger, crushed red pepper, and onions; cook until the onions are soft, about 5 minutes. Add the tomatoes and cook 5 minutes more, until they become saucy.
2. Season the sauce with salt and pepper and add the chickpeas; cook 5 minutes more. Sprinkle with chopped cilantro, if desired. Serve with basmati rice and Indian breads, such as Chapati *(page 124).*

Wild Rice Vegetable Pancakes

Crunchy, earthy-tasting wild rice cakes satisfy a comfort-food-loving part of the soul. They're easy to make and can be kept at room temperature for hours before serving. Try them with Braised Red Cabbage (page 158), or as an appetizer, with a light Asian soy-vinegar dipping sauce.

Serves 6–8

4 ounces wild rice
1 cup julienne carrots (see "Mandolin: Prep Cooks' Secret Weapon")
1 cup julienne celery
1 cup julienne white onion
3 scallions, chopped

2 eggs
½ cup flour
Kosher salt and freshly ground black pepper
Olive oil for frying

1. Boil the wild rice in 2 quarts of lightly salted water until very tender and most grains have burst open, about 40 minutes. Drain, reserving liquid, and cool the rice by spreading it on a platter or pan. Toss the rice with the carrots, celery, onion, scallions, egg, and flour. Season with salt and pepper. Moisten with a few drips of rice-cooking liquid to help the mixture adhere to itself.
2. Heat 2 tablespoons olive oil in a nonstick skillet over medium heat until a piece of onion sizzles when added, about 2 minutes. Place quarter-cup mounds of rice mixture into the pan; shape them into rough-hewn pancakes. Cook without moving them until they brown on the first side and are visibly cooked around the edges, about 5 minutes. Flip the pancakes with a spatula, and cook until lightly browned. Drain. Serve.

Mandolin: Prep Cooks' Secret Weapon

A slim metal or plastic board with a planelike blade, known as a mandolin, makes cutting delicate julienne strips and paper-thin slices into child's play. Available in fine houseware stores, kitchen supply shops, and department stores like Macy's, these once-rare tools have become widely available and much simpler than they used to be. I recommend compact, inexpensive Japanese models, like the Benriner, which usually sell for about $25, and slips into a knife drawer easily.

How to Julienne

Matchstick-shaped cuts called "julienne" are not rocket science. They just require you to use a system. For hard vegetables like carrots, first cut two-inch lengths, then slice those lengths into thin slices, then lay the slices flat and crosscut them into thin strips.

I used to hate julienning curved vegetables like celery, but an Italian chef helped me let go of that anger. He said that vegetables are a natural product, and that all pieces aren't identical in nature, so if your julienne are uneven, no big deal. Hey, it's only food! Cut two-inch lengths, slice the lengths into planks as flat as you can make, starting with the top of the arched back part of the celery (Step 1), then crosscut just as you would a carrot (Step 2).

Of course, julienne of onions will be curved. Cut off the polar ends of the onion and halve it through the root end. Separate two or three petals at a time, and cut them into as close a semblance of ⅛-inch sticks as you can. That's all Julia Child would do.

For the easiest, most uniform julienne, shave off the blade of a mandolin. Mandolins are flat boards with cutting blades and crosscutting blades. You just slide your vegetable across these blades (using the plastic hand guard for safety!) and clean, uniform julienne tumble onto a waiting plate below. Inexpensive Japanese mandolins, which cost about $25 at a kitchenware shop, are about an inch thick, and as long as a wine bottle.

Step 1

Step 2

Wild Rice with Apples and Almonds

For extra texture with an Indian curry dinner, such as Aloo Gobi (page 150) or Curried Parsnips (page 102), serve them in a ring of this chewy, crunchy mixture of nuts and fruits.

Serves 8

½ cup wild rice
½ cup shelled almonds, whole or
   in slivers
1 tablespoon oil
1 large onion, roughly chopped
1 Rome or Golden Delicious apple,
   peeled, cored, and diced

¼ cup raisins
Salt and freshly ground black pepper
   to taste
1 tablespoon olive oil (**or** butter)
¼ cup chopped cilantro **or** parsley

1. Boil the rice in 2½ quarts salted water until tender, about 40 minutes; drain, saving cooking liquid. Crisp the almonds by toasting them dry until fragrant and visibly shiny (see "Toasting Nuts for Fresher Flavor and Crispness," page 313). Heat the oil in a large skillet or Dutch oven over medium heat for 1 minute. Add onions; cook until softened, about 5 minutes. Add the apples, raisins, and a splash of the rice cooking liquid. Cook 5 minutes more, until the apples are translucent.
2. Combine the cooked rice, the apple mixture, the nuts, and salt and pepper. Stir in olive oil (or butter), if desired, and serve garnished with cilantro or parsley.

Saving Cooking Liquids as "Stock"

Water and broth from boiled wild rice, simmered beans, blanched vegetables, soaked dry mushrooms, and other cooking processes are free gifts. These no-work byproducts come packed with flavor, nutrients, and body, ready to use in any soup, stew, or dish that calls for "water or stock." Freeze them in portion-size plastic tubs for use anytime. I even save the juices from stir-fry dinners, which are concentrated, so they add wonderful vegetal flavor without watering down other flavors.

Egyptian Lentils and Rice   [V]

Amino acids in the lentils and rice combine to form complete proteins, making this warming, comforting dish nutritionally powerful.

Serves 8

1 tablespoon olive oil
¼ teaspoon cumin seeds
1 medium onion, roughly chopped
1 cup rice
½ cup brown **or** green lentils

2 teaspoons juice plus ½ teaspoon
   zest from a lemon
1 teaspoon salt
3 cups vegetable stock **or** water

Heat the oil and cumin seeds in a medium saucepan over medium heat until the seeds are fragrant, about 30 seconds. Add the onion; cook until translucent, about 5 minutes. Stir in the rice and lentils, mixing with a wooden spoon until well coated. Add the lemon juice, zest, salt, and stock. Cover tightly and simmer until all water is absorbed, about 20 minutes. Remove from heat and allow to stand for five minutes before fluffing with a fork and serving. Goes great with a dab of Egyptian chili sauce ("harissa") or other chili paste.

Rinsing Rice

To make perfect rice, start by washing the grains thoroughly under running water. I usually pour as much rice as I plan to use into the pot I plan to cook it in, and run cold water on it, agitating it with my hand until the water is no longer cloudy, but runs clear. This washes off excess starch on the outside of the grains, eliminates any pesticides that may have been used wherever the rice was warehoused (especially important with Indian basmati rice), and rinses off that weird-tasting multivitamin spray that American makers put into "enriched" rice (such supplements are of negligible nutritional value, and are mainly a way for companies to fill out the government-mandated nutritional charts on the packaging).

Mexican Rice

*This rice combines nicely with Mexican Frijoles Refritos (page 143)
for an excellent lunchtime meal.*

Serves 6

1½ cups long-grain white rice
1 large tomato, peeled, seeded, and chopped
⅓ medium white onion, roughly chopped
1 clove garlic, peeled and roughly chopped
*⅓ cup peanut **or** safflower oil*
3½ cups vegetable stock
2 teaspoons salt
½ carrot, peeled and finely chopped
⅓ cup green peas (frozen are okay)

1. Soak rice in hot water for 15 minutes, then rinse and drain. Purée the tomato, onion, and garlic in a blender.
2. Fry the rice in the oil, in a large saucepot, until it turns light gold in color, about 10 minutes. Pour off excess oil. Stir in the tomato purée and cook until almost dry, about 3 minutes.
3. Add stock, salt, carrots, and peas, cover, and simmer over low heat for 18 minutes; liquid should be absorbed and rice tender. Remove from heat and let stand 5 minutes, then fluff with a fork.

Cuban Black Beans and Rice
(Moros y Cristianos)

V

Use the black beans in this recipe for many other uses, including Huevos Rancheros (page 276) and Black Bean Burritos (page 138).

Serves 8

Prepare the Beans:

1½ cups black beans, soaked
   overnight, drained
6 cups water
2 tablespoons vegetable oil
2 cloves garlic, minced
½ Spanish onion, finely chopped
¼ teaspoon ground cumin
¼ teaspoon oregano
1 bay leaf
1 teaspoon salt
¼ teaspoon fresh ground black pepper
½ cup chopped fresh cilantro leaves
   and stems

1. Simmer beans in water until very tender (about 90 minutes).
2. Meanwhile, heat the oil. Add the garlic, onion, cumin, oregano, bay leaf, salt, and pepper and sauté until onions are soft. Add this mixture to the beans and simmer 20 minutes more. Stir in cilantro.

Prepare the Rice:

1 clove garlic, peeled and crushed
   with the side of a knife
4 teaspoons vegetable oil
1½ cups long-grain white rice,
   rinsed and drained
2 cups water
1½ teaspoon salt

1. Sauté garlic gently in 3 teaspoons oil until it begins to brown. Add rice and stir to coat.
2. Add water and salt; bring to a boil, and cover. Lower heat and simmer 20 minutes.
3. Remove from heat; pour in remaining oil, and fluff to separate grains. Serve topped with a ladle of Cuban black beans.

Black Bean Burritos

It's probably no accident that these burritos (which can be made vegan by substituting soy cheese for the cheddar and Monterey jack) are a source of complete protein, since their origins are hot Mexican lands, where many local residents considered animal protein a luxury.

Serves 4

1 tablespoon oil
1 cup chopped onions
*4 large (12-inch) flour **or** whole wheat tortillas*
*1 cup shredded cheese, such as a combination of cheddar and Monterey jack **or** soy cheese*
*2 cups cooked brown **or** white rice, such as Mexican Rice (page 136), hot*

*1½ cups cooked black beans in sauce (such as Cuban Black Beans, page 137), hot, **or** 1 can of black beans (15 ounces), heated with some cumin and garlic*
½ cup Salsa Fresca (page 64) or chopped tomatoes and onions
1 ripe Hass avocado, peeled and sliced
½ cup fresh cilantro sprigs
Tofu Sour Cream (page 87, optional)

1. Brown the onions in the oil until soft. Soften a tortilla over a gas burner or in a hot oven (see "Softening Store-Bought Tortillas," page 52); place on a clean work surface. Spoon a quarter of the hot onions into a line, one-third the way up on the tortilla; sprinkle on a quarter of the shredded cheese. Immediately spoon on ½ cup hot rice; this should be hot enough to melt the cheese. Ladle on a quarter of the beans, including some of its sauce; top with the salsa, avocado slices, and cilantro.
2. Fold edge nearest to you up to cover the fillings. Fold side flaps in, to seal ingredients into a pocket. Roll the burrito away from yourself, keeping even tension, and tucking with your fingers as you roll. Repeat with remaining tortillas.

Easy Saffron Vegetable Risotto

This is about the fastest risotto you can make, and still achieve the creamy, saucy, flavorful dish of Northern Italy. The key is the gradual addition of hot liquid while stirring, which extracts natural starches in the short-grain rice, thickening the sauce. The dish is even better if you use freshly sautéed veggies, but frozen are a suitable convenience.

Serves 6

3 pinches saffron
*10 cups vegetable stock (**or** 5 cups canned vegetable broth combined with an equal amount of water)*
2 tablespoons olive oil
1 onion, roughly chopped
*1 pound short-grain Italian rice for risotto, such as arborio, carnaroli, **or** roma*

½ cup dry white wine
1½ cups grated Parmesan cheese
*1 pound frozen mixed vegetables, **or** an equal amount of sautéed fresh vegetables*
Salt and freshly ground black pepper to taste
1 tablespoon unsalted butter
Lemon wedges (optional)

1. Combine the saffron with 1 cup of the stock and let steep for 10 minutes; heat the remaining stock separately until hot but not boiling. Heat the oil in a heavy-bottomed saucepan over medium heat; add the onion and cook until translucent, about 5 minutes. Stir in the rice and mix with a wooden spoon until rice is well coated and begins to change color, about 5 minutes.
2. Add the white wine; cook until all wine is absorbed. Add the saffron mixture; cook, stirring, until the liquid is absorbed. Begin adding the hot stock in 1-cup increments, stirring each time until all the liquid is absorbed before adding the next cup, until rice is soft and creamy, and you have only 1 cup of liquid left. Fold in the cheese, vegetables, salt, pepper, and butter. Stir until well combined; remove from heat. Adjust consistency with remaining stock. Rice should have a saucy consistency and be soft, but still have a little bite. Serve with lemon wedges.

Wild Mushroom Risotto with Truffles

The earthy taste of wild mushrooms and the musky perfume of truffles marry incredibly well with the natural richness of risotto. This recipe works as well using dried wild mushrooms (see "True Grit," page 56), which are easier to find out of season. Practice with cultivated "exotics" like shiitake, cremini, and oyster mushrooms before delving into the $28-per-pound chanterelles.

Serves 8

4 tablespoons unsalted butter, divided
*6 shallots **or** 1 large onion, roughly chopped (about 1½ cups)*
1 pound assorted wild and exotic mushrooms (see "Fungus among Us," page 63)
*1 pound short-grain Italian rice for risotto, such as arborio, carnaroli, **or** roma*

½ cup dry white wine
10 cups Mushroom Vegetable Stock (page 71)
1½ cups grated Parmesan cheese
Salt and freshly ground black pepper to taste
*Fresh **or** canned truffle for shaving (optional)*
Lemon wedges (optional)

1. Melt 3 tablespoons butter in a heavy-bottomed saucepan over medium heat; add the shallots and cook until translucent, about 2 minutes. Add the mushrooms; cook 5 minutes more until they have wilted and given up some juices. Stir in the rice and mix with a wooden spoon until rice is well coated and begins to look chalky white, about 5 minutes.

2. Add the white wine; cook until all wine is absorbed. Start adding the hot stock in 1-cup increments, stirring each time until all the liquid is absorbed before adding the next cup, until rice is soft and creamy and you have only 1 cup of liquid left. Fold in the cheese, salt, pepper, and remaining 1 tablespoon of butter. Stir until well combined; remove from heat. Adjust consistency with remaining stock. Rice should have a saucy consistency and be soft, but still have a little bite. If using, shave white or black truffles over the finished plates at the table. Serve with lemon wedges.

Beet Risotto Cakes

Serves 10

2–3 medium-size beets (about
   1 pound), peeled and diced
   (¼-inch) **or** 2 cans (14.5 ounces
   each) beets, diced, liquid reserved
1 tablespoon red wine vinegar (if
   using fresh beets)
3 tablespoons butter, divided
1 large onion, chopped

1 pound Italian arborio short-grain
   rice for risotto
½ cup red wine (optional)
Vegetable stock **or** water
Kosher salt and freshly ground black
   pepper
1 cup grated Parmesan cheese
Cornmeal
Olive oil **or** butter for frying

1. If starting with fresh, cook the diced beets in enough water to cover them, along
   with the vinegar and a pinch of salt. Drain, reserving the cooking liquid. Combine
   the cooking or canning liquid with enough water to total 8 cups. Melt 2 tablespoons of butter in a large, heavy-bottomed saucepan; add the onions and cook
   until soft, about 5 minutes. Stir in the rice, and cook over medium heat until it
   attains a chalky, cooked color, about 5 minutes.
2. Add the wine to the cooking rice; stir constantly with a wooden spoon until all
   liquid is absorbed. Gradually start to add the stock mixture in ½-cup increments,
   stirring constantly, waiting until all liquid is absorbed before adding the next cup.
   Continue until rice is saucy, but still slightly "al dente." Season with salt and
   pepper; stir in the Parmesan, cooked beets, and remaining 1 tablespoon of butter.
   The risotto is now ready to be served as a soft entrée, garnished with Parmesan
   shavings. If using for Risotto Cakes, transfer mixture into a buttered 9" × 13" glass
   baking dish; set aside to cool. Refrigerate at least 4 hours or overnight, until risotto
   is firm to the touch.
3. Using a 3-inch cookie cutter or other shaping device (a 15-ounce can with both
   ends removed works quite well), cut out as many round cakes as you can (ball up
   and reflatten all the remaining bits). Heat a large nonstick skillet over medium heat;
   add 2 tablespoons olive oil or butter. Dip the flat surfaces of the risotto cakes in
   cornmeal, and fry them until a crisp crust forms and they are golden brown on the
   outside, hot on the inside, about 4 minutes per side. Serve hot or warm.

Polenta with Butter and Cheese

Delicious as a base for stews and ragouts, such as chunky tomato sauce, sautéed wild mushroom ragout, or a vegetable stew, polenta is also excellent when allowed to chill, then grilled or fried.

Serves 4

*4 cups water **or** stock, boiling*
1 teaspoon salt
*1 cup coarse yellow cornmeal
  (polenta)*

½ cup grated Parmesan cheese
1 tablespoon butter

1. Add salt to the boiling water. Whisking constantly with a stiff wire whisk, gradually pour cornmeal into water in a steady stream, whisking out any lumps. Continue whisking constantly until mixture thickens noticeably.
2. Lower heat to a very low simmer. You should see only the occasional bubble plopping up through the polenta—beware: The polenta is molten lava at this point, and spattering can be hazardous. Stir regularly with a wooden spoon until full thickening is achieved, about 25 minutes. Stir in cheese and butter; remove from heat. Serve immediately, or allow to cool for grilling or frying.

First Things Last

To make a meal in the shortest time possible, approach a menu by deciding what items you absolutely have to save until the last minute, and those that you absolutely must do first. For example, if you'll be serving Grilled Marinated Portobello Mushrooms (page 227), Polenta with Butter and Cheese, and a Warm Spinach Salad (page 31), you know that the warm salad will be the last thing you'll do, because it will wilt sorrowfully if you go on to do another project after making it. You know from reading the recipe that the polenta sits on a burner for a substantial time, and will stay hot for a very long time even after leaving the stove, so you'll put that on first. Everything else will fall into place after that. Generally, starches like rice, polenta, mashed potatoes, and grain pilafs go on first and green vegetables go on last.

Mexican Frijoles Refritos (Refried Beans)

The sweet-corny taste of pinto beans is favored by Mexican for this rich prepa-
ration, which is usually made with bacon fat, but sometimes with vegetable oil
instead for economical reasons.

Serves 6

Prepare the Beans:
½ pound pinto beans, washed
¼ white onion, roughly chopped
1 tablespoon oil
1 teaspoon salt

Bring beans to a boil with onions, oil, salt, and 5 cups water in a 2½-quart pot.
Lower flame and simmer 2½–3 hours, until very tender, skimming occasionally
and adding water if necessary to keep it brothy.

Fry the Beans:
½ cup chopped white onion
6 tablespoons olive oil
The cooked beans (about 4 cups with broth)

1. Cook the onions in the oil until translucent in a 10-inch skillet (iron is best), then
   add the beans (broth included) 1 cup at a time, mashing with a wooden spoon
   over high heat.
2. Constantly mash and stir until beans dry out and sizzle around the edges. They
   should start coming away from the surface of the pan. Rock the pan back and
   forth to make sure they loosen, and turn them out, omelet style, onto a warm
   serving platter.
3. Garnish with radishes, lettuce, shredded *queso blanco* (a fresh Mexican cheese
   sold in most Hispanic food sections) or feta cheese. Accompany with Mexican Rice
   (page 136).

Hummos bi Tahini with Sprouts and Cherry Tomatoes in a Pita Pocket Ⅴ

These beautiful, healthful sandwiches are colorful and attractive to serve when afternoon guests arrive. They're quick to make.

Serves 4

1 (15.5-ounce) can chickpeas (garbanzos), drained and rinsed
2 tablespoons tahini (sesame paste)
1 tablespoon ground cumin
Juice of 1 lemon (about 2 ounces)
⅓ cup, plus 1 tablespoon, olive oil
Coarse salt and freshly ground black pepper
4 (7-inch) loaves pita bread
1 cello box alfalfa sprouts
12 ripe cherry tomatoes, washed and halved

1. To make the *hummos* (hummus), purée together the chickpeas, tahini, cumin, and half of the lemon juice at high speed in a food processor. While machine is running, gradually add ⅓ cup olive oil. Adjust flavor to taste with salt, pepper, and remaining lemon juice.
2. Make an opening at the top of each pita, and slather each generously with hummos. Into each pocket, stuff a tuft of alfalfa sprouts the size of a golf ball, and 6 cherry tomato halves. Drizzle remaining olive oil over contents of all sandwiches. Serve with *pepperoncini* or other spicy pickles.

The Great Tahini

That hard-to-define, slightly smoky, slightly nutty dimension to many Middle Eastern foods is a fine-ground sesame seed paste called tahini. It's excellent in dressings, and combines beautifully with anything containing chickpeas for both wonderful flavors and complete proteins.

Granola

This crunchy, healthful cereal is a delicious snack, and travels well. Consider keeping some in your "emergency travel kit" (see "Feed Bag," page 87) for occasions where you might not be offered suitable vegetarian foods.

Serves 8

3 cups rolled oats (such as Quaker quick oats)
1½ cups wheat germ
*1 cup chopped walnuts, almonds, peanuts, **or** a combination*
1 cup shredded coconut
½ cup sesame seeds
½ cup nonfat dry milk
¼ cup oil
½ cup honey
1 cup brown sugar
1 cup raisins

1. Heat oven to 350 degrees. Spread the oats onto a baking sheet; bake for 15 minutes. Lower oven to 325 degrees.
2. In a large mixing bowl, combine the toasted oats with wheat germ, nuts, coconut, sesame seeds, nonfat dry milk, oil, honey, and brown sugar. Mix well with your hands. Transfer to a baking sheet; spread into a single layer. Bake for 10 to 15 minutes, until lightly browned. Toss with raisins. Cool to room temperature before serving.

Storing Nuts

Squirrels freeze their nuts under the cold ground in winter. Maybe they're not so stupid after all. Nuts go rancid within a couple of months at room temperature. Store them in the freezer, in airtight containers.

Green Rice Pilaf

Green with fresh herbs, this rice is a great stuffing for vegetables, base for curries, or accompaniment to a hearty vegetable stew.

Serves 4

3 tablespoons butter
2 cups chopped onion
2 cups long-grain rice
½ cup (packed) mixed chopped herbs, such as chives, chervil, tarragon, parsley, and dill
4 cups vegetable stock
Salt and pepper to taste
1 bay leaf

1. In a medium saucepan, melt the butter over a medium flame. Add the onion; cook until translucent, about 5 minutes. Add the rice; cook, stirring often, until the rice is well coated and becomes golden.
2. In a blender, combine the herbs, stock, salt, and pepper; blend until herbs are finely chopped. Add to the rice; bring to a boil, add the bay leaf, and then lower to a very slow simmer. Cover tightly; cook until rice has absorbed all liquid, about 25 minutes. Fluff with a fork, then cover and let stand for 5 minutes before serving.

Chapter Six

Leafy Greens and Cruciferous Vegetables

Artichokes in Court Bouillon with Lemon Butter

The elegant artichoke stands on its own as a self-contained snack or appetizer. Few foods offer the Zen-like feeling of methodically savoring them, leaf by leaf, until you reach the buttery, tender prize at the heart. Each part has its own character, from the earthy bits of meat on the outer leaves, to the sweet, wholly edible, purple-tinged inner leaves, to the vegetal bottom. This court bouillon is a standard cooking medium for artichokes.

Serves 4

4 whole artichokes (preferably pointed-leaf, not "globe" artichokes)

4 lemons

2 tablespoons whole coriander seeds

2 tablespoons salt

8 ounces salted whole butter

1. Trim the stems of the artichokes to about 2 inches. Bring 5 quarts water to a rapid boil. Halve 3 of the lemons, squeeze them into the boiling water, and toss the squeezed lemon fruits into the water, along with the coriander seeds and salt. Boil 5 minutes.

2. Place the artichokes in the cooking liquid and cover with a heavy plate or other object to keep them from floating. Boil until a paring knife, inserted where the stem meets the bottom, comes out very easily, about 15 minutes. Meanwhile, melt the butter in a microwave for 30 seconds on high, then mix with the juice of the remaining lemon.

3. Serve each person a whole artichoke, accompanied by a ramekin of butter sauce and a large bowl for discarded leaves. Eat the artichoke leaf by leaf, starting by dipping them in the butter and nibbling at the tender bits at the bottoms of the outer leaves, gradually reaching fully edible inner leaves. When you reach the hairlike "choke," scoop it out with a spoon, discard it, and carve the prized "heart" at bottom into pieces for easy consumption.

Spinach and Tomato Sauté

The subtle addition of coriander brings this dish an understated elegance, perfect for a dinner main course. Always wash spinach twice, submerging it in fresh water each time and agitating it well by hand. Growing low to the ground, spinach usually hides plenty of soil in its crevices.

Serves 4

3 teaspoons butter
6 plum tomatoes, roughly chopped
1 teaspoon coriander
2 bunches flat-leaf spinach, washed very thoroughly
½ teaspoon salt
Freshly ground black pepper

In a large skillet or heavy-bottomed Dutch oven, melt 2 teaspoons of the butter over medium-high heat. Add the tomatoes and coriander; cook until softened, about 5 minutes. Add the spinach in handfuls, allowing each handful to wilt before adding the next. Season it well with salt and pepper. Finish by swirling in the remaining butter.

Nonreactive Pots: Welcome to the Steel and Glass Generation

Aluminum and copper, commonly used materials in pots and pans, react with (and alter the flavor and color of) acidic foods. Always use pans with a stainless steel or glass cooking surface to avoid sour tomato sauce, discolored green beans, and "off"-tasting soups. For the lightweight and even heat of aluminum and copper, combined with the nonreactive property of steel, buy aluminum or copper alloy pots clad to a steel "jacket" (inner lining).

Aloo Gobi
(Cauliflower and Potato Curry)

V

This classic North Indian curry is a hearty main course. It's also an excellent filling for wraps known as roti. It's a natural with basmati rice and Indian Chapati Pan Bread (page 124).

Serves 8

1 large head cauliflower
2 pounds potatoes
3 tablespoons oil
2 large onions, finely chopped (about 5 cups)
4 jalapeño or other chili peppers, finely chopped
1 (1-inch) piece fresh ginger, finely chopped
3 tomatoes, finely chopped
1¼ teaspoons chili powder

1 teaspoon turmeric
1 teaspoon coriander
2 teaspoons kosher salt
1 teaspoon garam masala (spice mixture available at specialty stores—**or** make your own by combining 1 teaspoon each of ground cardamom, cumin seed, cloves, black pepper, and cinnamon)
Cilantro **or** parsley, chopped

1. Cut the cauliflower and potatoes into large chunks. Heat the oil in a heavy skillet over medium-high heat, and cook the onions, chilies, and ginger until brown, about 10 minutes. Add the tomatoes, chili powder, turmeric, coriander, and salt; cook 5 minutes more, until spices are fragrant and evenly disbursed. Mix in the potatoes and cauliflower, plus enough water to come halfway up the vegetables.
2. Cover the pan and cook for 20 minutes, stirring occasionally, until the potatoes and cauliflower are very tender. Add the garam masala powder; cook 5 minutes more. Serve garnished with cilantro.

Stir-Fried Asian Greens

$\boxed{V}$

Heaping ceramic bowls of jasmine rice with portions of this stir-fry consti-tute Asian "comfort food" at its best. This may require two large pans, or need to be cooked in two batches.

Serves 8

1 bunch (about 1 pound) collard greens, thinly sliced

1 small head (about 1 pound) Chinese cabbage (barrel-shaped napa cabbage), thinly sliced

1 bunch watercress, stem ends trimmed

2 tablespoons peanut oil

1 package (10 ounces) white **or** cremini mushrooms

1 large "horse" carrot **or** 2 cello carrots, peeled, sliced thinly on the bias (diagonal)

¼ pound snow peas, halved diagonally

1 medium red onion, halved and sliced with the grain

2-inch piece ginger, julienne

3 cloves garlic, finely chopped

Salt and white pepper to taste

2 tablespoons soy sauce

1 tablespoon Chinese cooking wine **or** dry sherry (optional)

1 teaspoon Asian sesame oil

Black sesame seeds **or** toasted white sesame seeds for garnish (optional)

Mix together the collards, cabbage, and watercress; wash thoroughly and dry. Heat the peanut oil in a large skillet (13 inches) over high heat until it is shimmery, but not smoky. Add the mushrooms, carrots, snow peas, onion, ginger, and garlic; sauté 2 minutes, stirring frequently, allowing some parts to brown. Season it well with salt and white pepper. Add the greens, soy sauce, wine, and sesame oil. Toss or stir; cook only 1 minute, until the greens begin to wilt. Serve immediately, with jasmine rice and a sprinkling of sesame seeds.

Shanghai Bok Choy with Garlic and Black Bean Sauce

V

Miniature jade green heads of Shanghai bok choy, often labeled "baby bok choy," are increasingly available in groceries where Asian greens are sold. If you can't find these attractive miniature heads, regular bok choy is fine, with stems and leaves cut into three-inch lengths.

Serves 4

8 heads Shanghai ("baby") bok
　　choy
2 cups Mushroom Vegetable Stock
　　(page 71) **or** other strong
　　vegetable stock
1 teaspoon sugar
1 tablespoon Chinese fermented black
　　bean sauce, **or** 1 teaspoon
　　Chinese fermented black beans
　　(both available from Asian
　　specialty stores, or check our
　　resources Appendix, page 325)

2 teaspoons hoisin sauce (available
　　in the Asian section of most
　　supermarkets)
2 teaspoons cornstarch, dissolved in
　　¼ cup cold water
2 teaspoons peanut **or** other oil
2 teaspoons (about 3 cloves)
　　chopped garlic
Salt to taste
Dash of Asian hot chili paste
　　(optional)

1. Halve the bok choy heads lengthwise, and blanch in rapidly boiling salted water for 3 to 4 minutes, until crisp tender (see "It's Easy Being Green," page 44). Drain and plunge immediately into ice water to stop the cooking. In a saucepan, bring the stock to a boil. Whisk in sugar, bean sauce **or** beans, and hoisin sauce. Simmer 10 minutes, then whisk in cornstarch slurry to thicken; cook 5 minutes more, covered. It should have the consistency of honey. Taste for seasoning.
2. Heat the oil in a skillet, over medium heat. Add garlic, and allow it to sizzle until it *begins* to turn golden brown. Immediately add the blanched bok choy, season lightly with salt, and cook until vegetable is warmed through. Add chili paste if desired. Transfer to a serving platter, and spoon on the black bean sauce, reserving any extra to be served on the side at the table.

Braised Swiss Chard

Handsome, broad-leafed, and cool, Swiss chard has come back into vogue in recent years, thanks in great part to the devotion of gourmet chefs and nutritionists who have rediscovered the striking beauty (especially of the red-veined varieties) and unearthed its cancer-fighting possibilities. The juicy stems and tender leaves are cooked separately.

Serves 4

*1 large bunch red **or** green Swiss chard (about 1½ pounds)*
*1 cup strong vegetable stock, mushroom stock, **or** liquid from cooking beans*
Salt and freshly ground black pepper to taste
1 tablespoon olive oil
2 medium shallots, finely chopped (about ¼ cup)
1 tablespoon unsalted butter
Lemon wedges

1. Wash the chard thoroughly under running water, and shake dry. Using your hands, tear the leafy parts away from the stems; set aside. Cut the stems into bite-size pieces. In a nonreactive skillet (see "Nonreactive Pots: Welcome to the Steel and Glass Generation," page 149), bring the stock to a boil; add the stem pieces. Season with salt and pepper; cook until tender. Transfer them to a bowl or plate, reserving their cooking liquid. Wipe out the skillet.

2. Return the skillet to the heat and add the olive oil and shallots. Cook 1 minute until they sizzle and soften slightly. Add the chard leaves, and cook only until they wilt. Add back the stems, plus 2 tablespoons of their cooking liquid. Bring to a simmer, and swirl in the butter. Taste for seasoning. Serve with lemon wedges.

Cabbage Stewed in Tomato Sauce

Hearty winter food like stewed cabbage goes beautifully with seasoned brown rice and some Mini Lentil-Scallion Pancakes (page 53).

Serves 8

2 tablespoons olive oil
1 medium onion, roughly chopped
1 small head green **or** *red cabbage (about 2 pounds, chopped)*
1 teaspoon caraway seeds
Salt and freshly ground black pepper
2 cups Basic Fresh Tomato Sauce (page 185) **or** *tomato sauce of your choice*
2 teaspoons brown sugar

Heat the oil in a large Dutch oven. Add the onions, and cook until they are translucent, about 5 minutes. Add the cabbage, caraway seeds, and a little salt and pepper; cook over medium heat until soft and saucy, about 5 minutes more. Stir in tomato sauce and brown sugar. Lower flame to a simmer, and cook covered, stirring occasionally, for 1 hour, until the cabbage is very tender and has taken on color from the sauce.

Spinach with Pine Nuts (Pignolia) and Garlic

V

Based on a Roman dish, this antioxidant-rich spinach dish picks up nuttiness not just from the pignolia, but also from the toasted garlic.

Serves 4

¼ cup pine nuts (pignolia)
3 tablespoons extra-virgin olive oil
2 cloves garlic, finely chopped
2 pounds washed spinach leaves, stems removed
Salt and freshly ground black pepper
Lemon wedges

1. Gently toast the nuts in a dry sauté pan until they start to brown. Set aside. In a very large pan, heat the olive oil and garlic over medium heat until it sizzles and starts to brown.
2. Add ⅓ of the spinach, and the pine nuts, and sauté until it's wilted, and lets off some liquid. Add the rest of the spinach in batches, seasoning with salt and pepper as it cooks. Serve with lemon wedges.

The Incredible Shrinking Spinach!

Leafy green vegetables look huge when they're taking up cubic yards of refrigerator space, but seem to shrivel into mouse-size portions when you cook them. They shrink to one-sixth their raw volume upon cooking. Stem trimmage also means they're less voluminous than you'd think. Figure on a half pound of raw greens per person (slightly less if the stems are eaten, as with Swiss chard).

Basic Buttered Brussels Sprouts

Brussels sprouts are an excellent fall and winter vegetable, which hold very well for a long time, making them perfect for busy working people who can keep them on hand in the refrigerator for whenever they're needed.

Serves 4

1 pint Brussels sprouts
2 ounces (½ stick) unsalted butter
Salt and white pepper
Pinch nutmeg (optional)

1. Remove outer leaves from sprouts, and trim the stems so that they're flush with the sprout bottoms. Halve the sprouts by cutting through the stem end.
2. Boil in small batches, in 4 quarts of well-salted, rapidly boiling water. Drain.
3. In a medium (10-inch) sauté pan, over medium heat, melt the butter, and add the cooked sprouts, tossing with the seasonings to coat. Serve with lemon wedges.

Where Vegetarians Shop

Seek out your nearest natural foods and/or "gourmet" specialty food shop. That's where you'll find the delectable grains, spices, chilies, and whole foods essential to healthy vegetarian life. Mainstream supermarkets carry most or all of what you'll see in this book, but you'll be surprised at the difference in quality (and sometimes, believe it or not, lower prices) you'll find at these stores.

Smoky Spiced Collard Greens with Turnip [V]

The smokiness in this dish comes from the chipotle chili, a smoked jalapeño pepper, available dried or canned in most supermarkets in the Mexican foods section, or at Latino specialty markets. For milder greens, remove the seeds and veins from the chili before use. Collards are high in usable calcium, essential in the vegetarian diet.

Serves 4

1 bunch collards or turnip greens
1 medium white turnip, peeled and diced into 1/4-inch pieces
1 medium onion, chopped
1 chipotle chili, dried or canned, cut in half
1 teaspoon salt
1 tablespoon olive oil
*1 cup vegetable stock **or** water*

1. Wash greens and remove the stems. Cut leaves into long thin strips (julienne).
2. In a heavy-bottomed pot, sauté the turnip, onion, and chili in olive oil until the onion is translucent. Add the greens and salt, and sauté a few minutes more, until greens are wilted.
3. Add stock or water, bring to a boil, and reduce heat to simmer for 20 minutes, or until greens are very tender and turnips are soft.

Braised Red Cabbage
(Chou Rouge à la Flamande)

This classic European winter dish pairs marvelously with Crisp Potato Pancakes (page 107) and a helping of Wild Rice with Apples and Almonds (page 134). Cruciferous vegetables, such as cabbage, broccoli, radishes, and collard greens, contain phytochemicals that may help to protect against some of the most deadly cancers.

Serves 8

1 small head red cabbage (about 2 pounds)
1 teaspoon salt
Pinch of grated nutmeg
1 tablespoon oil
1 tablespoon red wine vinegar
4 Granny Smith (pippin) apples, peeled and cut into ¼-inch slices
1 tablespoon brown sugar

Wash cabbage and discard tough outer leaves; quarter, core, and thinly slice it (julienne). Sprinkle shredded cabbage with salt and nutmeg. Heat oil in a large Dutch oven or ovenproof casserole dish with a tight-fitting lid; add cabbage and red vinegar. Cover and cook over a low heat for at least 1 hour, either on the stovetop or in a low (325 degree) oven. Add the apples and sugar; cook for another 30 minutes, until cabbage is very tender and apples are mostly dissolved.

Scented Escarole with Fennel

Serves 6 as an appetizer,
3 as a main dish

2 tablespoons extra-virgin olive oil
2 cloves garlic, finely chopped
1 small onion, finely chopped
12 cups coarsely chopped escarole
1½ teaspoons fennel seeds, lightly toasted in a dry pan
Salt and freshly ground black pepper
1 tablespoon grated Parmesan cheese (Parmigiano Reggiano)

1. Heat the oil over a medium heat. Add the garlic, and cook about 1 minute, until it starts to brown. Add onion, and cook to translucent, about 5 minutes.
2. Add the escarole and fennel seeds, season with salt and pepper, and cover. Cook until escarole is wilted, and simmer in its own juices. Remove cover, raise heat to medium-high, and cook to evaporate most of the liquid, about 5 minutes. Serve garnished with grated cheese.

More Than Milk? Calcium in Leafy Greens

It'd be great if all the good things said about leafy greens were true, but beware: While it's true that beet greens, spinach, chard, and rhubarb provide more calcium than dairy products, it is in a form that your body cannot use. A better source comes from fortified soy beverages, tofu processed with calcium, broccoli, nuts, legumes, and certain leafy greens such as kale, collards, and mustard greens.

Broccoli Florets with Lemon Butter Sauce

White butter sauce, or beurre blanc, is a simple, smooth base, which can be tailored to whatever it is served with—whole-grain mustard, herbs and/or various citrus flavors.

Serves 4

2 small shallots, finely chopped
¼ cup white cooking wine
Juice of 1 lemon
8 ounces cold, unsalted butter, cut into small pieces

Salt and white pepper
1 large head broccoli, broken into florets

1. Place the shallots, wine, and half of the lemon juice in a small saucepan, over a medium heat. Simmer until almost dry. Reduce heat to very low, and stir in a few small pieces of butter, swirling it in with a wire whisk until it is mostly melted. Gradually add the remaining butter, whisking constantly, until all is used, and sauce is smooth. Never boil. Season the sauce with salt, white pepper, and remaining lemon juice to taste. Keep in a warm place, but not over a flame.
2. Wash the broccoli and boil in 4 quarts of rapidly boiling, salted water. Drain, and serve with lemon butter sauce.

Antioxidants

Antioxidants are vitamins and other substances that help your body expel "free radicals," harmful byproducts of cellular oxygen use. Antioxidants are believed to have cancer-fighting properties, aid in heart regulation, and strengthen immune systems. Dark, leafy greens are high in antioxidants such as beta-carotene (which your body turns into vitamin A), selenium, and vitamins C and E. Scientists are still unsure exactly which antioxidants work on which parts of the body, so a balanced diet is still the best diet.

Creamed Spinach

To add richness and silky texture to a meal, add a spoonful of this savory classic vegetable dish to the plate. It works especially well as a counterpoint to crunchy foods like Crisp Potato Pancakes (see page 107) or toasted crostini (bread rounds).

Serves 4

2 pounds spinach, stemmed and washed
½ cup heavy cream
½ teaspoon salt
Grated nutmeg
Freshly ground black pepper

1. Heat a large nonreactive skillet or Dutch oven over medium heat, and cook the spinach with a few drops of water until just wilted. Drain, rinse, and squeeze dry in a colander. Chop the spinach finely.
2. In a skillet, bring the cream to a boil; add the salt, nutmeg, and pepper. Stir in the spinach; cook until most of the water has cooked out, and the spinach is thick. If desired, purée in a food processor.

Microbaked Potatoes

I've heard chefs malign microwaves for years, but I think not having one in your home today is slightly akin to not having a telephone. It's just wasteful to heat up the whole oven to warm a tiny plate of leftover lasagna. That said, I think there's plenty of microwave abuse going on, too. Heating bread in a microwave should be prohibited by law. It creates leathery chew sticks not fit for animal consumption. Jasper White, my mentor, said the microwave was best for drying flowers and softening ice cream that's too hard to scoop. But I think it's an excellent way to cook baked potatoes, especially if they're to be used for another recipe. The microwave is also one of the better methods for cooking small amounts of green vegetables—preserving color, flavor, and nutritional value.

Stuffed Cabbage

V

Comfort food like these neat little packets of rice feel like Thanksgiving all over again. This recipe is time-consuming, so plan on making it a day ahead, or on a leisurely day in the kitchen. They freeze well.

Serves 6

*1 head green cabbage (about
    1½ pounds), stem core cut out
2 tablespoons olive oil
1 large onion, roughly chopped
1 bunch of scallions, chopped
1 bunch of basil, leaves picked,
    washed well, and cut into julienne
½ cup chopped Italian parsley
1 teaspoon oregano*

*½ teaspoon thyme
Kosher salt and freshly ground black
    pepper
1 cup of cooked barley, spelt,
    brown rice **or** other whole grain
¼ cup puréed silken tofu
¼ cup vegetable stock
2 cups tomato sauce*

1. Bring a large stockpot of water to a boil; submerge the cabbage in it for about 5 minutes. Peel off the first few softened leaves, then put the cabbage back in to soften some more. Repeat this process until you have 12 softened leaves; cut the thick vein from their stem ends. Finely shred the remaining cabbage.
2. Heat the olive oil in a large skillet over high heat for 1 minute; add the chopped cabbage, onions, scallions, basil, parsley, oregano, and thyme. Season thoroughly with salt and pepper. Cover and cook until vegetables are tender, about 15 minutes, stirring occasionally; drain. Combine with cooked barley and puréed tofu. Taste for seasoning, adding more salt if necessary—it should be highly seasoned.
3. Place the softened cabbage leaves on a work surface, with the stem end closest to you. Distribute the filling onto the leaves, placing it closest to the stem end. Fold the sides in to envelop the filling, then roll away from yourself, providing even tension to keep the rolls plump. Place the rolls in a baking dish; add the vegetable stock. Bake 30 minutes at 350 degrees. Make small pools of tomato sauce on 6 plates, and serve 2 rolls atop the sauce for each portion.

Gai Lan (Chinese Broccoli) with Toasted Garlic

V

Darker, leafier, and more slender-stemmed than Western broccoli, gai lan is nonetheless a cousin in the Brassica family, which also includes most cabbages, cauliflower, mustard greens, and bok choy. It's worth seeking out in Asian grocery markets, but if you can't find it, this recipe will work just as well with regular broccoli or broccoli raab.

Serves 4

*1 pound gai lan (Chinese broccoli) **or** other type of broccoli*
2 tablespoons peanut oil
5 cloves garlic, finely chopped
Pinch of crushed red pepper flakes (optional)
Kosher salt and freshly ground black pepper
Lemon wedges

1. Prepare a deep bowl full of salted ice water; set aside. Bring a large pot of salted water (it should be as salty as tears) to a rapid, rolling boil. Trim any frayed ends from the stems of the gai lan. Cook it by handfuls (see "It's Easy Being Green," page 44), only until crisp-tender; plunge immediately into the ice bath. Drain.
2. In a large skillet or wok, heat the oil over a medium heat until it is hot. Add the garlic and red pepper (if using), and cook without stirring, until the garlic begins to turn golden brown. Immediately add the blanched vegetable, and toss gently to stop the garlic from browning further. Cook until the vegetable is thoroughly hot. Season well with salt and pepper. Serve with lemon wedges.

Swiss Chard Rolls with Root Vegetables

This dish is particularly attractive with red Swiss chard, though green is fine.

Serves 4

8 large leaves Swiss chard,
   thoroughly washed
3 tablespoons olive oil, divided
2 cups roughly chopped red onion
2 carrots, roughly chopped
2 sweet potatoes (about ½ pound),
   peeled and finely diced
8 cups chopped root vegetables
   (such as celery root, parsnips,
   turnips, and white potatoes—try
   Latino roots, such as yuca, **or**
   cassava, **or** taro)

¼ cup roughly chopped Italian
   parsley
2 teaspoons chopped cilantro
   (optional)
Kosher salt and freshly ground black
   pepper
Juice of 2 limes (about
   4 tablespoons)
1 cup stock **or** water

1. Remove the stems from the chard; chop them finely. Heat 2 tablespoons of the olive oil over a medium flame in a heavy-bottomed Dutch oven or large skillet. Add the chard stems, red onion, carrots, sweet potatoes, root vegetables, parsley, lime juice, and cilantro; season well with salt and pepper.
2. Bring a large pot of salted water to a boil. Blanch the chard leaves for 3 or 4 minutes, then drain and cool. Spoon ¼ cup of filling onto the stem end of a chard leaf. Fold in the sides to envelop the filling; roll away from yourself, keeping even tension so the rolls remain plump. Line the rolls up in a greased skillet; add 1 cup of water or stock, season lightly with salt. Cook 10 minutes; serve garnished with remaining filling.

Spinach Pancakes with Cardamom

I first saw these cakes in a café in Kreuzberg, Berlin, where they were one of several vegetarian choices. I had them with a cracked wheat pilaf, caramelized onions, and a glass of Sprite or white Riesling wine on a hot August midday. Cool . . .

Serves 4

1 tablespoon olive oil
2 teaspoons finely chopped garlic
2 pounds fresh spinach, washed and stemmed
4 pods cardamom, cracked open, **or** *½ teaspoon ground*
1 teaspoon salt
Freshly ground black pepper
2 ounces egg substitute
1 cup plus 2 tablespoons breadcrumbs
Oil for frying
Lemon wedges

1. Heat the olive oil in a large skillet or Dutch oven over high heat; add the garlic. Cook for 30 seconds, until garlic becomes clear and fragrant; add the spinach, cardamom pods, salt and pepper to taste. Cook just until spinach is wilted; transfer to a colander to cool.

2. Squeeze all excess water from spinach. Combine with egg substitute and 2 tablespoons of breadcrumbs; mix well. Form into four pancakes; dredge in remaining breadcrumbs. Heat fry oil in a heavy-bottomed skillet, and fry cakes until browned on both sides, and hot in the center. Serve with lemon wedges.

Spinach-Stuffed Vegetables

The little child in all of us loves stuffed things. Maybe it's the sense of something hidden, mysterious. Or maybe it's just the sneaky feeling that we're getting two things instead of just one. But the best reason to treasure this colorful cornucopia is that they're easy.

Serves 4

1 tablespoon olive oil
1 tablespoon whole coriander seeds
3 medium shallots, roughly chopped
¼ teaspoon crushed red pepper flakes (optional)
2 pounds spinach, washed and stemmed
½ teaspoon salt
¼ cup crumbled feta cheese (optional, not vegan)

4 plum tomatoes, tops cut off, insides scooped out
1 medium zucchini, cut into 4 (2-inch) cylinders
1 medium yellow squash, cut into 4 (2-inch) cylinders
4 large stuffing mushrooms, stems removed
Lemon wedges

1. Heat the olive oil and coriander seeds in a small pan until very hot but not smoking—the coriander seeds should become fragrant, but not brown. Strain the oil into a large skillet or Dutch oven; discard the seeds. Over a medium heat, cook the shallots and crushed pepper, if using, for 1 minute—they should sizzle but not brown. Add the spinach all at once; season with salt and cook, stirring, just until spinach is wilted. Transfer to a colander to cool.
2. Chop the spinach roughly on a cutting board. Add the feta cheese, if using. Trim the bottoms of the tomatoes just enough to help them stand straight. Using a small spoon or melon-baller, scoop enough of the seeded center from the zucchini and yellow squash to form a teaspoon-sized pocket. Season all the vegetables liberally with salt and white pepper. Spoon the spinach mixture into them, mounding slightly on top. Any extra spinach may be used to line the plates when serving.
3. Arrange the vegetables in a steamer basket. Steam over rapidly boiling water just until the zucchini becomes tender, about 6 minutes. Serve hot or at room temperature, along with remaining spinach filling and lemon wedges.

Spinach and Feta Pie

Every June on Manhattan's Ninth Avenue, there's an International food festival. The owners of a Greek bakery near 46th Street set up one of my favorite booths, which features spinach and feta pie to die for.

Serves 8

1 bunch fresh spinach (about 4 cups)
3 tablespoons olive oil
1 yellow onion, chopped
1 cup grated Swiss cheese
2 eggs
1¼ cups light cream
½ teaspoon salt
¼ teaspoon freshly ground black pepper
Pinch of nutmeg
¼ cup grated Parmesan cheese
1 (10-inch) deep-dish pie crust, prebaked 5 minutes at 375 degrees
6 ounces feta cheese, crumbled
2 medium tomatoes, sliced (optional)

1. Heat oven to 350 degrees. Wash and stem the spinach; steam until wilted. Squeeze out excess water and chop. Heat the olive oil in a small skillet, and cook the onion until golden, about 7 minutes; toss with the spinach. Stir in the Swiss cheese.

2. Combine the eggs, cream, salt, pepper, nutmeg, and Parmesan cheese in a blender. Blend 1 minute. Spread the spinach mixture into the crust. Top with feta cheese and decorate with tomatoes if desired. Pour on the egg mixture, pressing through with your fingers to make sure it soaks through to the crust. Bake 45 minutes, until a knife inserted in the pie comes out clean. Serve hot or room temperature.

Grilled Radicchio

Though it's usually thought of as a salad leaf, radicchio, a bitter-sweet purplish red head lettuce, mellows and becomes juicy when it's lightly dressed and cooked on a grill or in a grill pan. Select tight round heads that are heavy for their size, without wilted leaves or blemishes.

Serves 4

4 heads radicchio
1 tablespoon extra-virgin olive oil
1 lemon, halved
Salt and pepper to taste

1. Quarter the radicchio heads through the root end. In a mixing bowl, drizzle the olive oil over the pieces, squeeze on the lemon juice, and season with salt and pepper; toss to coat.
2. Heat a grill or stovetop grill pan to medium heat. Lay the radicchio, cut-side down, across the grill ribs. Cook until wilting is visible from the sides, only about 2 minutes. Turn to the other cut side and cook for 1 or 2 minutes more, pulling it from the grill before it goes completely limp. Serve with extra lemon wedges on the side.

How to Make Lemon Wedges

Waiters and bartenders drive chefs nuts when they try to get artistic with citrus. Chopping off the ends of the lemons, cutting wedges super thin, cutting the limes into slices instead of wedges—these unnecessary steps all lead to inconvenient and messy squeezes. Select lemons and limes that are as elongated as possible for wedges. Then, just halve, quarter, and eighth the fruit lengthwise. Flick out only the seeds you see on the surface of the wedges, using the tip of a small knife. Don't bother mining for deep seeds—it'll only yield sloppy wedges.

Kale with Garlic and Thyme [V]

Antioxidant-rich dark leafy greens like kale are nutritional power-houses loaded with calcium, beta-carotene, and vitamin C. They're also high in fiber and phytochemicals. One could say they're the liver of the vegetable world!

Serves 4

2 pounds kale, stems and ribs removed
1 tablespoon olive oil
1 medium red onion, chopped
1 tablespoon chopped garlic
Pinch of crushed red pepper
*2 teaspoons chopped fresh thyme leaves **or** ½ teaspoon dried*
*¼ cup dry sherry **or** white wine*
Salt and fresh ground black pepper
Grated Parmesan cheese (optional; not vegan)

1. Bring a large pot of well-salted water to a rolling boil. Add the kale, and cook for 10 minutes, until it has lost its waxy coating and the leaves are tender. Transfer to a colander to drain, reserving about ½ cup of the cooking liquid. Roughly chop the kale.
2. Heat the oil in a large skillet or Dutch oven. Add the onion, garlic, red pepper, and thyme. Cook over medium heat until the onions are soft and starting to brown around the edges. Splash in the sherry; cook for 5 minutes until all alcohol has evaporated. Add back the kale; cook 10 minutes more. Season with salt and pepper. Serve sprinkled with grated Parmesan cheese if desired.

Szechuan Stir-Fried Cabbage with Hot Peppers [V]

One private client I cooked for had traveled throughout China from end to end. When I heard of her travels, I commented that she must've tasted lots of interesting things. "Cabbage," she replied, "Everywhere I ate cabbage. They have so much of it they hang it outside their doors." While I can't help feeling she missed something, Chinese cabbage dishes are so delectable that they can make you forget about other things.

Serves 4–6

¼ cup plus 2 tablespoons peanut or
   other neutral oil

8 dried red chili peppers, quartered
   and seeded

1 (1-inch) piece fresh ginger, peeled
   and finely chopped

1 medium head cabbage (preferably
   Chinese cabbage, but any variety
   is okay), washed and chopped
   into 2-inch pieces

½ teaspoon cornstarch

1 tablespoon soy sauce

1 teaspoon dry sherry **or** Chinese
   cooking wine

1 teaspoon sugar

1 teaspoon rice wine vinegar

1 teaspoon Asian sesame oil

1. Heat ¼ cup of the oil in a wok or skillet over high heat. Stir in the peppers and fry, stirring, for 1 minute, until the peppers darken in color. Transfer the peppers and oil to a bowl and set aside.

2. Pour remaining 2 tablespoons of oil into the wok; add the ginger and cook for a few seconds until fragrant. Add the cabbage all at once. Fry, stirring, for 1 minute. Combine the cornstarch, soy sauce, and sherry together in a small bowl. Add to the wok. Stir until the cornstarch cooks and forms a thick sauce; add the sugar and vinegar. Sprinkle in the sesame oil and pour in the red peppers and their oil. Stir to combine well. Transfer to a serving bowl.

Garlicky Broccoli Raab

The key to the toasty flavor of this dish is to brown the garlic to a golden color before adding the blanched raabs. Their moisture stops the garlic from cooking, preserving its browned, but not burned flavor.

Serves 4

1 pound broccoli raab, bottoms trimmed
2 tablespoons good quality olive oil
2 tablespoons finely chopped garlic
Pinch of crushed red pepper flakes (optional)
Salt and freshly ground black pepper
Lemon wedges

Blanch the raabs in rapidly boiling salted water (see "It's Easy Being Green," page 44); shock in ice water and drain. Heat the olive oil in a large, heavy-bottomed skillet over medium heat for 1 minute. Add the garlic and red pepper flakes, if using, and cook stirring with a wooden spoon until garlic is golden. Add all of the raabs at once; toss to coat. Season well with salt and pepper (make sure to taste as you season, remembering that the raabs should have been blanched and shocked in salted water!). When the vegetable is hot, serve with lemon wedges on the side.

Spicy Variations

In place of or in addition to pepper flakes, substitute toasted cumin seeds, fennel seeds, anise, or chopped fresh ginger for different character.

Collard Greens with Tomatoes and Cheddar

The assertive vegetal taste of collards benefits from marriage with equally gutsy tomatoes and cheddar cheese. Try this with a grain pilaf, such as soaked bulgur wheat, for a chewy textural contrast. White cheddar from Vermont is my favorite.

Serves 4

2 pounds collard greens, stems and ribs removed
2 tablespoons olive oil
1 tablespoon finely chopped garlic (about 2 cloves)
*4 ripe red or yellow tomatoes (**or** a combination)*
1 teaspoon salt
1 teaspoon oregano
4 ounces cheddar cheese, shredded

Bring a large pot of salted water to a rolling boil. Cook the greens until tender, about 10 minutes; drain and roughly chop. Heat the oil in a large, heavy-bottomed skillet over medium-high heat. Add the garlic; allow it to sizzle for 30 seconds before adding the collards, tomatoes, salt, and oregano. Cook for 4 minutes, just until the tomatoes are hot. Serve topped with the shredded cheese.

Tomatoes and Other Vegetables

Cumin-Roasted Butternut Squash   V

Choose butternuts with a large cylindrical barrel, and small bulbous bottom, so you yield the most squash and fewest seeds. Since the squash is peeled for this dish, the longer barrel means easier preparation.

Serves 8

1 medium butternut squash (2–3 pounds)
2 tablespoons ground cumin
2 tablespoons olive oil
Salt and coarsely ground black pepper
1 tablespoon roughly chopped Italian (flat-leaf) parsley

1. Cut the butternut in two, crosswise, just above the bulbous bottom. Place the cut side of the cylindrical barrel down on a cutting board, and peel it with a knife or potato peeler, removing all rind. Repeat with the bottom part, then cut bottom in half and remove seeds.
2. Dice squash into 1-inch chunks. In a large mixing bowl, toss squash with cumin, oil, salt, and pepper.
3. Spread into a single layer on a doubled baking sheet, and roast in a 375-degree oven for 40 minutes, turning after 25 minutes, until browned and tender. Serve sprinkled with chopped parsley.

Mushroom-Stuffed Tomatoes ⊻

Use any ripe tomato you prefer for this dish. Late in the season, roma plum tomatoes are usually the best choice, since they keep a long time even when ripe. If using a processor to chop the mushrooms, "pulse" them in small batches, stopping before they clump.

Serves 6 as an appetizer or side dish, or up to 12 as a tasty garnish

4 shallots, chopped fine
2 tablespoons olive oil, divided
1 pound white mushrooms, washed and chopped fine
1 teaspoon salt plus 2 pinches
Splash of white wine (about ¼ cup)

¼ cup finely chopped parsley
Freshly ground black pepper
6 large ripe plum tomatoes, halved crosswise, bottoms trimmed flat
3 tablespoons bread crumbs

1. Sauté chopped shallots with 1 tablespoon olive oil in a large skillet over medium heat. Add chopped mushrooms (if some don't fit, you can add them later, when the rest have wilted down) and 1 teaspoon salt, and raise heat to high. Cook, stirring occasionally, until mushrooms have given up their water, and most of it has evaporated.
2. Add the white wine, and cook until it has mostly evaporated. Stir in chopped parsley, remove from heat, and season with freshly ground black pepper.
3. Scoop the innards from the tomatoes, and season the tomato cups with 2 pinches salt. Fill each tomato with mushroom filling so that it mounds slightly, topping each with a sprinkle of bread crumbs. Line into a baking dish, and drizzle with remaining olive oil. Bake 25 minutes, until soft, at 350 degrees.

Herbed Red and Yellow Tomatoes on Honey-Nut Bread

V

Golden or yellow tomatoes have a sweet, mellow flavor that, at its best, is grassy like fresh garden tomatoes, but without excessive tartness. The combination of two colors of tomatoes makes this a very festive summer sandwich.

Serves 4

¼ cup extra-virgin olive oil
¼ cup balsamic vinegar
1 tablespoon Dijon mustard
*½ bunch fresh oregano **or** marjoram, roughly chopped*
½ bunch Italian parsley, roughly chopped
1 small bunch chives, chopped

*2 ripe beefsteak **or** other sweet variety red tomatoes, sliced ½-inch thick*
2 yellow acid-free tomatoes, sliced ½-inch thick
*8 slices "Branola" **or** other type sweet-dough bread containing whole grains, ½-inch thick*
Coarse salt and black pepper to taste

1. Whisk together oil, vinegar, and mustard in a small steel bowl. Fold in chopped herbs.
2. Lay tomato slices in a single layer into a glass (nonreactive) dish, and pour most of the dressing over them, reserving about 2 tablespoons. Allow to marinate at room temperature for about 10 minutes.
3. Toast the whole grain bread and drizzle with remaining dressing. Shingle tomatoes in alternating colors. Season with coarse salt and freshly ground black pepper.

Fried Green Tomatoes
with Remoulade Sauce

*These classic tart, flavorful American favorites go particularly well
with the light summer salads such as Succotash Salad (page 11)
and Mixed Baby Greens with Balsamic Vinaigrette (page 30).*

Serves 4 as an appetizer or side dish

1 cup mayonnaise (preferably homemade)
1 hard-boiled egg, finely chopped
1 tablespoon capers, chopped
1 tablespoon chopped cornichons **or** *dill pickle*
1 teaspoon chopped parsley
Dash of hot pepper sauce, **or** *cayenne*
3 large green tomatoes, sliced ½-inch thick (should total
*   12–14 slices)*
Flour for dredging
6 beaten eggs, diluted with ½ cup milk
4 cups plain or seasoned bread crumbs, preferably homemade
3 cups light oil, such as canola **or** *peanut, for frying*

1. Make the remoulade sauce: Combine mayonnaise with chopped egg,
   capers, pickle, parsley, and hot sauce. Taste for seasoning and
   refrigerate.
2. Dredge each tomato slice in flour, then eggs, then bread crumbs,
   pressing the bread crumbs to ensure adherence. Fry in small batches
   over low-medium heat (325 degrees oil temperature), until they feel
   tender when tested with a fork. Season with salt, and serve immediately with remoulade sauce.

Tomato Confit with Fine Herbs   V

The term "confit" refers to items cooked in their own liquid, which these tomatoes do inside their skins. Oven roasting intensifies the sweetness of tomatoes by cooking out some of their water. These slow-cooked summer jewels benefit from the essence released by herbs steaming in the tomatoes' juices. They keep, refrigerated, for four days.

Serves 5 as a side dish, or up to 10 as a tasty garnish

5 large ripe but firm beefsteak tomatoes, cored, halved crosswise, seeded

12 big sprigs assorted fresh herbs like thyme, oregano, rosemary, parsley, etc.

3 tablespoons olive oil

1 teaspoon salt

1. Preheat oven to 275 degrees. Toss the tomatoes gently with the herbs, olive oil, and salt, then arrange cut-side down in a baking dish, so that the herbs are under and touching them.
2. Bake 2 hours, until flesh is very soft to the touch, and skin looks wrinkled.
3. Cool until you can touch them, and carefully remove the skins. Serve warm.

Red and Yellow Plum Tomato Chutney V

This summer salsa accompanies fried tofu very well, and is also a great base for grain salads, such as the Quinoa Salad with Tomatoes and Cilantro (page 118).

Yields about 3 cups

⅓ cup sugar
Juice of 1 lemon
6 ripe red plum tomatoes, seeded and roughly chopped
6 ripe yellow plum tomatoes, seeded and roughly chopped
¼ cup finely diced red onion
¼ cup fresh cilantro, roughly chopped (optional)

Mix sugar with ½ cup water in a medium saucepan. Cook over high heat until water is evaporated and molten sugar begins to turn golden brown. Pour in lemon juice to stop the sugar from cooking and bring it up from the bottom of the pan. Add the chopped tomatoes and red onion. Simmer for no more than 5 minutes (this is to warm the tomatoes, not cook them). Remove from heat. Allow to cool in a colander, letting the excess water released from the warmed tomatoes drain out. Stir in chopped cilantro.

Chopping Tender Herbs

Keep fresh herbs looking neat and clean by cutting them with a slicing action rather than a chopping motion. Even though recipes call for "chopped" leafy herbs, it's best to bunch gentle leaves like basil, oregano, or mint into small piles or stacks, then slice them against the cutting board with the sharpest knife you can find. If your knives are dull, snipping with scissors is a gentler action than chopping. Chopping can result in unattractive black edges, clumps, and rapid spoilage. Heartier herbs, such as fresh thyme, parsley, and rosemary can stand up to a rough chop.

New Mexico Chili Sauce

This tomato-based Southwestern sauce is the ultimate salsa for Black Bean Burritos (page 138), a wonderful accompaniment to scrambled eggs or omelets, and the base for the sauce in Chilaquiles (page 181).

Yields 3 cups

1 teaspoon olive oil
1 medium onion, roughly chopped
5 New Mexico chilies, seeded, soaked, and puréed (see "It's Not Hot, It's Chili" Tip below)
1 jar (28 ounces) roasted-garlic-flavored marinara sauce
½ teaspoon ground cumin
½ teaspoon dried oregano

Heat the oil in a saucepan over a medium flame. Add onion; cook, stirring occasionally, until translucent, about 5 minutes. Add chili purée; cook 3 minutes more. Add the marinara sauce, cumin, and oregano. Simmer 10 minutes. Purée in a blender until very smooth.

It's Not Hot, It's Chili

Fruity, smoky, citrusy, woodsy . . . These are just a few words to describe the flavors of various chilies. Make dried chilies ready for use by toasting them in a 350-degree oven for five minutes, until they soften, become fragrant, and smoke lightly. Then, soak them in enough water to cover for one hour, and purée in a blender with just enough soaking liquid to make a thick purée circulate in the blender vase. For less "heat," remove the seeds before soaking.

Chilaquiles (Tortilla Stew)

Pronounced "chill-uh-KILL-ehs," these softened tortilla chips are a favorite hearty breakfast item in Mexico. They're perfect for brunch, because they only take a few minutes to throw together once the ingredients are assembled.

Serves 2

4 cups tortilla chips (any color)
2 cups vegetable stock
1 cup New Mexico Chili Sauce (page 180) or spicy tomato sauce
4 large eggs (optional)
2 tablespoons sour cream **or** *Tofu Sour Cream (page 87)*
Chopped cilantro

Place the chips in a large skillet over a high flame. Add 1 cup of vegetable stock and the New Mexico Chili Sauce. Bring to a boil, then lower to a simmer, adding more stock as needed to keep the mixture soupy. Cook until the tortillas are well softened, but not mushy. If desired, fry the eggs in a little butter. Serve the chilaquiles on 2 plates, topped with fried eggs, a dollop of sour cream, and a sprinkling of chopped cilantro.

Avocado Sashimi with Miso Dressing $\boxed{V}$

Serves 2

1 ripe Hass avocado, halved, seeded, and peeled
1 lemon
1 teaspoon white **or** *yellow miso*
1 teaspoon grated ginger root
1 teaspoon light soy sauce
1 teaspoon sugar
1 teaspoon sesame oil
Wasabi paste for garnish
Pickled ginger for garnish

1. Place the avocado halves cut-side down on a board; score them at ⅛-inch intervals, leaving the stem end connected to hold them together. Squeeze the lemon over the scored avocados to prevent browning. Fan the avocados onto 2 small plates.
2. Whisk together the miso, ginger, soy sauce, sugar, and sesame oil until the sugar is dissolved. Spoon some of the dressing over the avocadoes. Serve garnished with wasabi and pickled ginger.

Ratatouille

A classic Provencal dish, this is a perfect way to make the most of summer's harvest.

Serves 6

2 tablespoons olive oil
1 large onion, diced
2 medium zucchini, diced
2 medium yellow squash, diced
1 small eggplant, diced
1 bell pepper, diced
1 tablespoon flour
3 tomatoes, seeded, and cut into 6 pieces
*2 teaspoons dried Herbes de Province (***or*** a combination of*
   oregano, thyme, rosemary, marjoram, savory and/or lavender)
1 teaspoon salt
Freshly ground black pepper
Fresh basil leaves, chopped (optional)

1. Heat the olive oil in a heavy-bottomed Dutch oven until hot, but not smoky. Add onion; cook until translucent, about 5 minutes. Combine the zucchini, yellow squash, eggplant, and bell pepper in a large paper bag; dust with flour, fold bag closed, and shake to coat. Add floured vegetables to the pot, along with the tomatoes, herbs, salt, and pepper.

2. Reduce heat to a simmer, cover, and cook gently for 1 hour, until all vegetables are tender. Serve hot or at room temperature. Garnish with freshly chopped basil, if desired.

Quick Tomato and Oregano Sauté Ⓥ

This versatile pan stew accompanies steamed, baked, or sautéed mushrooms as easily as it does grilled tempeh or fried tofu. It also works beautifully as a simple pasta sauce.

Serves 4

1 tablespoon olive oil
2 cloves garlic, finely minced
2 tablespoons chopped fresh oregano, **or** *½ teaspoon dried*
2 cups chopped tomatoes (any variety)
Scant ½ teaspoon salt

1. Heat olive oil in 10-inch skillet over medium flame. Sprinkle in chopped garlic, and stir with a wooden spoon for only a moment, until the garlic whitens, and releases its aroma. Do not allow it to brown.
2. Add chopped tomato, salt, and, if you are using dried oregano, add that now. Simmer 10 minutes, until most water has evaporated, stirring occasionally.
3. Season with fresh ground black pepper, and if you are using fresh oregano, stir it in and simmer 1 minute more.

Basic Fresh Tomato Sauce

August and September are tomato harvest season in the East, when thousands of cooks pack summer's bounty into jars of fruity tomato sauce to last them the whole year. This sauce freezes well, and can also be canned.

Yields 1 quart

4 pounds tomatoes, preferably roma plum tomatoes, but any variety will do
2 tablespoons olive oil
1 large onion, roughly chopped
5 cloves garlic, chopped (about 2 tablespoons)
1 teaspoon sugar
2 tablespoons tomato paste
1 cup washed fresh basil leaves, stems removed (optional)
Salt and freshly ground black pepper

1. Halve the tomatoes and squeeze out as many seeds as you can. Dice the tomatoes. Heat the olive oil in a large saucepan or Dutch Oven (pan should be enamel, steel, or glass-lined—see "Nonreactive Pots: Welcome to the Steel and Glass Generation," page 149) over medium heat until hot enough to sizzle when a piece of onion is added. Add the onions; cook until soft and beginning to brown slightly, about 10 minutes. Stir in the garlic, sugar, and tomato paste; cook 2 minutes more, stirring constantly. Add the tomatoes; cook 10 minutes until mixture becomes brothy.
2. Uncover, lower flame to a slow simmer, and cook 30 minutes more, until all tomatoes are fully softened; season to taste. If you prefer chunky sauce, add the basil, if desired. For smooth sauce, purée and strain, then add the basil leaves at the end.

Quick Tomato Sauce

This sauce can be assembled in 20 minutes from ingredients right in the house. It is an excellent all-purpose red sauce for pasta or any recipe calling for tomato sauce.

Yields 1 quart

2 tablespoons olive oil
1 medium onion, chopped
2 tablespoons chopped garlic
(about 5 cloves)
1 teaspoon dried oregano
(optional)
1 tablespoon tomato paste
1 teaspoon sugar
1 can (28 ounces) crushed toma-
toes (use a domestic brand like

Redpack, Progresso, Hunt's, or
Muir Glen Organic—most
imports in supermarkets are
old and sour)
1 can (14 ounces) diced tomatoes
in purée
Salt and freshly ground black
pepper

Heat the oil in a medium saucepan for 1 minute over medium heat. Add onions, garlic, and oregano if using; cook 5 minutes, until onions are translucent. Stir in tomato paste and sugar; cook, stirring, 5 minutes more. Add crushed tomatoes, diced tomatoes, salt, and pepper. Simmer 10 minutes.

Being Creative with Your Tomato Sauce

There are many options available to you when preparing a tomato sauce. Try replacing the oregano with a bay leaf or some basil. Try a finely diced pepper or even cilantro in place of (or in addition to) the onion. Another idea is to look around the grocery store at what types of tomato sauces there are and take a crack at incorporating some of those varieties in your own sauce. Vodka and cream are also popular flavorings these days. Be sure to steam off any alcohol after adding vodka to tomato sauce.

Zucchini "Lasagna"

Layered and baked like the beloved Italian-American pasta dish, this wheat-free casserole is best made a day in advance, and cut while cold, then warmed before serving. If you don't have a mandolin or slicing machine, the deli counter person is usually glad to slice your zucchini at the store.

Serves 8

3 cups tomato sauce
4 large zucchini, sliced very thin on
    a mandolin **or** slicing machine,
    about ⅛-inch thick
Kosher salt and freshly ground black
    pepper
1 pound ricotta cheese

1 pound provolone, fontina,
    mozzarella, **or** cheese of your
    choice, shredded
2 cups sautéed onions and
    mushrooms, **or** 2 cups frozen
    mixed vegetables, thawed

1. Heat oven to 350 degrees. Spread 1 cup sauce onto the bottom of a 9" × 13" baking dish. Arrange a layer of zucchini slices into the pan, overlapping the pieces by a third.
2. Dot the zucchini layer with half of the ricotta, distributing teaspoonfuls evenly around the casserole. Layer on ⅓ of the shredded cheese, and half of the vegetables.
3. Arrange another layer of zucchini, and repeat fillings, using remaining ricotta, vegetables, and another third of the shredded cheese. Add a final layer of zucchini on top, and spread on 2 more cups of tomato sauce.
4. Sprinkle top with remaining cheese; bake 1 hour until casserole is bubbly and cheese is lightly browned. Cool to room temperature, and then refrigerate until cold. Cut into portions, and reheat in the oven or microwave until hot.

Zucchini Lasagna Twist

Try replacing about half the zucchini in this recipe with an equal portion of eggplant. Be sure to use thin, flat slices that are very lightly dusted on one side with salt.

Eggplant Rolatine

These spinach-and-ricotta-filled roulades make a very beautiful dinner presentation served atop a heap of tomato-sauced linguine, garnished with a sprig of fresh basil. They were one of the first dishes I learned, when I was working as a dishwasher and prep cook in high school. Have the deli counter at your super-market slice the eggplant for you on their machine—it's almost impossible to do with a knife. The finished rolatine keep well for several days, and are delicious at room temperature or as sandwich fillings.

Serves 8

1 large eggplant, sliced lengthwise into even ⅛-inch slices (as thick as the cover of a hardcover book)
Flour for dredging
Egg wash of about 6 beaten eggs, mixed with ½ cup water
4 cups breadcrumbs
Oil for frying
1 pound ricotta cheese

8 ounces shredded mozzarella cheese
*½ cup grated Parmesan (good quality, like Parmigiano Reggiano **or** Grana Padano)*
Salt and pepper
*1½ pounds fresh spinach, washed and cooked, **or** 1 pound frozen spinach, thawed*
4 cups tomato sauce

1. Bread and fry the eggplant: Dip a slice of eggplant in the flour to coat both sides; shake off excess flour, submerge in egg wash, shake off excess, and coat in bread-crumbs, pressing to make sure they adhere well. Place on a holding tray, and repeat with remaining slices. Heat oil to about 350 degrees (a piece of vegetable should sizzle visibly when dropped into the oil). Fry the breaded eggplant slices, dripping any excess oil off before stacking them between layers of paper towels.

2. Fill and roll: Heat oven to 350 degrees. Combine the 3 cheeses in a mixing bowl, and season lightly with salt and pepper. Place 1 teaspoon of cooked spinach and a generous teaspoon of cheese mixture at the wide end of a fried eggplant slice. Roll away from yourself, jellyroll style, and place into a baking dish, with the seam on the bottom. Repeat with remaining eggplant and fillings, lining the finished roulades close together in the baking dish. Bake until cheeses are visibly hot, and the edges begin to brown lightly. Serve on a pool of tomato sauce, garnished with basil leaves. One piece per appetizer portion, 2 per main course.

Simple Salsa

This simple condiment pairs magnificently with burritos, tacos, empanadas, tortilla chips, and all kinds of other Mexican savories.

Yields 1 cup

2 large tomatoes
1 small onion, finely diced
1 or 2 jalapeño peppers, finely chopped
½ teaspoon fresh-squeezed lime juice

Salt and freshly ground black pepper
½ teaspoon chipotle purée (optional—
see "¡Hola! I Must Be Going:
Mexican Specialty Foods," page 61)

Quarter the tomatoes. Cut out the inside viscera; reserve. Cut the remaining petals into a fine dice. Purée the insides in a food processor until smooth. Toss together with the tomato dice, the diced onion, jalapeños, lime juice, salt, pepper, and chipotle if using. Keeps in the refrigerator for 2 days, but is best used the day it's made.

———————

Stir-Fried Snow Peas with Cilantro

Serves 4

*2 tablespoons peanut **or** other*
light oil
1 cup thinly sliced scallions
1 cup snow peas
½ cup strong vegetable stock
2 teaspoons cornstarch

½ cup finely chopped cilantro leaves
(a.k.a. "Chinese parsley" or
"coriander leaf")
Dash of soy sauce
Pinch of sugar

1. Heat oil in a large skillet until very hot, almost smoking. Add scallions and snow peas, tossing or stirring quickly to coat them with oil. Add stock, cover the skillet, and cook for 2 minutes. Meanwhile, mix the cornstarch with 2 tablespoons of cold water and the cilantro.
2. Stir the cornstarch mixture quickly into the peas, stirring constantly until the sauce thickens; season with soy sauce and sugar. Serve immediately. The entire cooking time for the peas should not exceed 5 minutes.

Eggplant Parmigiana

My grandmother, Sally, used to make eggplant parmigiana by top-ping raw rounds of sliced eggplant with sauce and cheese and baking it until the cheese was brown. It was good, but I've since learned that to make these basic ingredients sing, the eggplant needs to be precooked.

Serves 8

Oil for frying
1 medium eggplant (about 1 pound), sliced thin
1 cup flour
*3 eggs, beaten, mixed with ½ cup water **or** milk*
3 cups breadcrumbs
*Four cups Basic Fresh Tomato Sauce (page 185) **or***
*   1 (28-ounce) jar store-bought sauce*
1 pound part-skim mozzarella cheese, shredded
*Chopped Italian parsley **or** whole fresh basil leaves*

1. Heat the oil in a heavy skillet or fryer (about ½" deep) until a piece of vegetable sizzles when added. Dip a piece of eggplant in the flour and shake off excess; dip it in the egg mixture and shake off excess; then press it into the breadcrumbs. Repeat with remaining slices of eggplant. Fry the slices until golden, about 3 minutes each; drain on a rack or on paper towels.
2. Heat oven to 350 degrees. Line the slices into a baking dish. Top each with a teaspoon of tomato sauce, and a small mound of shredded cheese. Bake until cheese is melted, browning and bubbly, about 15 minutes. Serve with additional tomato sauce on the side, gar-nished with chopped parsley or leaves of fresh basil.

Steamed Asparagus with Hollandaise Sauce

Hollandaise is what the French call a "mother sauce," meaning that it can be transformed into other sauces by adding just a few ingredients (tarragon, pepper, and shallots—béarnaise; mustard—Dijonnaise; orange concentrate—maltaise, etc).

Serves 6

3 egg yolks
Juice of 1 lemon (about ¼ cup), divided
1 tablespoon plus a few drops of cold water

8 ounces (2 sticks) melted butter
Pinch of cayenne
¼ teaspoon salt
1 bunch asparagus, woody bottoms trimmed off

1. In a large, steel mixing bowl over a pot of simmering water, or in a double boiler over a very low flame, whisk together the yolks, half of the lemon juice, and 1 tablespoon cold water. Whisk vigorously until the yolks attain a lemon-yellow color and become thick (about the consistency of creamy salad dressing). Be careful not to let the eggs cook into lumps—keep whisking all the time, and remove the bowl from the heat if it starts getting too hot. Once yolks are ready, set the bowl they are in onto a damp towel on a firm surface. Whisk in a few drops of cold water, then a few drops of the melted butter. Gradually whip in the melted butter in small increments, making sure that each addition is thoroughly incorporated before adding any more. Season with cayenne, salt, and remaining lemon juice.
2. Steam the asparagus for 5 minutes, until tender but still brightly colored. Divide onto plates; spoon hollandaise over the middle of the stalks.

With Asparagus, Thin Ain't Always In

Fat-n-sweet or thin and delicate, asparagus are one of the most sensuously delicious foods known to man. Contrary to popular belief, thick, voluptuous asparagus are not always woody and tough. In fact, they can have much more natural juiciness, sweetness, and silky texture than the pencil-thin variety. Check the cut bottoms of asparagus for freshness, making sure they're plump, moist, and recently cut. Wrinkled asparagus of any girth are no good.

Eggplant and Tomato Sauté

Serve this as an eggplant sauce with pasta or chilled as a summer salad with bulgur wheat pilaf or another grain salad.

Serves 8

1 medium eggplant (about 1 pound), cut lengthwise into 8 wedges
Kosher salt
3 tablespoons olive oil, divided
2 medium onions, sliced thickly (about ½-inch)
¼ teaspoon crushed red pepper flakes
1 tablespoon chopped garlic (about 3 cloves)
2 cups chopped plum tomatoes
*¼ cup chopped fresh oregano **or** parsley*

1. Sprinkle the eggplant wedges liberally with kosher salt; set aside for 10 to 15 minutes, until water visibly pools under the wedges (this extracts some bitter juices, making the eggplant especially mellow for this recipe). Dry the eggplant off with a towel. Heat 2 tablespoons of olive oil in a large, heavy-bottomed skillet until a piece of vegetable sizzles when added. Fry the eggplant wedges until they are lightly browned and bubbling with juice. Transfer to a cutting board and cut into large (2-inch) pieces.
2. Put remaining olive oil in the skillet, and heat 1 minute over medium heat. Add onions, crushed pepper, and garlic; cook, stirring occasionally, until onions are very soft, about 10 minutes. Add tomatoes, and cook just until they begin to break down into a chunky sauce. Add the eggplant and chopped oregano or parsley. Bring to a simmer; remove from heat. Season to taste.

Asparagus-Shallot Sauté

V

Asparagus are loaded with beneficial insoluble fiber, which aids in digestion, sweeping unwanted potentially harmful items through the system before they can do damage.

Serves 6

1 bunch asparagus
Kosher salt
*1 tablespoon olive oil (**or** butter;*
*   not vegan)*
½ cup finely chopped shallots
*   (about 4 shallots)*

Pinch of roughly cracked black
*   pepper (see tip below)*
*1 tablespoon dry white wine **or***
*   sherry*
Lemon wedges

1. Bring a large pot of water to a rolling boil, and cook the asparagus according to directions in "It's Easy Being Green," (page 44), shocking them in salted ice water when they are fully cooked but tender. Transfer to a cutting board, and cut on a diagonal angle into 2-inch pieces.
2. Heat the olive oil in a large skillet; add the shallots and black pepper. Cook until translucent, about 3 minutes; add the wine and asparagus; cook until heated through. Season to taste. Serve with lemon wedges on the side.

Roughly Cracked Black Pepper

Release inner tension while liberating black pepper's inner fruitiness, perfume, and fresh taste by cracking against a counter or board with the bottom of a pan. Like many seeds, black pepper's best flavor remains locked inside until it's smashed. Place ten peppercorns at a time on a flat, hard surface. Using a small saucepot or small skillet, apply pressure with the heel of your hand to break the seeds a few at a time. Roll logs of goat cheese in this exceptionally fresh seasoning, or use it as you would ground black pepper.

Roasted Vegetables

As an appetizer, main course, or an ingredient in Basic Pasta Salad (page 267), or as a spread with crackers, this mélange of roasted veggies, accented by sweet balsamic vinegar and mellow roasted garlic, is easy comfort food. Cut everything into one-inch cubes. You'll probably need two roasting pans or baking dishes for this recipe.

Serves 8

1 small eggplant (about 1 pound), cubed

1 small butternut squash (about 1½ pounds), peeled and cubed

1 pound red potatoes, cubed

3 large "horse" carrots, cut into 1-inch pieces, or approximately 1 pound of cello carrots

12 cloves garlic, peeled

2 large white onions, cut into 1-inch cubes

1 medium zucchini and 1 yellow squash, cubed

10 ounces mushrooms

3 tablespoons olive oil

1 teaspoon kosher salt

½ teaspoon freshly ground black pepper

*½ cup mixed chopped herbs, such as rosemary, thyme, oregano, parsley, chives, **or** less than ¼ cup of dried mixed herbs*

¼ cup good quality balsamic vinegar (see "Choosing Balsamic Vinegar," page 26)

1. Heat oven to 350 degrees. In a large bowl, combine eggplant, squash, potatoes, carrots, garlic, onions, zucchini, yellow squash, mushrooms, olive oil, salt, pepper, and mixed herbs; toss to coat.
2. Spread into a single layer onto 1 or 2 roasting pans, jellyroll pans, or baking dishes. Cook 1 to 1½ hours, until vegetables are very tender and browned lightly. Sprinkle with balsamic vinegar, and set out to cool.

Chinese Wrinkled String Beans

Chef Geh Yah Yin, my Chinese chef-instructor at the Culinary Institute of America, said, "Don't think too much—your face will shrink early." Then he taught me this recipe for green beans.

Serves 4

Oil for deep-frying
1 pound fresh green beans, stem ends snipped off
2 tablespoons peanut oil
½ cup chopped scallions
1 (1-inch) piece fresh ginger, peeled and finely chopped
1 tablespoon chopped garlic
1 teaspoon sugar
1 teaspoon white vinegar
Salt
Asian sesame oil

1. Heat 2 inches of oil in a wok or deep skillet to 350 degrees (a piece of vegetable should sizzle vigorously, but the oil should not smoke). Carefully fry the green beans in 4 small batches. They will shrivel as they cook—they take about 5 minutes per batch. Leave time in between batches to let the oil come back up to temperature.
2. In a separate skillet, heat the peanut oil. Add the scallions, ginger, garlic, sugar, and vinegar. Cook 1 minute, until the garlic turns white. Add the green beans; toss to coat. Season with salt and Asian sesame oil.

Green Beans and Pine Nut Sauté

The key to keeping this attractive dish vibrant is to select only exquisitely fresh, plump, unblemished green beans, and cook them in small batches just until tender, shocking them to lock in color, flavor, and nutrients (see "It's Easy Being Green," page 44).

Serves 6

2 tablespoons extra-virgin olive oil
*½ cup finely chopped shallots **or** red onion*
¼ cup pine nuts
1 cup diced tomatoes
1 pound fresh green beans, blanched in salted water and shocked
Salt and freshly ground black pepper

Heat the oil in a large skillet over medium heat; add the shallots and pine nuts. Cook until the pine nuts begin to brown lightly, 3–4 minutes. Add the green beans, tomatoes, salt, and pepper. Cook only enough to warm through and soften the tomatoes slightly. Serve hot or at room temperature.

Chapter Eight

The Onion Family

Jumbo Beer-Battered Onion Rings

One regular customer at Restaurant Jasper in Boston would order a glass of whiskey and an extra-large steak, and sit at the bar smoking cigars. When Jasper offered him some of these delicious onion rings the guy would say, "Just the steak. Tobacco's my vegetable."

Serves 4

1 bottle (12 ounces) beer
2 extra-large eggs, beaten
½ cup peanut oil
2 cups cornstarch, plus extra for dredging
½ teaspoon salt
*2 very large Spanish **or** Bermuda onions*
Peanut oil for deep-frying

1. Whisk together the beer, eggs, ½ cup oil, cornstarch, and salt until it makes a thick batter. Cut the onions into 1-inch thick slices; separate into rings. Heat the fry oil to 360 degrees in a medium saucepan. Dredge the onion rings in cornstarch, dip into the batter, and fry. Do not overcrowd the pot. Add rings one by one to the pot, making sure the first has started to sizzle before adding the next (this prevents them from sticking together).
2. Drain on paper towels and sprinkle with salt before serving.

Stuffed Onions

French chef Georges August Escoffier, founder of the Ritz Hotel in Paris, and one of the great chefs of all time, codified many of the classic recipes of France at the turn of the twentieth century. This is one of them, which is still taught to young chefs today.

Serves 4

4 medium Spanish onions
3 teaspoons butter, divided
1 chopped shallot
1 cup very finely chopped mushrooms
1 tablespoon dry white wine

1 tablespoon finely chopped
   parsley
Salt and freshly ground black
   pepper
2 cups strong vegetable stock

1. Heat oven to 375 degrees. Trim the tops from the onions, and cut the roots off, but leave the root core in to hold the onion together. Peel the skins. Blanch the onions in lightly salted boiling water for 10 minutes. Scoop out the insides, using a melon-ball scoop or spoon, leaving ⅓-inch walls. Chop the scooped insides, and sauté them in 1 teaspoon of the butter.
2. Melt the remaining 2 teaspoons of butter in a skillet; add the shallots. Cook over medium heat until they are translucent, about 5 minutes; add the mushrooms. Cook until mushrooms have wilted, and most liquid has evaporated; add the wine, cook to almost dry. Remove from heat; add the chopped parsley. Season well with salt and pepper. Combine the mushroom mixture with the chopped onion insides, and fill into the onion shells. Place in a small buttered baking dish with the vegetable stock. Cover with foil.
3. Bake for 1 hour, basting once. Remove the lid halfway through to allow the onions to brown.

Braised Leeks

V

Silky, delicate braised leeks are juicy and light, making them an excellent foil for spicy dishes and fried foods. Broth from braising leeks is an excellent vegetable stock, so keep it for use in soups, stews, and risottos. Remember to wash leeks very well, twice even, as they often contain lots of sandy grit (see "Cleaning Leeks" Tip below).

Serves 4

5 black peppercorns
5 parsley stems
1 bay leaf
1 onion, halved
2 carrots, thinly sliced

1 rib celery, sliced
4 leeks, cleaned, halved lengthwise
1 tablespoon extra-virgin olive oil
*Chopped chives **or** parsley*

1. Combine peppercorns, parsley stems, bay leaf, onion, carrots, and celery in a non-reactive pot (see "Nonreactive Pots," page 149) with 3 quarts of water and 2 teaspoons salt. Bring to a boil; lower to a simmer. Add the leeks; simmer very gently for 15 to 20 minutes, until leeks are very tender.
2. Remove leeks from the broth; arrange them cut-side up on a platter. Drizzle with olive oil and sprinkle with chives.

Cleaning Leeks

Leeks tend to trap a lot of earth, sand, and grit in between their layers. It's important to wash leeks twice before using them. For dishes where the leek will be used unchopped (such as Braised Leeks), trim the roots leaving the root core still attached to the leek. Fan through the leek layers with your thumb and middle finger while running the leek under cold, clean water. Repeat several times.

Chopped leeks should be submerged in a large amount of clean water, rubbed together with your hands, and then skimmed off. Rinse the bowl of any accumulated grit, and wash the leeks this way again. Make sure to agitate the water vigorously with your hands to dislodge stubborn sand.

Grilled Leeks with Tarragon and Lemon Ⓥ

Some vegetables are best grilled after a light blanching. Leeks achieve a tender, silky texture and mild vegetal sweetness on the grill when they've been steamed or blanched in boiling water before they hit the barbecue. Always leave the root core attached to hold cooking leeks together.

Serves 4

4 leeks, cleaned, split lengthwise
3 tablespoons extra-virgin olive oil, divided
Kosher salt and freshly ground black pepper
1 teaspoon Dijon mustard
2 teaspoons freshly squeezed lemon juice (about ½ of a lemon)
*1 tablespoon freshly chopped tarragon, chervil, chives, **or** Italian*
   parsley

1. Heat a grill or stovetop grill pan. Steam or blanch the leeks in boiling salted water for 5 minutes. Shock them by plunging them into ice-cold water; drain well. Lightly brush them with olive oil, top and bottom; lightly season them with salt and pepper. Grill the leeks on both sides until dark brown grill marks appear. Transfer to a platter.
2. Whisk together the mustard and lemon juice. Gradually whisk in the remaining olive oil; season the dressing with salt and pepper. Drizzle this dressing over the grilled leeks. Sprinkle with chopped tarragon (**or** other herb of your choice), and serve hot or at room temperature.

Scallion Pancakes

V

A Chinese takeout favorite, these delicious, crunchy pancakes are excellent with garlicky sautéed Asian greens, such as Gai Lan (page 163), Shanghai Bok Choy (page 152), or Stir-Fried Asian Greens (page 151) and steamed jasmine rice.

Serves 4

2½ cups all-purpose flour
1½ teaspoons salt
1½ tablespoons peanut oil
1 cup water, boiling

4 teaspoons Asian toasted sesame oil
1 cup chopped scallion greens
½ cup corn oil for frying
All-Purpose Asian Dipping Sauce (page 122)

1. In a large mixing bowl, combine 2 cups flour, salt, peanut oil, and 1 cup boiling water. Mix with a wooden spoon to form workable dough, adding more flour if necessary. Knead the dough on a lightly floured surface until smooth, about 5 minutes; wrap it in plastic film, and allow it to rest for 20 minutes.
2. Divide the dough into 4 parts. Roll out 1 part into a 6" × 8" rectangle. Brush with sesame oil and sprinkle with ¼ cup of scallions. Roll, jellyroll style, into a cylinder; flatten the cylinder slightly, and crimp the ends. Coil the cylinder into a disk, and crimp or pinch to seal. Repeat with remaining dough. Roll the disks into 8-inch pancakes.
3. Heat a skillet over medium heat; add 3 tablespoons of corn oil. Fry the pancakes 1 at a time, adding more oil when necessary, and keeping finished cakes warm in the oven. Serve with All-Purpose Asian Dipping Sauce and a sprinkling of chopped scallions.

Leek Tart

In keeping with the tradition of pies at Thanksgiving, add this savory tart to your holiday table. Leeks are available year-round.

Serves 6

½ recipe Basic Pie Dough (page 92)
2 tablespoons unsalted butter
2 pounds leeks, sliced ¼ inch, washed very thoroughly
½ teaspoon salt
Freshly ground black pepper
2 large eggs
½ cup cream **or** half-and-half
¼ teaspoon ground nutmeg

1. Heat oven to 400 degrees. Roll the dough to fit a 9-inch tart or pie pan. Set the dough in the pan; refrigerate until ready to use.
2. Melt the butter in a skillet and cook the leeks over low-medium heat until very soft, about 30 minutes, seasoning with ½ teaspoon salt and black pepper to taste. Do not brown. Whisk together the eggs, cream, and nutmeg; season with salt and pepper. Combine the leeks and the egg mixture, and pour into the pie shell. Bake until golden, about 25 minutes. Allow to rest 10 minutes before cutting.

Caramelized Pearl Onions

You can use frozen pearl onions, which are already peeled, for this recipe. But the sweetness and crunch of fresh ones elevates the dish, so use them when you have the time and patience to peel for twenty minutes or so.

Serves 40

1 bag (2 cups) peeled pearl onions	*¼ teaspoon salt*
*2 teaspoons sugar **or** brown sugar*	*1 tablespoon butter **or** olive oil*

In a heavy-bottomed skillet over medium heat, combine onions, sugar, salt, and butter with 1 cup cold water; bring to a simmer. Cook gently until all water is absorbed, and onions are coated in a light glaze, about 5 minutes. Lower heat to low; cook slowly until glaze browns and onions attain golden brown appearance, about 5 minutes more.

Alternative Method: Once liquid is reduced to a glaze, put the entire pan in a 350 degree oven, and roast until browned.

When Are Onions "Translucent," "Soft," and "Caramelized"?

Practically every recipe calls for getting onions to do *something*! Translucent? Soft? Golden? Caramelized? The point of most of these techniques is to extract the natural juices that are trapped in the raw onions' cell walls. By adding heat, these walls break down, releasing sugars and flavors, which add complexity and dimension to food. Simply adding the raw onion to foods will achieve little, since it is the slow stewing in a medium such as oil or butter that draws out those flavorful elements.

After a few minutes of sizzling gently in oil or butter, onions wilt as their cell walls collapse, giving up their juices. This gives the once-opaque raw onion a watery, "translucent" appearance. The edges, once rough and sharp, are then "soft." As the water evaporates from the juices, the onions' natural sugars concentrate on the exterior of the pieces, and brown in the heat. The first stages of this transformation give onions a golden appearance. Since browned sugar is known as caramel, the browning of onions is often referred to as "caramelizing."

Onion Tart

With a lightly dressed salad, this makes an excellent lunch. Experiment with your own herb combinations to make this tart your own.

Serves 8

½ *recipe Basic Pie Dough (page 92)*, **or** *1 (9-inch) frozen pie crust*
2 tablespoons unsalted butter
3 cups thinly sliced onions
3 teaspoons chopped fresh thyme leaves, **or** *other herb, such as oregano or tarragon*

1 tablespoon flour
¾ *cup half-and-half*
¼ *cup sour cream*
2 large eggs, beaten
¾ *teaspoon salt*
½ *teaspoon freshly ground black pepper*

1. Heat oven to 400 degrees. Roll the dough out to a 10-inch disk, and fit into a 9-inch tart pan or pie plate, cutting any excess from the edges or crimping in an attractive way; prick the bottom lightly with a fork in several places. Place a sheet of waxed paper on the pie shell; fill with pie beads or dried beans and "blind bake" until lightly browned, about 15 minutes; cool on a rack. If using a frozen pie crust, follow directions on the package to blind bake.

2. Lower oven to 350 degrees. Melt the butter in a skillet over medium heat. Add the onions and thyme; cook slowly until onions are soft and lightly browned, about 15 minutes. Stir in the flour and cook 1 minute more. Transfer to a mixing bowl; combine with the half-and-half, sour cream, eggs, salt, and pepper. Pour into par-baked pie shell; bake in center of oven until filling is set and lightly browned on top, about 35 minutes.

Roasted Sweet Onions

The easiest recipes are sometimes the best. Choose sweet onions such as Vidalia or Texas Sweets for the most otherworldly experience.

Serves 4

4 large sweet onions, all the same size

1. Heat oven to 350 degrees. Trim the visible roots from the onions, but leave the skins on and the tops untrimmed. Place the onions root-end down in a baking dish. Roast in center of oven until onions are very soft, and give easily to gentle pressure. They take between 60 and 90 minutes, depending on the size of the onions.
2. Peel the outer skin, but leave on the caramelized outer layers, which add extra flavor. Alternately, you could serve them in their skins and let guests unwrap them at the table.

Roasted Shallots

These sweet jewels pair surprisingly well with both Eastern and Western foods. The Thais actually use shallots as often as the French!

Serves 4

16 medium shallots, peeled, ends trimmed, root core left intact
1 teaspoon sugar
2 tablespoons olive oil

1. Heat oven to 350 degrees. Toss the shallots with the sugar to coat. Heat the oil in an oven-safe skillet over medium heat; add the shallots. Cook 1 minute, just to start the browning. Turn the shallots, and place the pan in the oven.
2. Roast for 30 minutes. Transfer to a plate to cool slightly. If necessary, peel off any leathery outer layers before serving.

Grilled Onions with Balsamic Glaze   Ⓥ

The key to perfect, sweet grilled onions is slow, even cooking. They're custom-made for the outer edges of the grill, or a grill pan over a whisper of a flame.

Serves 4

4 large sweet onions (about the size of a baseball)
2 tablespoons extra-virgin olive oil

Kosher salt and freshly ground black pepper
1 cup good quality balsamic vinegar

1. Leaving the skin on, cut off the polar ends of the onions, about a half inch from the root and sprout ends. Halve the onions laterally; a sharp knife will help keep the onion sections together, which makes flipping them on the grill easier. Brush them with olive oil and sprinkle them with kosher salt and black pepper to taste. In a saucepan over medium heat, simmer the balsamic vinegar until it has cooked down to syrup.

2. Heat a grill or stovetop grill pan to a low heat. Place the onion slices on the grill; cook slowly without moving them until dark grill marks appear, about 15 minutes. Turn once, using both tongs and a spatula to keep the rings together. Grill until the second side is well marked and juices begin to pool on the top, another 10 minutes. Brush with balsamic syrup 5 minutes before removing from the grill. Serve brushed with remaining syrup.

Sweet Onions

Part of the American culinary awakening of the past two decades has been the discovery of regional delicacies by people across the country. There's no better example than that of Vidalia onions from Georgia. These and other varieties of onion that are naturally high in sugar content and low in "burny" sulfurs have been part of Southern cuisine for generations.

Now these onions sweet enough to eat like apples are sold in mainstream supermarkets nationwide. Slice them on salads, cook them down into "onion jam," or chop them into spreads and salsas. They should not be substituted in stews and dishes that demand a full, "oniony" flavor, since they will fade into the background in highly seasoned preparations.

Grilled Scallions

Over brown rice, with a few Japanese pickles, this is an unconventionally flavored treat.

Serves 4

16 scallions
1 tablespoon pure maple syrup
2 teaspoons Asian toasted sesame oil
A few drops Tamari soy sauce
Assorted Japanese pickles, such as pickled daikon, baby carrots, or cabbage (Korean Kim Chi, fermented cabbage, is also a good choice)

Prepare a grill or stovetop grill pan over medium-high heat. Trim the root ends of the scallions, and cut off all but 5 inches of the green parts. Whisk together the syrup and the oil. Brush the scallions with the maple mixture. Place on the grill and cook, turning regularly, until they are golden brown and tender, about 5 minutes. Transfer to a platter; drizzle with soy sauce. Serve accompanied by Japanese pickles.

Onion Jam

The concentrated sweetness and naturally complex flavor of this caramelized onion spread come from slow cooking, which breaks down the cell walls of the onions, releasing one hundred percent of their flavor. Serve it with French bread slices or crackers as an hors d'oeuvre, or as a component of a dinner meal.

Serves 8

*6–8 large onions
2 tablespoons olive oil
2 sprigs fresh thyme* **or** *½ teaspoon dried (optional)
½ teaspoon salt*

1. Halve the onions through the root end, peel them, and slice them very thinly across the grain.
2. Heat the olive oil in a large, heavy-bottomed Dutch oven over medium heat until it shimmers, but does not smoke. Add the thyme and the sliced onions. Sprinkle with salt. Lower heat; cook slowly to wilt the onions completely, stirring gently with a wooden spoon. As the onions begin to caramelize (turn brown), use the wooden spoon to scrape dried-on juices from the bottom of the pot; stir regularly to incorporate as much of these browned juices as possible. Cook this way until onions are dark brown, and mostly disintegrated into a thick spread, usually about 40 minutes, depending on the water content of your onions. Cool to room temperature, or serve warm.

Leek Potato Cakes

With a dollop of crème fraîche, sour cream, or applesauce, these crisp disks are a texturally pleasing and comforting component of a complete meal. These are excellent with a small salad and a wedge of soft, ripened cheese such as Camembert.

Serves 4

2 cups finely chopped leeks, white part only
2 cups finely grated peeled potatoes
½ teaspoon dried sage
2 large eggs, beaten
2 tablespoons flour
1 teaspoon salt
¼ teaspoon freshly ground black pepper
Olive oil for frying

1. Wash the leeks very thoroughly to remove any grit. Combine the potatoes, leeks, sage, eggs, flour, salt, and pepper in a mixing bowl; mix well. Form into eight 3-inch pancakes.
2. Heat ¼ inch of olive oil in a heavy skillet over medium heat until a piece of leek sizzles when added. Transfer 4 of the pancakes into the pan, and cook gently, without moving them, until a crisp brown crust develops, about 5 minutes. Turn, and brown the other side; drain on paper towels, and repeat with remaining cakes.

Aïoli (Garlic Mayonnaise)

In Belgium, where "frites" (homemade French fries) is a national dish, ketchup is a rarity. Instead, the Belgians dip their fried potatoes in seasoned mayonnaises like aioli, flavored with fresh or roasted garlic. Once you've tried this luxurious flavor combination, you may never reach for ketchup again.

Serves 8

*2 large cloves garlic, finely chopped,
    or pushed through a press*
¼ teaspoon salt
2 large egg yolks

1 teaspoon Dijon mustard
*Juice of 1 lemon (about ¼ cup),
    divided*
1 cup extra-virgin olive oil

1. Mash together the garlic and salt in a large mixing bowl. Wet a cloth towel, wring it out, fold it in half, and set it onto a work surface (this will hold your bowl steady while you work). Set the mixing bowl on the towel, and mix in the yolks, mustard, and 2 teaspoons of the lemon juice.
2. Using a rapid whisking action, very gradually whisk ¼ of the olive oil into the yolk mixture. Add a few drops of room-temperature water in, to help incorporate the oil, then repeat with remaining oil, adding it in a slow, steady stream, while whisking vigorously. Season to taste with remaining lemon juice.

Roasted Garlic Variation

For a sweeter, more mature flavor, wrap one whole head of garlic in foil, roast in a 350-degree oven for one hour, and squeeze the resulting golden brown paste through a strainer. Substitute this roasted garlic purée for the fresh garlic cloves in the Aïoli recipe.

Garlic Bread

It is always advisable to crisp loaves of crusty bread in the oven just before serving. This simple step improves the texture and flavor of breads by slightly more than one thousand percent. By spreading some garlic and olive oil or butter on a split loaf, you can make the bread even more scrumptious at the same time.

Serves 6–8

*1 loaf Italian bread, **or** other crusty loaf such as a baguette*
*3 tablespoons extra-virgin olive oil, softened unsalted butter, **or** margarine*
2 cloves garlic, finely chopped (about 1 tablespoon)
Pinch of crushed red pepper flakes (optional)

Heat oven to 375 degrees. Laterally split the loaf of bread. Whisk together the olive oil (or butter or margarine) with the chopped garlic. Using a brush or a rubber spatula, generously slather both cut sides of the bread with garlic oil or butter. Sprinkle with some pepper flakes if desired. Place garlic bread halves on a sheet pan or baking dish, and bake in center of oven until crisp and lightly browned, about 20 minutes.

Note: When crisping whole loaves in the oven, it is not necessary to cut them unless you're making them into garlic bread.

Baked Peppers and Onions [V]

The fruity taste of good dark green olive oil pairs very well with the taste of peppers and onions, so don't skimp on this one—use only extra-virgin oil.

Serves 4

4 or 5 medium green and red bell peppers (about 1½ pounds)
1 pound small red potatoes
1 large yellow onion
¼ cup extra-virgin olive oil
Kosher salt and freshly ground black pepper

Heat the oven to 425 degrees. Wash the peppers and cut into 2-inch pieces. Scrub the potatoes and cut into 1 inch-slices or chunks. Peel the onion and cut into chunks. Place everything into a shallow oven-proof dish; pour the olive oil over the vegetables; toss to coat. Sprinkle with the salt and lots of pepper. Bake for about 30 minutes, until the potatoes are tender.

Keeping It Real: Seasoning at Every Stage of the Cooking Process

Imagine trying to teach a child everything from kindergarten to high school graduation in one year, when he or she is eighteen. Even if it were possible, you'd never be able to see whether the student was making progress, and there'd undoubtedly be important lessons skipped over. That's what seasoning all at once at the end of cooking is like. Competent chefs are constantly seasoning and tasting foods at every stage of the cooking process. That means starting the vegetables in a stew with a pinch of salt, tasting and seasoning the stock before it's added, and giving a final taste and adjustment just before serving the stew. It ensures that foods develop layers of flavor and complexity as they cook.

Vidalia Onion Salad

Sweet onion varieties like Vidalia, Maui, Walla Walla, and Oso Sweet are so low in sulfur that they have more of a fruity taste than an "oniony" one. That makes them perfect for eating raw. Thin shavings have a pleasing crunch without the teary pungency of yellow onions.

Serves 4

1 large Vidalia or other sweet onion (about 8 ounces)
2 tablespoons extra-virgin olive oil
1 lemon
¼ teaspoon celery seeds
Kosher salt and freshly ground black pepper to taste
French bread, or other crusty bread, warmed in the oven to crisp

Slice the onion into very thin rings, almost shavings. Arrange them in an attractive mound at the center of a serving plate. Drizzle them well with olive oil and a squeeze of lemon. Shower them with celery seeds, and season with salt and pepper. Allow them to rest for 30 minutes to an hour before serving with crusty bread.

Chive Dumplings

Serves 6

1 cup finely diced firm tofu
1 cup finely chopped chives
1 teaspoon sugar
1 teaspoon Asian chili sauce **or**
   ½ teaspoon ground white pepper

1 egg white, beaten
1 tablespoon soy sauce
1 teaspoon sesame oil
1 package wonton skins

1. Combine tofu, chives, sugar, chili sauce (or pepper), all but 1 teaspoon of the egg white, soy sauce, and sesame oil.
2. Place 2 teaspoons of filling onto a wonton skin. Use your finger to moisten the edge of the wonton skin lightly with a bit of the remaining egg white. Fold 2 opposite corners of the skin together to form a triangle shape. Seal edges together by pinching tightly with your fingers. Repeat with remaining filling and wonton wrappers, making as many triangle-shaped dumplings as filling allows. Place them on a plate dusted with cornstarch.
3. Bring 3 quarts water to a rapid boil. Boil the dumplings in batches. Serve with a dumpling sauce, such as All-Purpose Asian Dipping Sauce, page 122.

Peaks of Perfection

Floppy is soft, pointy is stiff. That's the basic rule when whipping cream, egg whites, or just about anything else that's required to be whisked into "soft peaks" or "stiff peaks." What that means is this: When the wire whisk is lifted from the bowl, it draws some amount of whatever is being whipped into a mound. The tip of that mound will either flop back upon itself when the whisk leaves the bowl, or it will stand straight up, pointing in the direction of the whisk.

Any item can be whipped too far. When cream is whipped too far, it coalesces into butter. When egg whites are beaten too far, they break down into a liquid state again. Soft peaks, therefore, are the most "stable," meaning they are unlikely to have any of the ill effects of overwhipping. They also have a more delicate, smooth mouth feel, so are more luxurious to taste by themselves. Since stiff peaks hold their shape better, they are better for decoration and as an ingredient in preparations where they're needed for structure, such as mousse and soufflé.

Pissaladiére

This Southern French version of pizza comes from Provence, the birthplace of tapénade, the olive and anchovy spread that is the flavor base for pissaladiére. This recipe makes six to eight individual pies, but you can just as easily make it as one large one, and cut pieces for your guests.

Serves 8

1 package active dry yeast
¾ cup hot tap water
2 tablespoons olive oil, divided
2 cups unbleached all-purpose flour
Salt
3 white onions, cut in half through
    root end, then sliced into thin strips
½ bunch thyme

¼ cup cornmeal
¼ cup tapénade **or** olive paste
    (available in specialty food
    stores)
3 tomatoes, seeds removed, cut into
    neat, fine dice (⅛-inch)
½ bunch parsley, chopped separately

1. Dissolve yeast in water, then add 1 tablespoon olive oil; gradually add flour, stirring with a wooden spoon and incorporating a sprinkling of salt, until dough can be worked on a board. Knead on floured surface until smooth. Allow to rise in an oiled bowl in a warm place until double in size (about 1 hour).
2. Sauté the onions with the thyme in 1 tablespoon olive oil until evenly browned (caramelized). Roll out dough very thin (1/16-inch thick) on a floured surface. Using a 5-inch diameter cookie cutter, or a coffee can, cut 8 disks of dough, and place them on a baking sheet generously dusted with cornmeal. Brush with olive oil. Spread about 2 teaspoons tapénade onto each disk, leaving a ½-inch border around the edge. Sprinkle on 2 tablespoons caramelized onions and a smattering of tomato dice.
3. Bake in very hot (450 degrees) oven until the crust is crisp and golden brown, about 20 minutes. Sprinkle with parsley and serve hot.

Pickled Red Onions

Crunchy and beautifully pink, these pair as perfectly with summer grain salads, such as Succotash Salad (page 11), as they do with polenta and a wild mushroom sauté.

Serves 8

2 large red onions, thinly sliced
1 quart boiling water
½ cup white wine vinegar
½ cup cold water
½ cup honey
1 teaspoon salt
1 teaspoon black peppercorns
½ teaspoon whole allspice (optional)

Place the sliced onions in a bowl; pour the boiling water over them and allow them to steep for 5 minutes; drain. Whisk together the vinegar, cold water, honey, salt, peppercorns, and allspice. Add the onions, and allow them to marinate for 10 minutes. Transfer to a jar, cover tightly, and refrigerate until very cold. These pickled onions will keep for several months, and get better with age.

Vegetarian Travel Destinations

The whole world is open to vegetarians. Considering some of the epidemics and spoilage concerns in many places around the globe, one might even suggest vegetarianism when traveling *just in case*! While some parts of the world present particular challenges (Eastern Europe, parts of South America, and the Caribbean for example), on the whole, it's easy to meet your nutritional needs and enjoy regional specialties all over the globe.

One billion people now reside in India, 80 percent of whom are vegetarian. Every region features its own typical masalas (spice mixtures) and local ingredients. Most of the spices used in modern cookery have their origins in this part of the world, and the inhabitants clearly continue to transform the simple to the sublime with the seeds, barks, roots, and rhizomes they use for seasoning. Among the more interesting culinary regions to visit is the western state of Gujarat. Vegetarians or not, plenty of people go to India specifically for the food. One caveat: Indian cookery uses a lot of dairy, including clarified butter (ghee), so vegans beware!

Most Asian destinations are good choices for vegetarians in search of a global graze. Vietnamese Buddhist monks follow a strict vegetarian lifestyle. And although many Vietnamese Buddhists are not strict vegetarians, they eschew meat during certain times of the year and during certain holidays. Thus, a rich vegetarian cuisine worth seeking out has evolved there. Some Buddhist sects made their way to Vietnam from China, which also has a great vegetarian realm, as do Taiwan and Tibet.

Europe defies its reputation as an unchanging block of culinary fiefdoms. Just as vegetarianism's evolution in the United States—formed from a fringe band of idealistic hippies into a mainstream lifestyle—has brought wholesale changes in food market offerings (raising the quality levels dramatically, I might add), so has it had an effect on restaurants and markets in the "Old World."

Domestically, we've got plenty to be proud of, with vegetarian sensibility becoming the norm in places you'd least expect it. But without a doubt, California and Hawaii are must-chews for the vegetarian gourmand. You could opt for a different vegetarian eatery every day in the San Francisco Bay area and never run out of new places for years. And Hawaii is, by far, the most delectable choice for meatless mawing. Organic farms on Oahu grow every conceivable vegetable and fruit— from tender baby lettuces, juicy beets and radishes, and carrots so full of nutrition and flavor that they're dark red. Local chefs know what to do with these incredible ingredients, many of which never leave the Islands.

Mushrooms and Truffles

Duxelles

This chopped mushroom spread is a classical French preparation. Chefs use it as a filling for turnovers, stuffed vegetables, savory strudels, and a zillion other things. It makes an excellent spread on crusts of baguette, and is fine in sandwiches.

Yields about 1 cup

1 tablespoon olive oil
3 shallots, chopped (about ½ cup)
½ teaspoon salt
1 package (10 ounces) mushrooms
¼ teaspoon freshly ground black pepper
¼ cup dry white wine
1 tablespoon finely chopped parsley

1. Chop the mushrooms finely (this is best done by hand, but may be done by pulsing them in batches of no more than 5 in a food processor until they're chopped, but not puréed).
2. Heat oil in a medium skillet over medium heat until a piece of shallot sizzles. Add the shallots and salt; cook until translucent, about 3 minutes. Add the mushrooms and black pepper; cook until the mushrooms have given up their liquid, and the pan is almost dry, 5–7 minutes. Add the wine, and cook until almost dry, about 3 minutes. Remove from heat; stir in chopped parsley.

Risotto with Portobello Mushrooms, Onions, and Garlic

Serves 4

*4 large portobello mushrooms
  with stems*
*6 tablespoons unsalted butter,
  divided*
*4 large white onions, finely
  chopped*
10 cloves garlic, finely chopped
1 cup arborio rice

5 cups vegetable stock **or** *water*
*2 tablespoons grated imported
  Parmesan cheese, preferably
  Parmigiano Reggiano*
1 bunch scallions, finely chopped
*Scented olive oil, such as truffle
  oil, garlic oil,* **or** *herb oil (or
  very good extra-virgin olive oil)*

1. Finely chop the stems of the mushrooms. Set the caps aside. In a large sauce pan, melt 5 tablespoons of the butter, and sauté the onions and garlic over medium heat until translucent, about 2 minutes. Add the chopped mushroom stems, and sauté a minute longer. Season with salt.

2. Add the rice. Stir well to coat, then add 1 cup of stock and stir until the liquid is mostly absorbed. Add another cup of stock, stirring constantly, and allow the rice to absorb it. Continue adding stock cup by cup, until all liquid is used, and rice is tender, but still a little firm to the bite in the middle (about 25 minutes). Stir in remaining 1 tablespoon butter and cheese, and season to taste with salt and freshly ground black pepper. Set aside.

3. Slice the portobello caps paper-thin. Divide risotto into 4 bowls, immediately sprinkle with the shaved portobellos, and garnish with scallions and a drizzle (about 2 teaspoons) of truffle oil (or other flavored oil).

Creamed Morels and Asparagus Tips in Vol au Vents

Serves 6

1 sheet (8 ounces), puff pastry cut into 8 rectangular pieces, brushed with egg wash
14 fresh morels, cut into small pieces
2 tablespoons chopped shallots
1 tablespoon unsalted butter
¼ cup Madeira wine
½ cup strong vegetable stock
½ cup cream
Salt and freshly ground black pepper
1 teaspoon chopped fresh chives
24–30 cooked pencil-thin asparagus tips

1. Arrange puff pastry rectangles on a baking sheet, spaced 1 inch apart. Bake at 400 degrees until highly puffed, and the domed top is golden brown, about 20 minutes; set on a rack to cool. Halve the cooked *Vol au Vents* (the puffed pastries) laterally.

2. Sauté shallots in butter over medium heat until translucent (3 minutes). Add morels, and cook for 5 minutes. Add Madeira. Simmer until volume is roughly halved, about 5 minutes more. Add stock, and cook until almost dry. Add cream; simmer until sauce consistency thickens to coat the back of a spoon. Season with salt and pepper. Sprinkle in chives. Set the bottom halves of the puff pastry *Vol au Vents* onto serving plates. Spoon creamed morels over each bottom, allowing some to overflow. Top each with 4 asparagus tips, and cover with pastry tops. Serve immediately so filling is hot.

Fettuccini with Morels and Spring Onions

Long pieces of onion pair nicely with the shape of this pasta.

Serves 4

1 sprig fresh rosemary
8 ounces fresh morels, halved
2 teaspoons olive oil
6 spring onions **or** *scallions cut into 1-inch pieces*
½ pound imported fettuccini, cooked al dente, drained and tossed
*   with a few drops of olive oil*
1–2 cups strong vegetable stock
1 tablespoon unsalted butter
1 tablespoon chopped Italian (flat-leaf) parsley

1. In a skillet large enough to hold all ingredients, sauté the rosemary and morels in olive oil over medium heat for 5 minutes, until soft. Add the spring onions and sauté another 1 minute.
2. Add the cooked fettuccine, 1 cup of vegetable stock, and the butter, and simmer until sauce is creamy, and adhering well to the pasta. Adjust consistency with remaining stock, season to taste, and serve sprinkled with chopped parsley. Pass Parmesan cheese if desired.

Polenta-Style Grits with Wild Mushroom Ragout

Cooked yellow cornmeal, known as "polenta," is still poured directly onto the center of the wooden table (tavola) in some farmhouses in Italy. It is then topped with a stew or ragout, and family members draw whatever portion they want from the common "pot."

Serves 4

*3½ cups Mushroom Vegetable Stock
  (page 71) **or** water*
1 cup grits
1 pound assorted mushrooms
*8 tablespoons (1 stick) butter, cut
  into small pieces*
1½ teaspoons plus 2 pinches salt
¼ of a small lemon
*2 teaspoons chopped fresh thyme
  (**or** ½ teaspoon dried)*

*2 teaspoon chopped fresh rosemary
  (**or** ½ teaspoon dried)*
*1 tablespoon cornstarch dissolved in
  ¼ cup cold water*
¼ cup grated Parmesan cheese
Freshly ground black pepper
*Roughly chopped Italian (flat-leaf)
  parsley*

1. Bring 3 cups of the stock to a boil, then stir in the grits in a steady stream. Lower flame, and set to simmer very slowly, stirring occasionally with a wooden spoon. Beware of splashing, since the stuff is molten lava at this point. Keep an eye on it while preparing the mushrooms. Should cook for about 30 minutes.
2. Clean mushrooms as best you can without running under water, using a brush or paper towel. Heat a heavy skillet over a high flame until very hot, then add the mushrooms to the dry pan. Toss in half of the butter, and allow it to melt under the mushrooms without shaking the pan (this helps them brown) for 2–3 minutes. Add 2 pinches of salt, a squeeze of lemon, the thyme and rosemary, and stir.
3. Add ½ cup stock to the mushrooms, and swirl in the dissolved cornstarch. Simmer 1 or 2 minutes to cook out the starch, then set aside, covered.
4. Finish the grits by stirring in the remaining half-stick of butter, grated cheese, and seasoning with 1½ teaspoons salt. A wooden spoon should stand up in the finished grits. To serve, portion grits onto 4 appetizer plates, make a depression on top of each portion, and spoon ¼ of the mushroom sauté onto each. Top with fresh ground black pepper and a sprinkling of chopped parsley.

Josh's Mushroom Dip

My friend Josh Martin is one of those cooks who make only about a dozen dishes, but he does them really, really well. This dip for raw vegetables is one of my favorites.

Serves 8

1 teaspoon olive oil
1 large portobello cap
1 package (10 ounces) white mushrooms
½ packet dried onion soup mix
1 pint sour cream
8 cups assorted raw vegetables, such as carrots, celery, mixed bell peppers, zucchini, and yellow squash, cut into sticks

1. Heat the olive oil in a small skillet over medium-high heat; cook the portobello until tender, about 5 minutes. Cool it, and chop it finely. Chop the white mushrooms finely, either by hand or by pulsing in a food processor in batches of 5 at a time.
2. Stir the onion soup mix into the sour cream. Fold in the chopped mushrooms. Transfer to a bowl, and serve surrounded by raw vegetables for dipping.

Portobello Pita with Buckwheat and Beans

While buckwheat is actually a seed, not a grain, it has an earthy taste and pilaflike texture that complete this earthy main-course sandwich.

Serves 4

4 medium-sized portobello
  mushrooms, stems removed
Kosher salt and freshly ground
  black pepper
1 tablespoon olive oil
4 pita pocket breads, medium-size
  (about 8 inches)

2 tablespoons mayonnaise **or**
  soy mayo
1 cup buckwheat groats **or**
  medium-granulation kasha,
  cooked according to directions
  on package
¼ pound cooked green beans

1. Brush the portobello caps clean (do not wash under water); season with salt and pepper. Heat oil in a large skillet until very hot, but not quite smoking. Cook the mushrooms top-side-down over high heat until cooked through, about 4 minutes. Small pools of juice should appear where the stem was removed.
2. Cut an opening in a pita; slather the inside with mayonnaise. Spoon in a layer of cooked buckwheat groats (or kasha), and add ¼ of the green beans. Stuff in 1 mushroom cap. Repeat with remaining pitas.

Ungrainly Grains

Sometimes things aren't what they seem. Most people think of couscous as a grain, but it isn't; it's pasta. Some consider buckwheat a grain; it isn't. It's the seed of a fruit completely unrelated to any kind of wheat. FYI: Wild rice isn't rice at all, but the seed of a native American grass. And while we're at it, next time a server tells you the choice of "vegetables" is corn or peas, remember that these are grain and legume, respectively.

Grilled Marinated
Portobello Mushrooms

Main course mushrooms like these go with anything from summer salads to wintry wild rice dishes. They're one of the best vegetarian dinners to pair with red wine. If you don't have a grill, bake the mushrooms on a sheet pan in a 400-degree oven for about ten minutes.

Serves 4

4 large portobello (4–6 inches in diameter) mushrooms, stems removed
1 cup extra-virgin olive oil
1 cup red wine vinegar
2 tablespoons soy sauce
1 tablespoon sugar
*½ cup chopped fresh herbs (such as parsley, chives, tarragon, oregano) **or** 1 tablespoon dried herbs*

1. Brush any dirt from the mushrooms, but do *not* wash them under water. Whisk together the olive oil, vinegar, soy sauce, sugar, and herbs. If using dried herbs, allow the mixture to steep for 15 minutes. In a shallow dish, pour the marinade over the mushrooms; marinate 10 minutes, turning occasionally.
2. Grill 2–3 minutes on each side. Serve whole or sliced. Sauce with leftover marinade, or save the marinade for another batch.

Mushroom-Spelt Sauté

Necessity is the mother of invention: I invented this mushroom-grain dish as a way to "use up" a number of items in my kitchen. Spelt, wheat berries (sold in Hispanic markets as trigo), or barley make great whole-grain alternatives to rice.

Serves 4

2 tablespoons extra-virgin olive oil
1 large onion, diced
2 cloves garlic, chopped
Kosher salt and fresh ground black pepper
1 package (10 ounces) mushrooms, sliced
¼ cup dry sherry **or** *white wine (optional)*
2 cups cooked spelt (available at health food stores) **or** *barley*

Heat the olive oil in a skillet over high heat until it shimmers, and a piece of onion sizzles in it. Add the onion and garlic; sprinkle with a little salt, and cook for 5 minutes, until translucent. Add the mushrooms, and cook, stirring occasionally, until some browning occurs, about 5 minutes; add the sherry, and cook until it has almost all evaporated, 2–3 minutes. Add the spelt and cook until heated through; season to taste.

Chinese Three Slivers ⊻

The silky texture of slender, white enoki mushrooms contrasts here with crunchy bamboo and "meaty" bean curd. Advertising idea-man Tuan Pu Wang, who introduced me to this dish, told me that the Chinese characters for it mean "three slivers." His creative touch was to serve the dish "taco style," wrapped in a crisp lettuce leaf.

Serves 4

2 tablespoons vegetable oil
1 can (4 ounces) sliced bamboo
   shoots, drained and rinsed
3 cakes (about 8 ounces) hard
   tofu, sliced into ¼-inch strips,
   patted dry with paper towel
1 package enoki mushrooms,
   roots trimmed, washed, and
   broken into individual strands

¼ cup Asian dumpling sauce
   (available in Asian markets),
   or All-Purpose Asian Dipping
   Sauce (page 122) plus ½ teaspoon sugar
½ teaspoon sambal **or** other
   Asian chili paste (optional)
1 tablespoon cornstarch dissolved
   in 2 tablespoons cold water
1 head iceberg lettuce

1. Heat the oil in a skillet or wok until very hot but not smoky. Add the bamboo shoots, and cook for 1 minute. Slide the tofu into the pan, and cook over high heat without stirring until lightly browned. Add the enoki mushrooms, dumpling sauce, chili paste, and cornstarch solution. Cook until thick, about 2 minutes. Transfer to a serving bowl.
2. Select 4 unbroken leaves from the lettuce head; wash thoroughly and tear them in half. Place the bowl of cooked Chinese vegetables in the center of a large serving platter, and arrange the lettuce pieces around it. Guests spoon filling into the leaves and eat the lettuce-wraps with their hands.

Chinese Black Mushrooms
with Jade Bok Choy

V

This is one of my favorite Chinatown dishes. The black mushrooms' smooth skin passes from soft to silky in the delicate sauce made from their soaking liquid, lending an almost sensual texture. Youthful, watery "jade," or "Shanghai," baby bok choy is increasingly available in produce markets, but plain old white bok choy is fine for its crunchy counterpoint.

Serves 4

20 dried black Chinese mushrooms, soaked overnight in 4 cups of water
1 tablespoon vegetable oil
3 cloves garlic, chopped (about 4 teaspoons)
¼ cup soy sauce
1 teaspoon sugar

*1 pound baby jade bok choy heads, halved, **or** regular bok choy, cut into 1-inch chunks*
2 tablespoons cornstarch dissolved in ½ cup cold water
Few drops Asian toasted sesame oil (optional)

1. Pour the soaking liquid through a strainer or cheesecloth; set aside. Discard the stems from the mushrooms.
2. Heat the oil in a skillet or wok until a piece of vegetable sizzles in it. Add the garlic and the mushrooms; sauté for 5 minutes. Add 2 cups of the mushroom soaking liquid; bring to a simmer, and cook 15 minutes over low flame. Add the soy sauce, sugar, and bok choy; raise heat and cook until bok choy is tender, about 5 minutes. Stir in the cornstarch solution; cook until thick, about 2 minutes more. Remove from heat and sprinkle with a few drops of sesame oil, if desired.

Taiwanese Mushroom Egg

Another home-cooking dish invented by Tuan Pu Wang, this dish uses only the egg whites, and a sweet "mayonnaise," also whites only.

Serves 4

6 perfect hard-boiled eggs (see "The Secret to Making Perfect Hard-
   Boiled Eggs," page 37)
2 teaspoons vegetable oil
12 shiitake mushrooms, stems removed, diced ¼-inch
1 egg white
1 teaspoon sugar
¼ teaspoon salt
½ teaspoon rice vinegar **or** white vinegar
⅓ cup peanut oil
1 tablespoon chopped fresh chives

1. Carefully halve the eggs lengthwise and discard the yolks; rinse out the whites. Heat the vegetable oil in a skillet, and cook the mushrooms until well wilted, about 5 minutes; transfer to a plate to cool.

2. In a food processor on high speed, combine the egg white, sugar, salt, and rice vinegar. With the motor running, gradually incorporate the oil until a thick white mayonnaise is formed. Mix 2 tablespoons of this white mayonnaise with the cooked mushrooms. Spoon this mixture into the egg halves, allowing the filling to mound generously. Sprinkle the tops with chopped chives. Serve 3 per person.

Spring Mushroom Risotto with Morels and Asparagus

Serves 6

½ pound medium-thick asparagus, woody lower parts removed, cut into 1-inch pieces

6 ounces fresh morels (**or** 2 ounces dried morels, soaked, liquid reserved), halved, and bottoms snipped

2 tablespoons butter, divided

Kosher salt and pepper to taste

1 medium onion, roughly chopped

6 ounces white mushrooms, sliced

2 cloves garlic, finely chopped

2 tablespoons olive oil

1½ cups arborio rice

½ cup dry white wine

5 cups hot Mushroom Vegetable Stock (page 71)

¼ cup freshly grated Parmesan cheese

1 lemon wedge

1 tablespoon chopped chives

1. Cook the asparagus pieces in boiling salted water until tender (about 4 minutes), drain, and set aside. Sauté morels in 1 tablespoon butter, seasoning liberally with kosher salt, until soft (about 5 minutes); set aside.

2. In a heavy-bottomed pot, gently sweat the onion, white mushrooms, and garlic in olive oil over medium heat until translucent, then stir in the rice with a wooden spoon until it is well coated with onion juices. Pour in the wine and stir constantly until it is absorbed.

3. Add 1 cup of the stock, and stir constantly until it is absorbed. Repeat with the remaining stock, 1 cup at a time, until the rice is mostly tender, and has a saucy consistency (about 20 to 25 minutes).

4. Remove from heat, stir in the cheese and the remaining 1 tablespoon butter. Stir in the morels, asparagus, and a squeeze of lemon. Season to taste, and serve sprinkled with chives and extra Parmesan.

Mushroom Bruschetta Ⓥ

About six years ago, I dined in a cozy restaurant outside Bologna, where the custom was to present each guest with a small plate of bruschetta to nibble on while perusing the menu. The one regret I have about not having a restaurant of my own is that I'm unable to pleasantly surprise nightly diners with this deliciously heartwarming gesture.

Serves 4

1 baguette **or** *crusty country bread*
4 teaspoons Aïoli (page 211) **or**
   mayonnaise mixed with
   chopped garlic
8 ounces white mushrooms, plus ¼
   pound mixed specialty mushrooms
   such as oyster, shiitake, enoki, **or**
   portobello (optional)
*2 tablespoons olive oil (***or*** butter;*
   not vegan)

1 teaspoon mixed dried herbs, such
   as thyme, oregano, rosemary,
   and basil
Juice of ½ lemon
Kosher salt and freshly ground
   black pepper
Fresh chopped parsley **or** *chives*
   (optional)

1. Heat a stovetop grill (or an oven to 400 degrees). Slice the bread on a diagonal into eight 1-inch thick oblong slices; spread the aïoli onto both sides of each slice. Grill or bake the bread slices until dark brown marks decorate their faces, top and bottom. Transfer to a serving plate.

2. Cut the mushrooms into large, uneven chunks and slices, and mix all the varieties together. Warm a large, heavy skillet over high heat. Add the mushrooms to the dry pan all at once, then add the olive oil
   (**or** butter); sprinkle the herbs on top. Cook without stirring for the first 4–5 minutes, allowing the mushrooms to get a brown crust. After 5 minutes, stir to mix in the herbs, and cook until the accumulating liquid is mostly evaporated. Season well with lemon, salt, and pepper. Spoon onto the grilled bread, and garnish with chopped parsley or chives if desired.

Mushroom-Barley "Risotto"

The saucy, resilient texture of risotto pairs with the nutty earthiness of barley, when the barley is prepared risotto-style like this.

Serves 4

3 tablespoons olive oil
1 large onion, chopped (about 2 cups)
½ teaspoon garlic powder, **or** *4 cloves garlic, finely chopped*
1 tablespoon chopped fresh rosemary, **or** *1 teaspoon dried*
1 pound cremini **or** *white mushrooms, sliced*
1 teaspoon salt, and additional salt to taste
1 cup pearl barley
½ cup white wine
5 cups Mushroom Vegetable Stock (page 71) **or** *other broth*
Juice of 1 lemon
Pepper to taste
Chopped chives **or** *Italian parsley*
Parmesan cheese (optional)

1. Heat the oil in a large Dutch oven or saucepan over medium-high heat; add the onion, garlic, and rosemary. Cook 5 minutes, until onions are translucent; add the mushrooms and salt. Cook 5 minutes more, until the mushrooms have wilted a bit; add the barley.
2. Cook, stirring regularly, until the barley is well coated. Add the wine; cook until alcohol has evaporated, about 5 minutes. Stir in 1 cup of stock; cook, stirring until it is absorbed. Repeat with remaining stock, adding it in 1-cup increments and cooking until it's absorbed—about 20 minutes. Adjust seasoning with lemon, salt, and pepper. Transfer to wide soup plates. Garnish with chopped chives or parsley. Pass Parmesan cheese on the side, if desired.

Oven-Roasted Mushrooms

Roasting intensifies the flavor of these savory herbed mushrooms, making them an excellent topping for whole grains like brown rice, barley, or wheat berries.

Serves 4

1 pound white, cremini, **or** *shiitake mushrooms*
1 tablespoon extra-virgin olive oil
1 tablespoon chopped fresh thyme, **or** *1 teaspoon dried*
½ teaspoon salt
Pinch of crushed red pepper flakes
1 teaspoon balsamic vinegar **or** *lemon juice*
Chopped Italian parsley

Heat oven to 400 degrees. If using shiitakes, remove stems. In a bowl, combine mushrooms, olive oil, thyme, salt, and red pepper flakes; toss to coat. Spread in a single layer into a roasting pan. Roast in center of oven for 30 minutes, until nicely browned. Toss with parsley and vinegar or lemon juice. Serve hot or room temperature.

What's a "Serving"?

For the purposes of this book, a serving is a unit of which two constitute a light meal (by itself), and three make up a substantial meal.

Vegetable-Stuffed Portobello Mushrooms

Fork-and-knife mushrooms like portobellos are attractive and easy to serve. These can be made up to one day in advance, and kept in the refrigerator before the final cooking step.

Serves 4

16 bite-size broccoli florets
2 tablespoons olive oil, divided
1 medium onion, chopped
10 ounces washed spinach leaves
Salt and pepper to taste

1 tablespoon heavy cream
1½ cups shredded Gruyère **or**
   emmenthaler cheese
4 large portobello mushrooms

1. Blanch the broccoli florets in boiling salted water and shock them in ice water (see "It's Easy Being Green," page 44). Heat 1 tablespoon olive oil over medium heat in a skillet, and cook the onion until translucent, 5 minutes. Add the spinach, season with salt and pepper, and cook until spinach is wilted. Transfer to a plate to cool, and then squeeze any excess water from the spinach. In a food processor or with a knife, finely chop the spinach, and mix in the cream and ⅔ of the cheese. Taste for salt.

2. Remove the mushroom stems; scoop out some of the dark ribs in the center of the caps. Divide the spinach-cheese mixture into the mushroom caps. Arrange 4 broccoli florets into a tight bouquet in the center of the cap, planting the stem deep in the spinach filling. Mushrooms can be cooked now, or refrigerated for cooking later.

3. Heat the broiler. Heat remaining 1 tablespoon olive oil in a large skillet. Transfer the stuffed mushrooms to the pan, cover, and cook over medium heat for 10 to 15 minutes, or until cooked through. Uncover, sprinkle with remaining cheese, and broil until cheese is molten and bubbly.

Creamed Mushrooms

For a decadent sense of luxury, nothing compares with the silky-rich taste of mushrooms in a mushroom-flavored cream sauce. This dish is delicious over polenta, poured over toasted bread for luscious open-faced sandwiches, or as part of a vegetarian sampler plate, with sweet glazed carrots, steamed snow peas, and crisp onion rings.

Serves 6–8

2 tablespoons unsalted butter
1 tablespoon finely chopped shallot **or** onion
10 ounces domestic or wild mushrooms (ceps, or porcinis, are
    exquisite prepared this way), sliced
½ teaspoon salt, and some pepper to taste
1 cup cream, plus 2 tablespoons
Lemon juice (optional)

1. In a heavy skillet, cook the shallots in the butter for 1 minute; add the mushrooms, salt, and pepper. Cook until mushrooms have given up their water, and most of it has evaporated.
2. Add the cream; simmer until the cream has reduced almost to nothing. Remove pan from heat; stir in remaining 2 tablespoons of cream. A drop of lemon juice may be added to accentuate the flavor, if desired.

Mushroom-Tofu Stir-Fry

Ⓥ

Dried Chinese black mushrooms make their own delicious stock when you soak them. In this recipe, I use this liquid for the sauce. If you choose to use fresh mushrooms, substitute Mushroom Vegetable Stock (page 71) or another strong veggie broth.

Serves 4

10 Chinese dried black
   mushrooms **or** ½ pound fresh
   shiitakes
1 medium onion, halved and
   sliced lengthwise
2 tablespoons vegetable oil
1 tablespoon chopped fresh ginger
1 bunch scallions, chopped
1 tablespoon chopped garlic
½ teaspoon salt

3 tablespoons hoisin sauce
   mixed with ½ teaspoon
   Asian sesame oil
½ teaspoon rice vinegar **or** white
   wine vinegar
1½ teaspoon cornstarch, dissolved
   in 1 tablespoon of mushroom
   soaking liquid **or** water
20 ounces of silken tofu, cut
   into cubes

1. Soak the mushrooms in 4 cups of hot water for at least 20 minutes, or overnight. Pour off and reserve the liquid. Remove the stems and slice the mushrooms thickly (¼ inch). Heat the oil in a large skillet; add the ginger, scallions, and garlic. Cook until the onions are translucent, about 5 minutes; add 1 cup of mushroom soaking liquid. Season with salt, hoisin, and vinegar; stir, and simmer 5 minutes. Stir in the cornstarch.
2. Spoon the tofu cubes onto the top of the cooking vegetables. Cover, and cook slowly until the tofu is hot, about 5 minutes. Serve with steaming hot brown rice.

Mushroom Turnovers (Empanadas)

Tailor these savory pastry pockets to your own taste. You may like to add cheese, or other sautéed vegetables—go ahead.

Serves 8

1 recipe Basic Pie Dough (page 92) **or** *1 package frozen puff pastry*
1 recipe Creamed Mushrooms (page 237) **or** *mushrooms from step 2*
  of Polenta-Style Grits with Wild Mushroom Ragout (page 224)
1 egg, beaten
¼ cup milk

1. Heat oven to 350 degrees. Roll the dough to medium thickness (about the thickness of the cover of a hardcover book). Use an empty can or other cutter to stamp out sixteen 5-inch diameter disks. Spoon 2 tablespoons mushroom filling onto the center of each disk. Moisten the edge of the disks *very slightly*, fold the disk to form a half-moon, and crimp shut with the tines of a fork. Combine the egg and milk, and brush this egg wash onto the tops of the turnovers. Transfer them to a baking sheet.
2. Bake for 25 to 30 minutes, until plump and golden brown.

Pickled Mushrooms

As a snack or as part of a dinner buffet, pickled mushrooms bring an attractive piquancy to the table. They keep refrigerated for weeks.

Serves 8

1½ pounds small white
   mushrooms, halved

3 medium carrots, peeled and cut
   into julienne

1 tablespoon olive oil

½ cup canned pimento (red
   peppers), cut into 1" × ½" strips

½ teaspoon oregano

½ teaspoon garlic powder

¼ cup cider vinegar

½ teaspoon salt

¼ teaspoon freshly ground black
   pepper

Boil the mushrooms and the carrots separately; drain. Heat the oil in a medium skillet. Cook the carrots in the oil for 3 minutes; add the mushrooms. Cook 3 minutes more; add the pimento, oregano, garlic powder, cider vinegar, salt, and pepper. Cook until everything is heated through. Refrigerate for 24 hours before serving.

What Are Truffles?

They're so special, only pigs and dogs can find them! Truffles are fragrant underground fungi related to mushrooms. Their musky aroma is heavenly to some, and hellish to others. Extremely expensive due to their rarity and inability to be cultivated, they are sold fresh, dried, or canned, usually imported from France or Italy. The Italian white truffle from Alba is the most highly prized, and is worth, literally, more than its weight in gold. Like black truffles from France, the Alba truffle is usually shaved paper-thin over simple foods like pasta, polenta, or eggs, the better to appreciate its rare character. Truffles are often served in combination with mushrooms, which accent truffles' heady aroma. For most of us nonbillionaires, gourmet stores sell olive oil infused with truffle essence, which imparts much of the same flavor for a fraction of the price.

Warm Oyster Mushroom Salad

This variation on a popular salad from New York's Orso restaurant can be served warm, or room temperature. If you can't grill or broil the mushrooms and onions, sauté them in very hot olive oil instead.

Serves 4

3 tablespoons extra-virgin olive oil, divided
1 tablespoon good quality balsamic vinegar
1 tablespoon finely chopped shallots
Kosher salt and freshly ground black pepper
2 medium red onions, peeled, cut into 12 1-inch rings
½ pound oyster mushrooms ("pleurots"), root ends trimmed, in small bunches
*6 ounces frisee, chicory, **or** other resilient salad green*

1. Whisk together 2 tablespoons olive oil, balsamic vinegar, and shallots; season with salt and pepper.
2. Heat a grill, stovetop grill pan, or broiler. Toss the oyster mushrooms and onions, separately, with the remaining 1 tablespoon olive oil. Season them with salt and pepper, and grill or broil separately. The mushrooms will cook quickly—in about 2 minutes. The onions will take longer—about 5 minutes. Spoon some of the dressing onto the hot mushrooms and onions, and use the rest to dress the greens. Arrange the hot vegetables atop the greens and serve.

Mushroom-Leek Tart

Savory pies are common in Italy and France, but with the exception of quiche, not too well known here. It's a shame, because they make beautiful presentations, and with the right ingredients they're unforgettable. This one is French in origin.

Serves 6

1 recipe Basic Pie Dough (page 92)
1 large egg
1 teaspoon milk
5 or 6 leeks, white parts only, chopped and washed twice
1 teaspoon sage
1 cup heavy cream
Kosher salt and freshly ground black pepper
1 package (10 ounces) white mushrooms, sliced

1. Roll out the pie bottom very thin, and press it into a 10-inch pie pan, leaving excess hanging over the rim of the pan. Roll out the pie top into an 11-inch round, and place onto a floured sheet pan. Refrigerate both parts until needed. Whisk together the eggs and milk.

2. Heat oven to 400 degrees. In a heavy skillet over medium heat, cook the leeks in a few drops of water until they're bright green, about 3 minutes; transfer to a plate to cool. In a bowl, combine the leeks with the cream, salt, pepper, and mushrooms; mix well. Fill the pie bottom with the vegetable mixture. Brush the rim with egg wash, and carefully place the top onto the pie (it's easiest if you fold it into quarters, then unfold it onto the pie). Brush the top well with egg wash, and cut a few vents with scissors or a knife. Bake in center of oven until golden and bubbly, about 35 minutes. Cool for 10 to 15 minutes before cutting into wedges.

Mushroom Barley

It took a long time for it to sink in when my mother told me there was no actual barley in "mushroom barley," one of my favorite traditional Jewish dishes at Bar Mitzvahs, weddings, and funerals. I got over it. You will too, once you taste this delicious dish of garlicky pasta with sautéed mushrooms.

Serves 8

1 mushroom-vegetable bouillon cube (Telma makes these—they're vegetarian, and usually sold with Jewish foods in the supermarket)
Kosher salt
1 package (12 ounces) barley-shaped egg noodle (both Goodman's and Manischewitz make this pasta, usually sold in the "Jewish Ingredients" section of the supermarket)
2 tablespoons olive oil
1 large onion, diced
1 teaspoon garlic powder
1 package (10 ounces) mushrooms, sliced

1. Bring 8 cups water to a boil; add the bouillon cube, 1 teaspoon salt, and the pasta. Cook until tender, about 10 to 15 minutes. Drain.
2. Heat the olive oil in a large heavy skillet for 1 minute over high heat; add the onion. Cook 5 minutes, until translucent. Add 1 teaspoon salt and the garlic powder; cook a minute more; add the mushrooms. Cook over high heat for 5 to 7 minutes more, until mushrooms have given up their liquid and most has evaporated. Toss the mushroom mixture with the cooked pasta.

Pasta Dishes

Basic Pasta

Use this dough to make your own ravioli, fettuccine, tagliatelle, lasagna, etc.

Yields just under 2 pounds

*3½ cups unbleached all-purpose
    flour
2 large eggs (egg substitute **or**
    ½ cup hot water will also work
    as a vegan alternative)*

*½ cup plus 2 teaspoons cold water
1 teaspoon salt
1 teaspoon olive oil*

1. Pulse the flour, eggs, water, salt, and oil in a food processor until blended, being careful not to overheat the dough. Knead it for 10 minutes on a clean work surface, until the dough is smooth and highly elastic. The dough will be very stiff, and kneading will take a little "elbow grease." Cut the dough into 4 pieces. It's best to let the dough rest 30 minutes before rolling it out.

2. If using a pasta-rolling machine (relatively inexpensive, around $20, and very liberating!), follow manufacturer's directions. If rolling by hand, proceed as follows: Flatten 1 of the dough pieces, place on a floured work surface, and roll from the center out, turning the circle a quarter turn every few moments. When the dough reaches a thickness of ⅛ inch, wrap ⅓ around the rolling pin, and draw it away from yourself, stretching it thin. Repeat this rolling and stretching process until the dough is thin enough to see your hand through. Repeat with remaining dough.

Stir Pasta Early

To prevent pasta from clumping and cooking unevenly, wait until water is boiling rapidly before adding dried pasta, and stir the pasta immediately to separate the pieces or strands. Pasta should boil vigorously in a large amount of water, uncovered.

Gemelli with Asparagus Tips, Lemon, and Butter

Butter thickens this sauce and helps it adhere to these short, twisted pairs of macaroni, which have become one of the most popular shapes introduced in the last five years.

Serves 4

*2 bunches medium asparagus, cut
    on bias into 1½-inch pieces*
½ pound gemelli pasta
*4 tablespoons unsalted butter,
    divided*

Juice and zest of 2 lemons
½ cup vegetable stock **or** *water*
Salt and black pepper to taste
Grated Parmesan

1. Par-cook the asparagus pieces in 3 batches, in 6 quarts rapidly boiling salted water, plunging them immediately into salted ice water as they are removed from cooking water (shock), then drain. Boil gemelli in the asparagus cooking water "al dente" (soft, but still slightly chewy in the center). Drain and rinse.
2. Melt 1 tablespoon butter in a skillet large enough to hold all ingredients (12-inch diameter), and add the lemon zest and asparagus pieces. Sauté on medium heat until asparagus are hot, then add the stock, toss in the pasta, and raise heat to high.
3. When pasta is steaming hot, swirl in the remaining butter, the lemon juice, and salt and pepper to taste. Serve in bowls, sprinkled with Parmesan.

Garlic Oil

This stuff is indispensable if you make Italian pasta dishes frequently. Combine one cup extra-virgin olive oil with ¼ cup finely chopped garlic. Stir. Keeps refrigerated for up to two weeks. When you sauté in it, just take from the top, which is pure flavored oil; stir it up to get little bits of garlic if you're adding it to already-cooking dishes.

Pumpkin-Spinach Lasagna

Use either "sugar baby" pumpkins or butternut squash for this recipe. The larger kind, used for jack-o'-lanterns, are not very flavorful, and are intended mostly for decoration. If you find Mexican pumpkin, called calabaza, use it.

Serves 8

1 pound lasagna
1 tablespoon salt
1 small pumpkin (2–3 pounds)
¼ teaspoon crushed red pepper flakes
¼ teaspoon ground nutmeg
2 tablespoons olive oil
3 cloves garlic, chopped

1 large bunch spinach (**or** cello bag), washed thoroughly
2 pounds ricotta
1 egg
4 ounces Parmesan, grated
4 ounces grated mozzarella **or** provolone cheese
2 cups tomato sauce

1. Cook lasagna according to directions on box (it's best to undercook a little). Rinse and drain. Toss with a drop of olive oil. Set aside. Refill pasta pot with 3 quarts water, add 1 tablespoon salt, and bring to a boil.
2. Peel pumpkin (I cut off the top and bottom and shave the outside with a knife, always shaving downward, toward the cutting board. You may find a potato peeler easier.), discard seeds, and cube into bite-size pieces. Boil pumpkin pieces 15 minutes, until tender, in salted water. Drain, and toss with crushed pepper and nutmeg.
3. In a 10-inch skillet sauté half of the garlic in 1 tablespoon olive oil, adding half of the spinach when garlic starts to brown. Allow spinach to wilt, then turn out onto a plate, and repeat with remaining spinach and garlic. Season with salt and pepper. Mix the ricotta, egg, and Parmesan together. Set aside.
4. Assemble the lasagna in layers, starting with noodle, then cheese mixture, then spinach and pumpkin. Make 2 more layers, making sure to save unbroken lasagna for the top layer. Sprinkle grated mozzarella or provolone on top.
5. Bake 30 minutes at 400 degrees until brown and bubbling on top. Let rest 15 minutes before serving with tomato sauce on the side.

Swiss Chard Ravioli

Serves 8

2 tablespoons olive oil

1 medium onion, finely chopped

1 tablespoon chopped garlic (2–3 cloves)

Pinch of crushed red pepper flakes
(optional)

1 large bunch (about 1½ pounds) red
or green Swiss chard, stems removed

12 ounces (1½ cups) ricotta cheese

½ cup grated Parmigiano Reggiano **or**
Asiago cheese (use top quality here)

1 tablespoon breadcrumbs

2 beaten eggs, divided

Salt and freshly ground black pepper

1 recipe Basic Pasta dough (page
246), rolled into 4 sheets **or** 4
(9" × 14") sheets of any pasta dough

1. Heat the oil in a large skillet over medium-high flame. Add the onions, garlic, and red pepper if using; cook 5 minutes until onions are translucent. Add the chard; cook until just wilted. Transfer to a colander to cool and drain. Once the chard has cooled, squeeze out excess moisture with your hands. Transfer to a cutting board and give it a rough chopping.
2. In a large mixing bowl, combine the chopped chard, ricotta, Parmigiano Reggiano, breadcrumbs, and half the eggs. Season to taste with salt and black pepper (season it highly, as you'll only use a little in each ravioli).
3. Place 12 evenly spaced, tablespoon-sized dabs of filling onto each of 2 pasta sheets. Using a pastry brush, paint in between the filling portions with the remaining egg. Loosely cover these pasta sheets with the remaining 2 sheets. Press down with your hands to squeeze out any air pockets, and press firmly to seal the filling in. Using a knife, or fluted pastry cutter, cut between the ravioli, separating them, and pinch the edges extra tight between your fingers. Allow them to dry for 15 to 30 minutes before cooking in rapidly boiling salted water.

Sauces for Your Swiss Chard Ravioli

These ravioli are excellent with Basic Fresh Tomato Sauce (page 185). Another delicious way to serve them is with exotic mushrooms in brown butter: Cook one stick of butter over medium flame until lightly browned, then add two cups sliced shitake mushrooms, ½ teaspoon of salt and cook two minutes. Squeeze in juice of ½ lemon, and spoon over the hot ravioli immediately before serving. Sprinkle with chopped Italian parsley.

White Lasagna with Spinach and Mushrooms

Serves 12

5 cups milk
1 large onion, roughly chopped
2 bay leaves
4 whole cloves
Pinch of nutmeg
6 ounces (1½ sticks) unsalted butter
¾ cup flour
Salt and white pepper
1 package (1 pound) no-boil
    lasagna noodles (**or** par-cooked
    regular lasagna)
1 pound ricotta

1 cup grated Parmigiano Reggiano
    or other top-quality Parmesan
    cheese
1½ pounds shredded provolone,
    Monterey jack, **or** mozzarella
    cheese
1 pound mixed mushrooms (white,
    shiitake, cremini, portobello, etc.),
    sliced, seasoned, and sautéed
1½ pounds fresh spinach (**or**
    1 pound frozen chopped spinach,
    thawed), cooked

1. Prepare the white sauce: Combine the milk, onion, bay leaves, cloves, and nutmeg in a small saucepan; simmer slowly for 10 minutes. In a medium saucepan, melt the butter, stir in the flour, and cook on medium light until it smells slightly nutty, bubbles slightly, but has not darkened in color at all, about 3 minutes. Strain the milk; gradually whisk the strained milk into the bubbling flour mixture, whisking out any lumps that may form. Simmer 10 minutes; season with salt and white pepper.

2. Assemble the lasagna: Heat oven to 350 degrees. Spread 2 cups of white sauce on the bottom of a 9" × 13" baking dish. Arrange a layer of lasagna noodles onto the sauce; dot it with spoonfuls of ricotta (half of total), and a sprinkling of each of the other cheeses (⅓ of each). Form another noodle layer on top of the cheese. Distribute all of the cooked mushrooms and spinach in a single layer, season with salt and pepper, and sprinkle with another third of the grated and shredded cheeses, and dot with the remaining ricotta. Top with a final layer of noodle, smooth on another 2 cups of white sauce, and sprinkle with remaining cheeses.

3. Bake until bubbly and browned on top, about 25 minutes. Rest at room temperature for 10 minutes before cutting into 12 servings. Serve the remaining white sauce on the side.

Ziti with Peppers and Marinated Mozzarella

While I can hardly taste the difference between a purple pepper and an orange one, I do love the festive look they give to plates of food. Certain peppers, like the very sweet red ones, and the slightly bitter fresh green ones are a must, from there you're on your own.

Serves 4

1 pound fresh mozzarella cheese **or** smoked fresh mozzarella, cut into ½-inch cubes

3 tablespoons olive oil, divided

½ cup mixed chopped fresh herbs, such as parsley, chives, oregano, mint, etc.

Pinch of crushed red pepper flakes

1 teaspoon red **or** white wine vinegar

Kosher salt and freshly ground black pepper

1 tablespoon chopped garlic (about 3 cloves)

2 cups sliced onions

3 cups sliced mixed bell peppers

2 cups Basic Fresh Tomato Sauce (page 185) **or** store bought tomato sauce

½ box (½ pound) ziti, cooked al dente

1 tablespoon unsalted butter (optional)

¼ cup grated Parmesan cheese

1. Combine the mozzarella, 1 tablespoon of olive oil, the herbs, pepper flakes, vinegar, salt and pepper. Marinate at room temperature for 30 minutes.
2. Combine remaining oil with chopped garlic. Heat a large skillet over high heat, and bring a pot of water to a boil to reheat the pasta. Add the garlic oil to the pan, sizzle 10 seconds until the garlic turns white, and add the onions and peppers. Cook, stirring occasionally, until the onions are translucent. Add the tomato sauce, and lower flame to a simmer. Dip the pasta in boiling water to reheat; transfer hot pasta to the sauce, allowing some of the pasta water to drip into the sauce and thin it. Season to taste with salt and pepper. Remove from heat.
3. Toss with marinated mozzarella, and butter and Parmesan if desired.

Fusilli (Spirals) with Grilled Eggplant, Garlic, and Spicy Tomato Sauce

Smoky, fruity flavors of grilled or roasted eggplant marry beautifully with tomatoes and garlic. Fusilli's deep crannies scoop up every drop of this complex-tasting sauce.

Serves 4

1 small eggplant (about ½ pound), cut lengthwise into 8 wedges

3 tablespoons olive oil, divided

Kosher salt and freshly ground black pepper

3 cloves garlic, finely chopped (about 1 tablespoon)

¼ teaspoon crushed red pepper flakes

½ cup roughly chopped Italian parsley

*4 cups tomato sauce (page 185 **or** page 186, **or** store bought)*

*½ box (½ pound) fusilli **or** other pasta shape, cooked "al dente"*

1 tablespoon butter (optional, not vegan)

¼ cup grated Parmesan cheese (optional, not vegan)

1. Heat grill, grill pan, or broiler. Toss the eggplant wedges with 1 tablespoon olive oil; season liberally with salt and pepper. Grill or broil it on the largest cut side for 4 minutes, until black marks show. Using tongs or a fork, turn to another side and cook 3 minutes more until it is bubbling with juices. Transfer to a cutting board to cool; cut into 1-inch pieces.
2. Mix remaining olive oil with garlic and red pepper flakes. Heat a large skillet over medium-high heat. Add the garlic mixture; allow to sizzle just 15 seconds, stirring with a wooden spoon, before adding the parsley. Cook 30 seconds; add the eggplant and tomato sauce. Bring to a simmer, add the cooked pasta, and cook until heated through; remove from heat. Finish by adding butter and cheese (if using), adjusting for seasoning, and tossing well to combine. Serve in bowls, sprinkled with additional chopped parsley. Pass additional cheese on the side if desired.

Farfalle (Bow-Ties) Fra Diavolo

This is a very quick, easy pasta.

Serves 8

2 tablespoons olive oil
1 tablespoon finely chopped garlic (about 3 cloves)
½ teaspoon crushed red pepper flakes
1 cup roughly chopped Italian parsley
4 cups Basic Fresh Tomato Sauce (page 185) **or** *1 jar*
    (28 ounces) store-bought sauce
1 pound farfalle, cooked "al dente"
Kosher salt and freshly ground black pepper

1. Bring a pot of water to a boil for reheating the pasta. Heat a large skillet or heavy-bottomed pot large enough to hold all the ingredients over high heat. Add the oil, garlic, pepper flakes, and parsley; allow these ingredients to sizzle for 30 seconds. Add the tomato sauce; bring to a simmer.
2. Using a colander or China cap (a funnel-shaped strainer), dip the cooked pasta into the boiling water for 1 minute to reheat. Transfer the reheated pasta into the sauce, letting the water that adheres to the pasta drip into the sauce and thin it a little. Toss to coat; adjust consistency with additional pasta water, and season with salt and pepper to taste. Serve sprinkled with additional chopped parsley.

Five-Minute Pasta Pesto

Serves 4

2 tablespoons olive oil
1 medium onion, sliced very thin
2 cups frozen peas
4 cups (about ½ box) par-cooked ziti
   (see "Precooking Pasta," page 255)
3 quarts rapidly boiling water

Salt and pepper
⅓ cup pesto sauce (page 81 **or**
   page 258)
1 cup chopped tomatoes
Butter and grated Parmesan cheese
   (optional)

1. Heat the olive oil in a large skillet over very high heat; add the onions and peas. Place the par-cooked ziti into the boiling water. When onions are translucent (3 minutes), use a slotted spoon or strainer to scoop the cooked pasta from the boiling water into the pan with the vegetables, allowing some of the pasta water to fall into the skillet along with it. Season well with salt and pepper.
2. Remove pan from the heat; add the pesto, chopped tomatoes, and butter and cheese if using. Toss to coat. Serve immediately.

Five-Minute Pasta 125 Ways

Create your own five-minute pasta dish using the chart below to tailor the basic recipe for Five-Minute Pasta Pesto. Simply substitute your choice of vegetables from column A for the onions and peas in the recipe, a pasta shape from column B, and a sauce from column C.

Column A	Column B	Column C
Shallots and mushrooms	Rigatoni	Tomato sauce
Garlic and peppers	Farfalle	Alfredo sauce
Steamed carrots and broccoli	Elbows	Garlic-infused olive oil
Thin-sliced eggplant and scallions	Fusilli	White cream sauce (béchamel)
Blanched green beans and	Orecchiette	Seasoned strong
yellow squash		vegetable stock

Fettuccine Alfredo

Rich enough to sate the hungriest guest, this creamy pasta was named for the famous Alfredo's restaurant in Rome.

Serves 4

8 ounces (½ box) fettuccine
½ cup butter
2 cloves garlic, minced
1 tablespoon flour
1½ cups whole milk
2 tablespoons cream cheese
1 cup grated Parmesan cheese, plus extra for garnish
Salt and freshly ground black pepper

1. Prepare the pasta according to package directions. Drain and keep warm.
2. In a large saucepan, melt the butter; add garlic and cook 2 minutes. Stir in the flour, then add the milk all at once, cooking and stirring over medium heat until thick and bubbly. Add the cream cheese; stir until blended. Add the Parmesan cheese; continue cooking until all cheese has melted. Toss with fettuccine; season with salt and pepper. Serve with extra Parmesan passed on the side.

Precooking Pasta

Restaurant chefs have developed a trick for making pasta ready-to-serve in a minute, but still pleasingly al dente. The key is to just par-cook it, boiling for less than four minutes, drain it, rinse it well in cold water, and toss it with a few drops of olive oil. It will not seem cooked when you drain it, but it will soften to the chewy consistency of fresh pasta as it sits. This can be done anywhere from an hour to a day before service. When you're ready to serve it, dip it for one minute in boiling water, and toss with sauce of your choice. This works best with small dried pasta shapes like penne, ziti, rigatoni, shells, or farfalle (bow-ties). Use this method to make any of the five-minute pastas on the facing page.

Spaghetti with Asparagus, Parmesan, and Cream

In the winter, asparagus are fatter and imported from the other side of the world. They're perfect for pastas like this, which rely on plump stems.

Serves 6

1 bunch asparagus (preferably
 chubby-stemmed)
2 teaspoons olive oil
2 medium shallots, sliced thin
¼ cup white wine
¼ cup vegetable stock **or** water
2 cups heavy cream
8 ounces (½ box) spaghetti, cooked
 al dente, drained, tossed with a
 drop of olive oil

¼ cup Parmigiano Reggiano cheese
 or other top-quality Parmesan
Juice of 1 lemon, plus 6 lemon
 wedges
Kosher salt and freshly ground black
 pepper

1. Trim the bottoms of the asparagus, and use a vegetable peeler to peel off the skin from the bottom half of the stalks. Cut the asparagus into bite-size (about 1-inch) pieces. Heat the oil in a large skillet over medium heat; add the shallots and cook 3 minutes to soften them. Add the asparagus and wine; cook until the wine is mostly evaporated, then add the stock (or water).

2. When the asparagus are mostly cooked, and the stock is mostly steamed out, stir in the cream, and bring to a boil; add the spaghetti. Cook until the spaghetti is hot, and the sauce is slightly thick; add the Parmigiano and remove from the heat. Season with lemon juice, salt, and pepper. If necessary, adjust consistency with additional stock or water. Serve with lemon wedges on the side.

Orecchiette with Roasted Peppers, Green Beans, and Pesto

Orecchiette are "little ears" of pasta—dime-sized concave disks that catch sauce very well, and have a substantial, hearty bite. If you can't find them, look for conchiglie (small shells), which are similar.

Serves 6

½ pound (½ box) orecchiette **or**
 other pasta shape
1 tablespoon olive oil
2 teaspoons chopped garlic
1 cup roasted peppers (see
 "Roasting Peppers," page 21) **or**
 store-bought roasted peppers,
 sliced
¼ pound green beans, blanched (see
 "It's Easy Being Green," page 44)

¼ cup dry white wine (optional)
¾ cup homemade pesto (page 81
 or *page 258)* **or** *fresh store-*
 bought pesto
¼ cup roughly chopped Italian
 parsley
Salt and pepper to taste
1 tablespoon unsalted butter
Parmesan cheese
Lemon wedges

1. Bring a pot of salted water to boil; cook the pasta until al dente (still a little chewy), drain it, but save a cup of the cooking water for later. Toss the pasta with a drop of olive oil; set aside.

2. Combine the olive oil and chopped garlic. Heat a large skillet for 1 minute over medium heat. Add the garlic oil; sizzle for 15 seconds, then add the roasted peppers and green beans. Sauté for 3 minutes; add the wine. Cook 1 minute until alcohol has evaporated. Add ½ cup pesto; stir. Add the cooked pasta, parsley, salt and pepper, and butter; simmer until heated through, adding a few drops of the reserved pasta water to make it saucy. Remove from heat; toss with Parmesan cheese. Serve with lemon wedges and a little extra pesto on the side.

The Best Pesto

Serves 8

5 cloves garlic, peeled
½ cup pine nuts, toasted to very light brown
1 large bunch basil, stems and veins removed, washed and dried
  thoroughly
2 cups extra-virgin olive oil
½ cup grated Parmigiano Reggiano cheese
Coarse salt and freshly ground black pepper

1. Pulse garlic in food processor until finely chopped. Add nuts and pulse a few times just to break them into pieces. Scrape the bowl to loosen anything stuck to the sides.
2. Pile in all of the basil. Pour half of the oil over the leaves, and pulse until basil is medium chopped (pieces about the size of cooked rice). Transfer to a mixing bowl.
3. Using a plastic spatula or a wooden spoon, fold in the Parmigiano cheese; season with salt and pepper, and thin to sauce consistency with the remaining olive oil. It will keep in the refrigerator for 1 week, in the freezer for up to 2 months. When using frozen pesto, do not thaw, but break off what you need from a frozen block.

Practical Pasta Picking

Certain shapes work best with certain sauces and garnishes. For thin brothy sauces, concave shapes like conchiglie (small shells) and orecchiette ("little ears") scoop up flavorful sauce with every bite. They also work best for dishes with small garnishes like peas or chopped vegetables. Longer pastas, which have plenty of surface area to adhere to, are right for thicker sauces, which will stick to long strands of spaghetti or linguine.

Linguine with Olives, Capers, and Tomatoes   [V]

Remember to use a boxed variety of pasta when looking for a vegan pasta dish. Most fresh and many frozen pastas are made with eggs. You should also check the ingredients of any dry pasta you buy, just to be sure.

Serves 8

2 tablespoons olive oil
1 tablespoon chopped garlic
½ cup assorted olives, such as
    Picholine, Ligurian, Kalamata, **or**
    niçoise, pitted
1 tablespoon small (nonpareil)
    capers
Pinch of crushed red pepper flakes
½ cup roughly chopped Italian
    parsley
2 cups chopped tomatoes

2 cups Basic Fresh Tomato Sauce
    (page 185) **or** *other tomato*
    sauce
Salt and pepper to taste
1 pound linguine, cooked al dente,
    drained, rinsed, and tossed with
    olive oil
2 tablespoons unsalted butter
    (optional, not vegan)
¼ cup grated Parmigiano Reggiano
    cheese (optional, not vegan)

1. Heat the olive oil and garlic in a large, heavy-bottomed skillet or Dutch oven until it sizzles; add the olives, capers, red pepper flakes, and parsley. Cook 2 minutes; add the tomatoes. Cook until the tomatoes soften into a chunky sauce; add the tomato sauce, season to taste, and bring back to a simmer.
2. Add the cooked linguine; cook until heated through. Remove from heat, adjust seasoning, and toss with butter and cheese if desired. Serve sprinkled with additional chopped parsley.

Skip the Oil in the Boil

I've never found adding oil to the pasta cooking water to do anything but make cleanup harder. Pasta added to oiled water still sticks together. The best way to prevent sticking is to stir the pasta immediately after adding it to a sufficient amount of rapidly boiling water. Stir again after a minute or two to catch any remaining clumps.

Polenta with Wild Mushrooms

Northern Italian comfort food like this was often placed directly onto the center of a wooden farmhouse table in Italy. Diners would draw portions from the center pile over to their plates. It's the perfect winter dinner.

Serves 4

1 recipe Polenta with Butter and
   Cheese (page 142)
1 tablespoon olive oil
1 pound assorted wild **or** exotic
   mushrooms, such as
   hedgehogs, shiitakes, oysters,
   and chanterelles (see "Fungus
   Among Us," page 63), sliced
   into large pieces
8 ounces white button
   mushrooms, sliced

2 tablespoons butter, divided
1 teaspoon salt
¼ cup chopped fresh herbs such
   as rosemary, thyme, oregano,
   and parsley, **or** 1 tablespoon
   dried
Juice of 1 lemon
Freshly ground black pepper
Grated cheese (optional)

1. Keep polenta warm over a very low flame on a back burner. Heat the olive oil until very hot, almost smoking, in a large skillet. Add the wild and white mushrooms, and 1 tablespoon of butter; do not stir. Cook mushrooms undisturbed over a high flame for 5 minutes, to give them a nice browning. Season with salt; add the herbs, stir, and cook until the mushrooms are wilted and juicy. Remove from heat and swirl in a little lemon juice and remaining butter.

2. Pour the hot polenta into a deep serving dish or bowl—it should be thick but liquidy. In a minute, make an indentation in the center of the polenta, and spoon in the mushrooms. Serve with a few grinds of fresh black pepper, and pass grated cheese if desired.

Fettuccine with Shiitake Mushrooms and Brown Butter

This is an easy, elegant pasta I learned at Orso, one of New York's legendary theater district dining spots.

Serves 4

4 ounces (1 stick) unsalted butter, divided
½ teaspoon kosher salt
*3 leaves fresh sage **or** a pinch of dried*
1 pound shiitake mushrooms, stems removed, sliced thin
¼ cup dry white wine
*¼ cup vegetable stock **or** water*
8 ounces (½ box) cooked fettuccine
¼ cup roughly chopped Italian parsley
Juice of 1 lemon, plus 6 wedges

Place all but 1 tablespoon of the butter in a large skillet with the salt. Cook over medium heat until the butter turns brown and has a smoky, nutty aroma—it should not turn black or smell burnt. Add the sage, and then the mushrooms. Cook without stirring for 5 minutes, to brown the mushrooms. Stir; cook until the mushrooms are wilted and juicy; add the wine. Cook 1 minute to steam out the alcohol. Add the stock, cooked fettuccine, parsley, and lemon juice. Remove from heat, add remaining 1 tablespoon butter, and toss to coat. Serve with extra lemon wedges.

Angel Hair with Broccoli Raab, Toasted Garlic, Fava Beans, and Pecorino Cheese

Highlight one of spring's most delicious flavors by using fresh fava beans in this dish. If fresh favas are unavailable, use fresh or frozen green peas instead. Pecorino is a semihard sheep's milk cheese, with a tangy bite. If unavailable, try ricotta salata (a pressed, dried ricotta) or feta cheese.

Serves 6

1 pound fresh fava beans, shelled (about 1 cup) **or** *1 cup fresh* **or** *frozen green peas*
1 tablespoon olive oil
2 cloves garlic, finely chopped
Pinch of crushed red pepper flakes (optional)
¼ cup black olives, such as niçoise **or** *Kalamata, pitted*

1 bunch broccoli raab, cut into bite-size pieces, blanched (see "It's Easy Being Green," page 44)
1 box (1 pound) angel hair (capellini—extra-thin spaghetti)
1 tablespoon butter
¼ cup grated Parmesan cheese
¼ pound block pecorino, feta, **or** *other semihard cheese*
Lemon wedges

1. Bring a large pot of salted water to a rolling boil. Drop the fava beans in for 2 minutes, then skim them out with a slotted spoon, and shock them by plunging them into ice-cold water. Peel off the outer leathery skin. Set them aside. Keep the water at a rolling boil.
2. Heat the oil in a large skillet over medium heat. Add the garlic, pepper flakes, and olives, and cook, stirring, until the garlic begins to brown. Add the broccoli raab; cook until heated through, about 2 minutes. Turn off flame.
3. Put the angel hair pasta into the boiling water, stir well to separate, and cook until tender, about 5 minutes—it cooks very quickly; drain, and add to the skillet, allowing some of the water from the pasta to drip into the pan. Toss with butter and Parmesan; season to taste. Divide onto serving plates. Using a swivel vegetable peeler, shave pecorino cheese liberally over pasta. Serve with lemon wedges.

Spaghetti with Sweet Corn, Tomatoes, and Goat Cheese

Late summer is the perfect time to scoop up sweet seasonal vegetables like scallions, corn, and tomatoes. When vegetables are ripe, they do all the work for you in a dish like this.

Serves 4

½ box (8 ounces) spaghetti
2 tablespoons butter **or** oil
4 scallions, chopped
2 cups fresh corn kernels (about 3 ears)
1 cup diced red bell pepper
1 jalapeño pepper, finely chopped
3 tomatoes, diced
¼ cup chopped cilantro
¼ cup water **or** stock
Salt and pepper to taste
2 ounces goat cheese, crumbled
1 lemon

1. Cook the pasta according to the package directions. Heat the butter (or oil) in a large skillet over medium heat. Add the scallions, corn, red bell pepper, and jalapeño. Cook 3 minutes; add the tomatoes, cilantro, and ¼ cup water (or stock). Season to taste.
2. Add the pasta. Sprinkle in the crumbled cheese, and toss to distribute. Divide into 4 portions, and garnish with additional chopped cilantro and lemon wedges.

Baked Ziti

Italian-Americans have a cuisine that is distinctly their own, based on adaptation of ingredients available to their immigrant forefathers when they arrived in the United States. This is a staple of the Italian-American table.

Serves 10

1 box (1 pound) ziti
Olive oil
1 quart tomato sauce
*1 pound whole milk **or** part-skim ricotta cheese*
*1 pound whole milk **or** part-skim mozzarella, shredded*
Chopped Italian parsley

1. Prepare ziti al dente according to package directions; drain, rinse, and toss with a few drops of olive oil.
2. Heat oven to 350 degrees. Line the bottom of a 9" × 13" baking pan with half of the tomato sauce. Distribute half of the cooked ziti into the pan. Distribute the ricotta by the tablespoonful onto the ziti, and then sprinkle on half of the shredded cheese. Layer on the remaining ziti. Cover the top with most of the remaining sauce, saving about ½ cup for later—the top layer does not need to be even— or use all the remaining sauce to cover the pasta completely. Sprinkle on remaining shredded cheese. Bake 25 minutes until cheese is bubbly and starting to brown. Serve with additional tomato sauce on the side, garnished with chopped parsley.

Spinach Manicotti

Everybody loves stuffed things, so give them some. Why not make it easy on yourself by making one of the easiest?

Serves 4–5

8–10 manicotti shells
5–6 ounces fresh spinach leaves, washed
1 pound ricotta cheese
½ cup grated Parmesan cheese
1 egg, beaten
½ teaspoon salt
¼ teaspoon pepper
2 cups tomato sauce
½ cup shredded mozzarella cheese

1. Cook the manicotti shells according to the package directions. Pick the stems from the spinach leaves. Steam or sauté spinach until just wilted. In a large bowl, combine the ricotta, Parmesan, egg, salt, and pepper; stir in the spinach.
2. Heat the oven to 350 degrees. Stuff the shells lightly (easy with a pastry bag or spoon); line them into a lightly greased 8" × 11" baking dish. Pour the sauce over all; sprinkle with mozzarella cheese. Bake uncovered 30–40 minutes, until bubbly in the middle.

Note: Use the same filling for jumbo stuffed shells, cannelloni, or other stuffed, baked pasta.

Raw Veggie Pasta Toss

While cooking unlocks nutrients in some vegetables, such as the vitamin A in carrots, many vegetables are at their peak of healthful elements before cooking. So eating raw vegetables in dishes like this isn't just refreshing—it's smart.

Serves 4

1 small yellow squash, diced
1 small zucchini, diced
¼ cup extra-virgin olive oil
3 ripe roma plum tomatoes, seeded and chopped
1 cup shredded broccoli (available at groceries as "broccoli slaw")
3 scallions, sliced
1 clove garlic, finely chopped
¼ cup chopped fresh basil
Salt and pepper to taste
8 ounces ziti **or** *penne pasta*
½ cup shredded mozzarella **or** *provolone cheese*
¼ cup shredded Parmigiano Reggiano **or** *other top quality Parmesan*

1. In a large bowl, combine the yellow squash, zucchini, olive oil, tomatoes, broccoli, scallions, garlic, basil, salt, and pepper. Allow to stand while you prepare the pasta.
2. Cook the pasta according to the package directions. Immediately after draining, toss with the cheese until it melts, then toss with the vegetable mixture. Serve warm.

Basic Pasta Salad

If you decide to par-cook the vegetables, simply throw them into the water with the pasta for one minute before draining.

Serves 6

8 ounces tricolor corkscrew (fusilli or spirali) pasta
*1 cup **or** more Italian salad dressing*
¼ cup sliced scallions
*1 cup chopped broccoli (raw **or** parboiled)*
*1 cup chopped cauliflower (raw **or** parboiled)*
*1 cup shredded **or** chopped carrots*
¼ cup sliced black olives
*⅓ cup shredded Gouda **or** other cheese*
⅓ cup cubed cheddar cheese
*⅓ cup shredded Parmigiano Reggiano **or** other top-quality Parmesan*
Salt and pepper

1. Cook the pasta according to package directions. While it's still warm, toss in a deep bowl with ¼ cup salad dressing; allow to cool to room temperature 30 minutes, stirring occasionally.
2. Meanwhile, combine all the other vegetables in a deep, narrow bowl or container. Add about ½ cup of dressing and stir to coat; add up to ¼ cup more if necessary. Marinate 30 minutes at room temperature, stirring occasionally. Chill, and marinate both bowls for at least 6 hours, or overnight. When ready to serve, combine the pasta and vegetables. Toss with cheeses and season to taste.

Roasted Vegetable Pasta

Picnic-lovers: You've gotta try this one. Depending on your choice of vegetables, it's a combination barbecue and summer afternoon in Northern Italy. And it's vegan! I like to cook my pasta all the way to soft (past "al dente") for this pasta salad.

Serves 12

1 recipe Roasted Vegetables (page 194) **or** *Grilled Vegetable Antipasto (page 20) cut into 1-inch pieces*
1 box (1 pound) good quality fusilli, penne, **or** *other small pasta shape, cooked according to package directions (okay, a little softer than the box says).*
2 tablespoons top-quality extra-virgin olive oil
2 teaspoons balsamic vinegar
Pinch of sugar
1 teaspoon kosher salt
¼ teaspoon freshly ground black pepper
½ cup roughly chopped Italian parsley

Place roasted vegetables in a bowl, and allow them to come to room temperature. Add the cooked pasta, olive oil, vinegar, and sugar. Toss to coat. Marinate 30 minutes. Season with salt and pepper; toss with parsley. Pack into picnic basket.

Freezing Baked Pastas

Baked pastas, such as cannelloni and lasagna, freeze very well. Portion them into airtight zipper plastic bags for convenience. Pastas with a lot of watery vegetables in them, such as carrots or zucchini, may lose some of their original texture, but will be fine to eat. Generally, the more rich items there are in the dish, such as cheese or cream, the better they will hold up in the freezer.

Small Shells with Grilled Vegetables, Olives, Oregano, and Tomatoes [V]

Make extra grilled vegetables next time you have the grill or the broiler on. See the recipe for Roasted Vegetables on page 194 for a selection of veggies to use. You'll be ready to make this simple pasta quickly, assuming you're comfortable cooking over a high flame.

Serves 8

1 box (1 pound) shell-shaped pasta (conchiglie)

*1 tablespoon olive oil **or** garlic oil (see "Garlic Oil" Tip, page 247)*

*¼ cup pitted black olives, such as Kalamata, Gaeta, **or** niçoise*

*4 cups Roasted Vegetables **or** store-bought grilled vegetables from a salad bar or deli counter*

*¼ cup chopped fresh oregano leaves, **or** 2 teaspoons dried*

1 cup roughly chopped tomatoes

*2 cups Basic Fresh Tomato Sauce (page 185) **or** other tomato sauce*

¼ cup roughly chopped Italian parsley

Salt and fresh ground black pepper to taste

*Vegetable stock **or** water*

1 tablespoon unsalted butter (optional)

¼ cup grated Parmesan cheese (optional)

Cook pasta according to package directions; drain, rinse, and toss with a few drops of oil. Heat olive oil in a large (13-inch) skillet or Dutch oven for 1 minute over a high heat; add olives and roasted vegetables. Cook 5 minutes, until hot; add oregano leaves. Cook 2 minutes more, until oregano is fragrant; stir in the tomatoes and the tomato sauce. Cook 1 minute more, then toss in the pasta, parsley, salt, pepper, and a splash of stock (or water) to keep it saucy. Cook until the pasta is hot. If desired, toss with butter and cheese.

Linguine with Gorgonzola, Asparagus, and Cream

Gorgonzola is a highly fragrant Italian blue cheese. You may prefer to make this dish using milder French Roquefort, English Stilton, or American Maytag blue cheese—all are delicious and work fine in this dish. The mildest is Danish blue, which is what is usually used in blue cheese salad dressing.

Serves 4

½ pound linguine, broken in half
1 tablespoon olive oil
1 teaspoon chopped garlic
1 pound cooked asparagus, cut into
   1-inch pieces
1 cup heavy cream

*1 cup crumbled Gorgonzola **or** other*
   crumbly cheese
1 tablespoon finely chopped chives
   (optional)
Lemon wedges (optional)

1. Cook linguine in a large pot of rapidly boiling, lightly salted water until it's soft but still slightly chewy; drain, retaining some of the cooking water, rinse under cold water, and toss with a few drops of olive oil. Set into a colander for later use. Put another pot of water on to boil for reheating the pasta.

2. Heat the oil for 1 minute over a medium heat; add the garlic and let it sizzle for 15 seconds, until it turns white. Add cooked asparagus. Sauté for 1 minute until heated through; add cream. Bring to a boil, then lower to a simmer, and cook until cream is thick enough to coat the back of a spoon, about 3 minutes; stir in the blue cheese. Cook, stirring, until cheese is mostly melted, but a few lumps remain, about 2 minutes. Using a colander or strainer, dip the pasta into boiling water to reheat it, then add the hot pasta to the cream; toss to coat. If sauce is too thick, add a splash of the pasta cooking water. Serve with a sprinkling of freshly snipped chives and lemon wedges, if desired.

Spaghetti Ai Pomodori ⬚V

The simplest pasta requires almost no cooking. Just toss the ingredients in a bowl with the cooked spaghetti.

Serves 4

½ pound spaghetti
2 cups diced plum tomatoes
2 tablespoons chopped fresh oregano leaves **or** *Italian parsley*
1 tablespoon extra-virgin olive oil
1 teaspoon finely chopped garlic
½ teaspoon salt
¼ teaspoon freshly ground black pepper

Cook the spaghetti according to the directions on the package; drain. Transfer the hot spaghetti to a large mixing bowl; add all other ingredients. Toss thoroughly.

"Fresh" Pasta

Pasta that has not been dried is called "fresh" pasta. Fresh and dried pastas are equally good, but have different textures. Most fresh pasta is used for stuffed varieties, like ravioli and tortellini, or for long pastas, like spaghetti or fettuccine. In most cities with Italian ethnic populations, there are stores where fresh pasta is made and sold by the pound. Supermarkets are increasingly carrying "factory fresh" pasta, which is mass-produced, and often of low quality. There is no substitute for homemade (see recipe, page 246), which, though time-consuming, is very easy to make. Small shapes, such as ziti, small shells, and elbows, are almost always sold dried, and are of excellent quality. Tip for supermarket shoppers: Buy imported dried pasta, and sauce it with domestic tomato sauce.

Tagliatelle Aglio e Olio

The name means "cuttings with garlic and oil." Tagliatelle is similar to spaghetti, but is cut rather than extruded (terms describe the method of manufacture), and is usually sold fresh, not dried. It's one of the easiest pastas to manufacture at home, using a home pasta-rolling machine (these inexpensive devices can enrich your food life).

Serves 4

½ recipe Basic Pasta (page 246), cut into thin strands **or**
   1 pound store-bought fresh tagliatelle, **or** ½ box dried linguine
2 tablespoons extra-virgin olive oil
2 teaspoons finely chopped garlic
Salt and freshly ground black pepper to taste
Butter and grated Parmesan cheese (optional, not vegan)
Italian parsley, chopped (optional)

Cook the pasta al dente; drain in a colander, reserving ½ cup of the hot cooking water. Combine the olive oil and garlic in a large skillet over high heat until the garlic sizzles and becomes fragrant, but does not brown. Add all the cooked pasta at once. Season to taste, add a few drops of cooking water, and toss to coat. If desired, toss with butter, cheese, and/or chopped parsley.

Buying Garlic

When buying fresh garlic, look for heads that are plump, firm, and heavy for their size. Any green shoots or spouts indicate that the garlic is old and will have an off flavor. Store whole bulbs in an open plastic bag in the vegetable drawer of your refrigerator. Markets now carry a variety of processed garlic options, from peeled cloves to fully chopped pastes. They are a great convenience, but buy these in the smallest containers possible, since they lose their fresh taste and become stale very quickly.

Cheese Soufflé

This virtually foolproof soufflé can be prepared in advance and kept in the refrigerator for up to an hour before baking, making it perfect for when guests come over. Serve it with a simple salad such as Mixed Baby Greens with Balsamic Vinaigrette, page 30.

Serves 6

½ cup unsalted butter
½ cup flour
½ teaspoon table salt
½ teaspoon paprika
Dash of cayenne **or** pepper sauce

2 cups milk
½ pound sharp cheddar cheese, diced
8 large eggs, separated

1. Heat oven to 475 degrees. Butter a 10-inch soufflé dish, and coat the inside with flour. Melt ½ cup butter in a double boiler or a steel bowl, set over a pot of simmering water. Add the flour, salt, paprika, and cayenne (or pepper sauce); mix well. Gradually stir in the milk with a stiff whisk or wooden spoon. Cook, stirring constantly, until the mixture has become very thick. Stir in the cheese, and continue stirring until all cheese is melted. Remove from the heat.
2. Beat the yolks until they are lemon-colored, then gradually stir them into the cheese sauce. In a very clean bowl, whip the egg whites until they are stiff, but not dry. Gently fold them into the cheese sauce, and then pour this batter into the soufflé dish. At this point, the soufflé may be covered and refrigerated for up to 1 hour, or baked right away.
3. Bake at 375 degrees for 10 minutes. Reduce heat to 300 degrees, and bake for 25 minutes more. Serve immediately.

Artichoke and Cheese Squares

These rich vegetable cakes are easy-to-serve, attractive savories that can be made ahead, up to three days.

Serves 8

1 (12-ounce) jar marinated artichoke hearts, drained, liquid reserved
1 small onion, finely chopped
2 cloves garlic, finely minced
4 whole eggs, beaten
2 tablespoons flour
½ teaspoon salt
¼ teaspoon each of pepper, oregano, and Tabasco sauce
8 ounces shredded Monterey jack cheese
2 tablespoons chopped parsley

1. Chop artichokes and set aside. Heat the marinade liquid in a medium skillet, and sauté the onion and garlic in it until translucent, about 5 minutes.
2. In a mixing bowl, combine eggs, flour, salt, pepper, oregano, and Tabasco. Thoroughly mix in cheese, parsley, artichokes, and onion mixture.
3. Turn into a 7" × 11" baking dish. Bake at 325 degrees for 30 minutes, until set. Cool to room temp. Cut into squares, and serve room temperature, or reheat at 325 degrees for 10 minutes.

Huevos Rancheros

Rich and delicious, this Mexican ranch breakfast will fuel your whole morning, even if you're climbing Mt. Everest that day. While this recipe calls for scrambled eggs, it works equally well with any style of eggs.

Serves 4

1 can Mexican-style black beans in sauce **or** Cuban Black Beans (page 137)

2 cups Rancheros Salsa (page 277) **or** store-bought Mexican salsa

8 large eggs

½ cup half-and-half

½ teaspoon salt

Unsalted butter

8 soft corn tortillas (8-inch diameter)

1 cup shredded Monterey jack **or** mild cheddar cheese

½ cup sour cream **or** Tofu Sour Cream (page 87)

Chopped cilantro

1. Heat the beans and Rancheros Salsa in separate pots over low flames. Scramble together the eggs, half-and-half, and salt. Melt the butter in a nonstick pan; cook the scrambled eggs over a low flame until soft and creamy, with small curds.
2. Soften the tortillas either by steaming or flash cooking over an open gas burner (see "Softening Store-Bought Tortillas," page 52). Place 2 tortillas onto each plate. Divide the hot black beans evenly onto these tortillas. Spoon the eggs onto the beans, then sauce with a ladleful of Rancheros Salsa. Garnish with cheese, sour cream, and cilantro. Serve immediately.

Rancheros Salsa

V

This salsa, the best part of Huevos Rancheros, freezes exceptionally well. Consider making a double batch and storing half for later.

Yields 4 cups

2 tablespoons olive oil
1 medium white onion, roughly chopped
1 red bell pepper, roughly chopped
1 green bell pepper, roughly chopped
4 plum tomatoes, seeded and roughly chopped
1 tablespoon chopped garlic (about 4 cloves)
1 can (14 ounces) diced tomatoes in tomato purée
1 can (7 ounces) tomatillos, drained

1 can (7 ounces) green chilies, rinsed, drained, and roughly chopped
1 teaspoon chipotle purée (optional)
1 jalapeño pepper, seeded, finely chopped
¼ cup chopped cilantro
1 tablespoon frozen orange juice concentrate
1 teaspoon ground cumin, toasted in a dry pan until fragrant
1 teaspoon dried oregano
¼ teaspoon ground cinnamon
Salt and pepper to taste

In a large, heavy-bottomed pot, heat the oil over medium-high heat until hot but not smoky. Add onion, peppers, and plum tomatoes; cook 5 minutes until onion is translucent. In a food processor, purée garlic, diced tomato, and tomatillos; add to onion mixture. Cook 5 minutes more. Add chilies, chipotle, jalapeño, and cilantro; stir in orange juice concentrate, cumin, oregano, cinnamon, salt, and pepper. Cook 5 minutes more.

Roasted Vegetable Frittata

This perfect brunch main course can be made ahead and served at slightly above room temperature. It's a perfect way to utilize leftover vegetables of all sorts—any vegetables will work.

Serves 8

1 medium zucchini, quartered
   lengthwise
1 medium yellow squash, quartered
   lengthwise
1 cup small white mushrooms
1 small (Italian) eggplant, **or** ¼ of
   a regular eggplant, cut into large
   chunks
2 tablespoons olive oil
9 eggs, beaten
¾ cup half-and-half

½ teaspoon salt
2 tablespoons unsalted butter
1 baked potato, diced
1 medium onion, chopped
Chopped Italian parsley **or** cilantro
½ cup diced tomatoes (about
   1 large)
1 cup shredded cheese (Monterey
   jack, cheddar, **or** Havarti, for
   example)
Black pepper to taste

1. Heat oven to 400 degrees. Toss zucchini, yellow squash, mushrooms, and eggplant with olive oil; spread into a baking sheet or roasting pan. Roast until tender, about 20 minutes (**Note**: This step can be done up to 2 days in advance). Raise oven temperature to 450 degrees.
2. In a bowl, whisk together the eggs, half-and-half, and salt. In an oven-safe, 10-inch nonstick skillet, melt the butter over medium heat. Add the potatoes, onions, and parsley (or cilantro); cook until the onions are softened and the potatoes are slightly browned. Add the roasted vegetables and the egg mixture. Cook, stirring with a wooden spoon, until the mixture begins to thicken, but is still mostly liquid. Stir in the cheese and tomatoes. Season with pepper. Place pan on center rack of oven, and bake until frittata puffs slightly and begins to brown on top, about 15 minutes. Remove from oven and transfer frittata to a serving plate. Allow it to rest 5 minutes before cutting into 8 wedges and serving, garnished with additional parsley or cilantro.

Boursin Omelet

An omelet, say the chefs at the Culinary Institute of America (CIA), is yellow, never browned, and cigar-shaped, not folded like a half-moon. Over the years, I've forgiven myself many times for my delicious slightly-brown, half-moon omelets, and occasionally jumped through the hoops necessary to make the ultimate CIA omelet. Both are beautiful in their own way.

Serves 1

3 large eggs
*¼ cup half-and-half **or** milk*
¼ teaspoon salt
*Pinch of white pepper **or** a dash of*
*   hot pepper sauce*

1 teaspoon unsalted butter
*2 tablespoons Boursin **or** other*
*   creamy, tangy cheese, such as*
*   goat cheese*
*1 teaspoon chopped chives **or** scallions*

1. Whisk together the eggs, half-and-half, salt, and pepper (or hot pepper sauce). Melt the butter in an 8-inch nonstick skillet over medium-low heat (this is a case where a truly nonstick skillet is really important). Swirl the pan to thoroughly coat it with butter; add the egg mixture. Allow the eggs to sizzle for a minute without disturbing them. Then, using a wooden implement or heatproof rubber spatula, scramble the still-liquidy eggs around in the pan; smooth out the top with your implement, and allow to cook, undisturbed, until the eggs are 90 percent set, but still glistening on top (residual heat will cook the egg the rest of the way when you fold it).

2. Crumble the cheese into the center of the omelet. Now, you have to make a choice: cigar-shaped or the easy way.

For a cigar-shaped ("French rolled") omelet:

a. Strike the handle of the pan with the heel of your hand to loosen the omelet and move it to the tip of the pan; use an implement to fold the third of the omelet closest to you into the center, covering the cheese.
b. Place a plate at a 90 degree angle to the tip of the pan.
c. Gently tilt the pan to the plate, allowing the omelet to "roll" into a cigar shape.
d. Sprinkle with chives; take a photograph of it before eating.

For a simple omelet:

a. Fold the omelet in half, slide onto the plate, sprinkle with chives and enjoy.

Spinach Quiche

There's no yummier way to get the iron, calcium and other goodness from spinach than this elegant, simple, savory pie.

Serves 6

1 batch Basic Pie Dough (page 92)
  or *1 store-bought unsweetened 9-inch pie shell*
¼ cup scallions, chopped
2 tablespoons unsalted butter
1 pound (1 package) fresh spinach, washed, stems removed, roughly chopped

Pinch of nutmeg
½ teaspoon salt
¼ teaspoon fresh ground black pepper
3 large eggs
*6 ounces half-and-half **or** milk*
*¼ cup shredded Gruyère **or** Swiss cheese*

1. Heat oven to 350 degrees. If using fresh pie dough, roll out a disk of 11 inches in diameter, and line it into an ungreased 9-inch pie pan. Crimp edges, gently place wax paper over the unbaked crust, and fill the cavity with dried beans or pie beads. Bake until golden brown, 15–20 minutes (this is known as "blind baking" the crust.). Cool on
   a rack; remove beans. If using a store-bought shell, bake according to package directions for "blind baking." Increase oven temperature to 375 degrees.
2. Heat the scallions and butter in a skillet until they sizzle. Add spinach, nutmeg, salt, and pepper; cook until spinach is wilted. Whisk together eggs and half-and-half in a bowl. Add the spinach mixture. Sprinkle half of the cheese into the pre-baked pie crust; add the spinach-egg mixture. Top with remaining cheese; bake 35 minutes, until the top is domed and beginning to brown.

Creamed Carrots

I believe there should be a dynamic array of colors, textures, and flavors in a meal. With their appealing color and gentle bite, these carrots supply both elements. Also, since the vitamin A in carrots is lipid-soluble, this ingredient combination aids in the release of this important nutrient.

Serves 4

1 pound carrots, peeled, quartered lengthwise, cut into 2-inch sticks
½ cup water
2 tablespoons unsalted butter
1½ teaspoons sugar
½ teaspoon salt
½ cup light cream
Pinch of grated nutmeg
White pepper (optional)

Combine the carrots, water, butter, salt, and sugar in a large skillet. Simmer over medium heat until most of the water has evaporated and the carrots are tender. Add the cream; simmer until it lightly coats the carrots and has a saucy consistency. Season carrots with nutmeg, and white pepper if desired.

Creamed Corn

Now that sweet corn of good quality is available for much of the year, celebrate with a rich, comforting dish of creamed corn accompanied by dark greens and Jumbo Beer-Battered Onion Rings (page 198).

Serves 4

6 ears sweet corn, shucked
1 tablespoon butter
*¼ cup finely chopped shallots **or** onions*
½ cup heavy cream
Salt and freshly ground black pepper
Freshly chopped chives (optional)

Using a knife, cut the kernels from the cob with a tip-to-stem slicing motion. You should have about 3 cups. Melt the butter in a skillet; add the shallots and cook until soft, about 3 minutes. Add the corn and cream; cook until thickened, about 2 minutes; season with salt and pepper. Garnish with chives, if desired.

Corn and Pepper Pudding

When I cooked at Restaurant Jasper in Boston in the late 1980s, Chef Jasper White used to make a luscious bread and corn pudding as an appetizer. Here, I've added a Southwestern touch.

Serves 6

2 tablespoons unsalted butter, melted
3 cups cubed bread, about ½-inch dice
*3 poblano **or** bell peppers, roasted and peeled (see "Roasting Peppers," page 21), and then diced*
6 ears sweet corn, shucked, kernels cut off with a knife (about 3 cups)
¼ cup chopped chives
1 teaspoon salt
½ teaspoon freshly ground black pepper
4 eggs
2 cups milk
¾ cup shredded jalapeño pepper jack cheese

1. Heat oven to 350 degrees. Combine the melted butter and bread cubes; bake in a single layer until lightly browned, about 10 minutes. In a mixing bowl, combine the roasted peppers, corn, chives, bread cubes, salt, and pepper. Transfer to a buttered 8" × 11" baking dish.
2. Whisk together the eggs and milk; pour over bread mixture. Allow to sit for 10 minutes, to let the bread absorb the custard; top with the shredded cheese. Bake until set in the center, and lightly browned on top, about 1 hour.

Stuffed Eggs

These filled eggs are a variation on deviled eggs, and are a great first course or garnish for a main-course salad. Their tops are attractively browned under the broiler.

Serves 8

8 hard-boiled eggs (see "The Secret to Making Perfect Hard-Boiled Eggs," page 37)
¼ cup Dijon mustard
3 tablespoons heavy cream
2 tablespoons finely chopped shallot
1 tablespoon rice wine vinegar
1 tablespoon chopped chives
1 tablespoon chopped tarragon
Salt and white pepper to taste
Unsalted butter

1. Heat the broiler. Peel and halve the eggs. Take out the yolks and combine them with the mustard, cream, shallot, vinegar, chives, and tarragon. Season with salt and white pepper. Transfer mixture to a piping bag, and pipe it into the egg whites (you could also use a spoon).
2. Place the filled eggs in a baking dish or broiler pan. Dot the tops with a tiny nugget of butter, and broil them until lightly browned, about 5 minutes. Serve warm.

Scrambled Egg Burritos

This innovative "wrap" was taught to me by Dona Abramson, co-owner of the Bright Food Shop, an Asian/Southwestern/Mexican fusion restaurant in New York City.

Serves 4

1 tablespoon unsalted butter
1 medium onion, finely chopped
   (about 1 cup)
½ cup sliced roasted peppers (see
   "Roasting Peppers," page 21)
9 extra-large eggs, beaten
½ cup half-and-half

Few dashes of hot pepper sauce
2 cups shredded jalapeño jack
   cheese
Salt and pepper to taste
4 (12-inch) flour tortillas
Salsa Fresca (page 64) **or**
   store-bought salsa

1. In a large skillet over medium heat, melt the butter; add the onions and sliced roasted peppers. Cook until the onions are soft and translucent, about 5 minutes. Combine the eggs and the cream, and add them to the pan. Cook, stirring constantly with a wooden spoon, until the eggs are about half cooked—still very runny; add the hot pepper sauce, cheese, salt, and pepper. Remove from heat. Eggs should be soft, creamy, and have small curds.

2. Soften the tortillas by placing them directly atop the stove burner on medium heat (see "Softening Store-Bought Tortillas," page 52); a few black spots are okay. Spoon ¼ of the egg mixture slightly off center on a tortilla. Fold the sides in upon the egg and roll the tortilla away from yourself, folding the filling in and tucking with your fingers to keep even pressure. Repeat with remaining tortillas. Serve with salsa.

Miso Eggs Benedict

Miso has a salty flavor that replaces the Canadian bacon used in traditional eggs Benedict. Have all of the ingredients ready to go, and set the English muffins to toast at the same time as you put the eggs in to poach, so you can place freshly poached eggs onto freshly toasted muffins.

Serves 4

3 tablespoons white vinegar
1 teaspoon salt
4 extra-large eggs
2 English muffins, split
Butter
½ teaspoon miso paste

½ cup homemade **or** store-bought
   hollandaise sauce (page 191)
Chives (optional)
Hot pepper sauce (optional)

1. Combine the vinegar and salt in a deep skillet with 2 inches of water. Crack each egg into its own cup. When water boils, lower flame as low as you can. Gently lower the eggs into the hot water, one by one, and pour them from the cups into the pan. Set the muffins to toast.
2. Poach the eggs for no more than 3 minutes, then remove them with a slotted spoon, allowing excess water to drain back into the skillet. Transfer poached eggs to a waiting plate. Mash together the butter and miso; spread this mixture onto the toasted muffins. Place 1 poached egg onto each. Spoon generous helpings of hollandaise sauce onto each, and serve immediately with a sprinkling of chives and hot pepper sauce on the side.

Note: Eggs can be poached up to a day in advance, and stored submerged in cold water. To reheat, gently place in fresh boiling water for a minute before using.

Two Cheese Strata

This savory bread pudding is the right choice for a dinner party or luncheon, since the assembled casserole has to rest overnight before baking anyway. Just pop it in the oven to bake an hour before the guests arrive.

Serves 6

Unsalted butter
4 large eggs
2 cups milk
1 teaspoon Dijon mustard
1 teaspoon salt
9–10 slices white bread, torn into
    bite-size pieces
8 ounces Gruyère, Havarti, **or**
    Emmental (Swiss) cheese, shredded

8 ounces ricotta, drained in a
    cheesecloth for 1 hour
¼ cup sun-dried tomatoes, roughly
    chopped
½ cup fresh basil leaves, torn into
    small pieces
Hot pepper sauce

1. Liberally butter an 8" × 11" baking dish. Whisk together the eggs, milk, mustard, and salt. Make a layer in the baking dish with ⅓ of the bread. Pour on a third of the egg mixture. Distribute ⅓ of the shredded cheese, half of the ricotta, half the dried tomatoes, and half of the basil into the dish. Season with a few dashes of hot pepper sauce. Repeat for a second layer, finishing with a layer of bread topped with shredded cheese. Cover with plastic wrap, and refrigerate for at least several hours, or overnight.
2. Heat oven to 325 degrees. Bake the strata for 1 hour, until a toothpick inserted in the center comes out clean, and the top is lightly browned. Rest at room temperature for 10 minutes before cutting into portions.

Crepes

Sweet or savory, filled or simply sauced, crepes are delicate, elegant, delicious, and very easy to make. When I need to make a dessert in a hurry, I whisk together this batter, make some crepes, and slather them with Nutella, an Italian chocolate-hazelnut spread.

Yields about 8 crepes

½ cup flour
3 large eggs
1 cup milk

1 tablespoon olive oil
¼ teaspoon kosher salt
Butter

1. Whisk together the flour and eggs until they form a smooth paste. Gradually whisk in the milk, olive oil, and salt.
2. Heat a 10-inch nonstick skillet over medium heat. Add some butter, and spread it around the pan with a brush or the corner of a towel. Add ¼ cup of batter to the pan. Swirl the pan around in a circular pattern to evenly distribute the batter.
3. Cook undisturbed until the edges become visibly brown. Using a wooden or rubber spatula, lift the edge of the crepe from the pan. Quickly flip the crepe using your fingers or a wooden spoon. Cook for 30 seconds on the second side, then slide onto a plate; keep warm while you repeat the procedure with remaining batter. Crepes can be stacked 1 atop the other for storage.

Leave Brown Enough Alone

Top tip for getting beautiful golden-brown color in a pan: Don't touch. The main culprit in washed-out looking sautéed foods is that the cook shook the pan, flipped the food, or stirred too early. To properly brown, "caramelize," or sear, the pan must be very hot, with a small amount of oil or butter, and the item being cooked must be left undisturbed until it has colored. I find that starting items, such as mushrooms, in hot oil, and then adding a nugget of butter partway through (without stirring!), browns best.

Great Crepe Fillings

Mushroom and Cheese Crepes: Spread 1 teaspoon condensed cream of mushroom soup onto a crepe. Add 2 tablespoons sautéed mushrooms and ¼ cup shredded Swiss cheese. Fold and heat in a lightly buttered pan until the crepe is slightly crisp and the cheese has melted.

Ratatouille Crepes: Spoon 2 tablespoons of warm homemade (page 183) or store-bought ratatouille or caponata onto each freshly-made crepe. Roll cigar-style, and serve with a little extra ratatouille on the side.

Poached Egg Crepes: Spread 1 tablespoon of homemade or store-bought cheese sauce, such as Alfredo sauce or béchamel with addition of shredded Gruyère cheese, onto each crepe. Top with a poached or over easy egg, and any of the flavored "compound butters" discussed on page 302. Fold into quarters and serve warm.

Banana-Chocolate Crepes: Spread 2 teaspoons Nutella or other chocolate-hazelnut spread (or chocolate icing) onto each crepe. Cover with 6 or 7 thin slices of banana. Fold crepe in thirds, forming a wedge shape. Serve dusted with powdered sugar and/or cocoa powder.

Hot Apple Crepes: Sauté 2 peeled, sliced Rome or Golden Delicious apples with 1 tablespoon sugar in 2 tablespoons butter until browned. Spoon apple mixture into 4 freshly-made crepes; fold in half. Wash out the pan with ¼ cup brandy, and ignite it with a match; pour the flaming brandy onto the crepes at the tableside.

Fricos (Cheese Crisps)

Lacy, cooked wafers of cheese make exquisite garnishes for salads, accompaniments to soups or sandwiches, and handy snack foods. Their Northern Italian origins usually dictate that they be made with Parmigiano Reggiano, but they're equally good made with Asiago, cheddar, or provolone.

Serves 4

*1 cup finely shredded Parmigiano Reggiano **or** other cheese*

Heat a nonstick skillet over medium heat. Sprinkle 1 tablespoon of cheese into a small mound on the pan. Cook until the bottom is nicely browned, then transfer to drain on paper towels. They are soft and oozy, and require a little practice to handle them properly, so have a little extra cheese ready in case the first few are "less than perfect."

Roasted Red Bell Pepper Purée

Add sweet splashes of brilliant color to plates with this simple, delicious sauce, which is perfect for Brie Timbales (page 293) or as an accent for garlic mayonnaise—see page 211—(I love this combination as a soup garnish).

Serves 8

4 roasted red bell peppers (see "Roasting Peppers," page 21), chopped
1 tablespoon tomato paste
Zest and juice of 1 lemon
2 tablespoons extra-virgin olive oil
Salt and pepper to taste

Combine all ingredients in a food processor or blender. Purée until smooth. Heat in a saucepan before serving.

Cottage Cheese Blintzes

Having grown up on frozen blintzes, I found my first freshly made ones an epiphany. Tender, not chewy, and runny with fresh, milky-sweet filling, they're a simple luxury.

Serves 4

1 cup cottage cheese
½ cup ricotta
2 tablespoons sugar
1 large egg yolk
12 crepes (see page 288)
2 tablespoons unsalted butter, melted
Jams, jellies, and confectioners' sugar

1. In a food processor, pulse the cottage cheese, ricotta, and sugar until smooth. Transfer to a bowl; whisk in the yolk.
2. Heat oven to 325 degrees. Butter a 9" × 13" baking dish. On a clean work surface, spoon a generous tablespoon of cheese filling onto the bottom third of a crepe. Fold in the sides, and fold the bottom up to envelop the filling; roll the crepe away from yourself. Repeat with remaining crepes; line them into the baking dish and brush them with the melted butter. Bake 10–15 minutes, until they have become visibly plump. Serve with a dusting of confectioners' sugar, and assorted jams and preserves on the side.

Tomato and Cheese Tart

Store-bought puff pastry makes this an easy, attractive brunch item. Always look for puff made with real butter rather than shortening—guests can tell.

Serves 4–6

*8 ounces store-bought (**or** homemade) puff pastry, thawed*
1 tablespoon olive oil
4 leeks, sliced and thoroughly washed
*3 sprigs fresh thyme leaves, picked (about 2 teaspoons), **or** a scant teaspoon dried*
Kosher salt and freshly ground black pepper
*6 ounces raclette **or** other semisoft cheese, such as Havarti **or** Gouda, sliced*
2–3 tomatoes, thinly sliced
Pinch of sugar

1. Heat oven to 375 degrees. Roll the pastry out to fit a 14" × 4" oblong rectangular tart pan (you can also use a 10-inch circular tart pan—adjust dough dimensions accordingly); prick the rolled dough with the tines of a fork in several places. Arrange the dough in the pan and refrigerate until ready to use.
2. Heat the olive oil in a medium skillet over moderate heat; sauté the leeks and thyme until the leeks are soft and translucent, about 5 minutes; season with salt and pepper, remove from heat and cool to room temperature. Spoon the leeks into the tart shell; cover with the cheese. Arrange the tomatoes in rows or concentric circles (depending on what type of pan you're using), and sprinkle them with a little sugar. Bake 40–45 minutes, until cheese begins to brown and the crust is golden.

Brie Timbales with Roasted Red Pepper Sauce

Timbales are molded shapes that look especially dynamic as individual por-tions. Usually, they're made in custard molds, which are upended and served atop a sauce, such as the red bell pepper purée in this dish.

Serves 8

4 teaspoons butter, melted
7 ounces Brie
6 ounces cream cheese
4 ounces sour cream
3 eggs
Pinch of cayenne

Salt to taste
*White pepper **or** hot pepper sauce*
  to taste
1 teaspoon butter
1 recipe Roasted Red Bell Pepper
  Purée (page 290)

1. Heat oven to 350 degrees. Bring 2 quarts water to a boil. In a food processor or blender, combine the melted butter, Brie, cream cheese, sour cream, and eggs; process until very smooth. Season with cayenne, salt, and pepper (or pepper sauce).
2. Butter 8 (4-ounce) ramekins or custard cups (small teacups will do fine also); fill with egg mixture. Place into a deep roasting pan or baking dish; put in the oven, and pour boiling water in until it reaches halfway up the sides of the cups. Bake until set, about 30 minutes. Allow the timbales to sit at room temperature for 10 to 15 minutes. Loosen timbales by running a knife around the inside of the cup, then inverting the cups onto small plates. Spoon red bell pepper sauce around.

Buying Brie and Other Soft-Ripened Cheeses

You've got to poke it to know it. Feel the ripeness of Camembert, Brie, St. André, and other cheeses that are meant to soften before serving, by applying gentle finger pressure in the center. If it feels like a block of cheddar, it's not ripe. If it feels like your cheek, it's too runny—overripe. It should feel as soft, yet firm, as the tip of your nose. This can be done perfectly well through the paper wrapping on most cheeses. You must, however, open the wooden box that many of these cheeses come in. Any proprietor who will not let you test for ripeness doesn't deserve your business.

Scrambled Eggs Masala

I don't know if these eggs were ever served in Bombay, but Chef Muré at the Culinary Institute of America called them "Indian Style." Authentic or no, they have a fragrant allure. Serve them with Indian breads for a special brunch.

Serves 2

2 tablespoons butter
¼ cup chopped onion
*¼ teaspoon cumin seed, toasted in a dry pan and crushed (**or** very fresh cumin powder, toasted a minute in a dry pan)*
¼ cup diced tomato
4 eggs, scrambled
Salt and white pepper to taste
4 teaspoons chopped fresh mint leaves

1. Melt the butter in a medium nonstick skillet over a moderate heat. Add the onions; cook 5–8 minutes, until soft. Add cumin and tomatoes; cook a minute more.
2. Stir in the eggs, salt, and pepper. Using a wooden spoon, constantly stir the eggs until they form soft, creamy curds; transfer to plates and serve immediately. Garnish with the mint.

Greek Salad Tacos

This fusion of Mediterranean and Central American fare is a wholly North American phenomenon.

Serves 4

8 (6-inch) corn tortillas
8 ounces feta, cut into 8 slices
*2 cups shredded romaine **or** iceberg lettuce*
8 thin slices ripe tomato
24 pitted Kalamata olives
¼ cup extra-virgin olive oil
1 teaspoon dried oregano leaves, preferably Mexican
Salt and freshly ground black pepper to taste

1. Soften the tortillas over a stove burner (a few black spots are okay. See "Softening Store-Bought Tortillas," page 52).
2. Place a slice of feta in the center of a tortilla, along with a pinch of lettuce, a slice of tomato, and 3 olives. Repeat with remaining tortillas. In a bowl, whisk together the olive oil, oregano, salt, and pepper. Drizzle the tacos with spoonfuls of dressing, and serve with remaining dressing on the side.

Pitting Olives

Why the Deity created olives with diamond-hard stones right in the juiciest part is one of the great unsolved mysteries of the universe. But at least they come out easily (if you know the trick)! The key is to use a tool that's as hard as the pits to get 'em out. Try the bottom of a small pot or pan. My favorite is a six-inch skillet. Put the olives on a cutting board in groups of three or four and put the bottom of the pan flat on top of them. With the heel of your hand, smash the olives between the pan and the board, using the curved edge of the pan for leverage. Once flattened, the olives'll give up their pits submissively.

Ricotta and Goat Cheese Crespelle

*Crespelle are Italian crepes—paper-thin pancakes filled with any-
thing that inspires you. Here, I use a savory two-cheese filing, but
you could just as well roll them with sautéed mushrooms, warm
ratatouille, or a dessert filling like fresh peaches, bananas, and
chocolate sauce, or berries and crème fraîche . . .*

Serves 4

*8 ounces ricotta, drained over cheesecloth **or** a fine strainer
4 ounces (one log) fresh goat cheese, softened at room temperature
¼ cup roughly chopped Italian parsley
1 egg, beaten
Salt and freshly ground black pepper to taste
8 crepes (page 288)
Butter
2 cups Quick Tomato Sauce (page 186) **or** other tomato sauce*

1. Heat oven to 350 degrees. Whisk together the ricotta, goat cheese,
   parsley, egg, salt, and pepper. Place 1½ tablespoons filling onto the
   bottom third of a crepe; roll away from yourself, forming a filled
   cylinder. Repeat with remaining crepes. Line them up in a buttered
   9" × 13" baking dish.
2. Bake for 20 minutes, until tops are slightly crisp. Warm tomato sauce,
   and make ½-cup pools onto the centers of 4 plates. Place 2 crespelle
   onto each plate. Garnish with additional chopped parsley or basil
   leaves, if desired.

Noodle Pudding

Baked side-dish puddings, which can do double duty as dessert, such as rice pudding, bread pudding, and noodle pudding, are some of the old-fashioned comfort foods from my father's generation that are making a comeback.

Serves 6

2 large eggs
¼ cup sugar
1 cup cottage cheese
½ cup sour cream
¼ teaspoon salt
¼ cup raisins, soaked for 15 minutes in a cup of hot tap water
2 cups dried wide egg noodles
3 tablespoons butter, at room temperature
Ground cinnamon

1. Heat oven to 350 degrees. Combine eggs, sugar, cottage cheese, sour cream, salt, and raisins; stir well. Cook noodles according to package directions, drain and toss with butter. Add noodles to cottage cheese mixture; toss to coat. Transfer to a buttered 9-inch square baking dish. Cover with foil.

2. Bake until fully set in the middle, about 45 minutes, uncovering halfway through. Dust with cinnamon and allow to rest 10 minutes before cutting into portions.

Challah French Toast

Challah is a braided egg-enriched bread, similar to French brioche, which is a traditional start to the Jewish Sabbath meal. Its richness and golden color make for the most luxurious and attractive French toast. The key here is to let the "royale" (egg mixture) soak all the way to the center of thick bread slices, and then cook slowly, so it gets cooked in the middle without overbrowning the outside.

Serves 4

½ teaspoon ground cinnamon
3 cups milk
6 extra-large eggs, beaten
1 teaspoon vanilla extract
3 tablespoons sugar

1 teaspoon salt
8 thick slices (1 inch thick) challah
  or other bread
2 tablespoons unsalted butter
Pure maple syrup

1. In a mixing bowl, make a paste with the cinnamon and a drop of the milk. Whisk in the rest of the milk, the eggs, vanilla, sugar, and salt. Transfer to a wide, deep dish, and submerge the bread slices in the egg mixture. Allow to soak for at least 10 minutes, pressing the slices gently under with your fingertips to keep them submerged, and turning them halfway through.
2. Heat a large, heavy-bottomed skillet (the best is a cast-iron "Griswold") over a medium-low flame. A piece of butter should sizzle but not smoke when it is added. Melt ¼ of the butter, and fry the soaked bread 2 pieces at a time (it's important not to crowd the pan) on both sides until they bounce back when poked with a finger, about 4 minutes per side. Serve them as they come out of the pan, or keep them warm in the oven. Do not reuse butter—wipe the pan after each batch. Serve with pure maple syrup.

Is There a Pancake Tree?

No. There isn't. But there is a maple, the source of the luscious, natural, woodsy-tasting syrup that pancakes live for. Pure maple syrup is about three times the price of "pancake syrup," which often contains no maple syrup at all. If you can choose natural, 100 percent maple syrup, do. It's made by an eco-friendly industry from renewable resources here in the United States.

Cheese Fondue

Like most families in the early seventies, mine had a fondue pot that would come out of the tippy-top closet once in a blue moon, bringing joy and mess to our dinner table. As a preteen, I'm not sure which I enjoyed more, dipping the veggies and bread cubes in the molten cheese, or playing with the Sterno, but now I'm in love with the communal, get-together nature of this way to dine.

Serves 6

1 garlic clove, halved
2 cups dry white wine
¾ pound Emmental (Swiss) cheese, shredded (3 cups)
¾ pound Gruyère cheese, shredded (3 cups)

1 tablespoon cornstarch
2 tablespoons kirsch
Assorted steamed vegetables such as carrot sticks, broccoli, cauliflower, and green beans
Cubes of French bread

1. Rub the inside of a medium saucepot with the cut side of the garlic. Discard the clove, or leave it in. Add the wine, and cook over medium heat until it simmers. Whisk in the cheese in small handfuls, making sure that the last addition has completely melted before adding the next. Combine the cornstarch and kirsch into a paste; whisk into cheese mixture. Simmer the fondue gently for 5 to 7 minutes to allow the cornstarch to thicken.
2. Transfer the cheese mixture to a fondue pot, and set a low flame under it—just enough to keep it at the border of simmering. Assemble a platter with the vegetables and bread cubes, and set the table with either long fondue forks or long wooden skewers.

Chinese Soy Sauce Eggs

These strikingly dark, double-cooked spiced eggs are an excellent first course with a salad of baby Asian greens dressed with a few drops of rice vinegar and sesame oil.

Serves 4

8 large eggs
½ cup soy sauce
2 tablespoons sugar

2 tablespoons Chinese 5-spice powder
  (available in supermarkets)
1 tablespoon chopped garlic

Hard boil the eggs, about 10 minutes; run them under cold water, and peel them. Bring 4 cups water to a boil in a medium saucepan. Add the soy sauce and sugar. Simmer 5 minutes; add the 5-spice, garlic, and peeled eggs. Cover; simmer slowly for at least an hour, until the soy sauce's color has penetrated well into the eggs, all the way to the yolk. Cool in the cooking liquid, and serve warm or room temperature.

Step Up from Cheez Whiz?

A beautifully composed cheese board is a great way to start or end a meal or dinner party. Three basic principles make selecting and displaying cheeses easy: various textures, various strengths, and various cuts.

Textures of cheese are based on firmness—Parmigiano Reggiano is hard, aged cheddar is semihard, Havarti and Gouda are semisoft, and Brie is soft. You should have at least three cheeses on a board, and they should be of different textures.

Strengths range from mild to very sharp. Sometimes very pungent cheese, such as raclette, is very mild in flavor. You should have at least one strong cheese, such as cheddar, blue, or goat cheese (chèvre), and one mild, like the beautiful Morbier (which is decorated with a central layer of ash).

Finally, some of the cheeses should be left whole, uncut, until all of the cut pieces are gone. This creates an especially nice look with cheeses bearing an attractive rind, such as Parmigiano Reggiano or Stilton (an English blue cheese). The rest may be cut into attractive slices, crumbled for easy access (as in Roquefort), or left alone (as with soft, ripened cheeses like Camembert or Brie). A basket of sliced French bread, crackers, and a bunch of grapes is all that's needed to complete the picture. All wine goes well with cheese.

Chapter Twelve

Desserts and Baked Goods

Compound Butters for Breads and Summer Grilling

Chefs have been melting flavored butters, called compound butters, over grilled items like portobello mushrooms for years, adding flavor and richness, while taking advantage of the savory natural juices cooked foods produce. They know that as the butter melts, it mixes with the intense char on the food's surface, making a sauce that capitalizes on the food's own unique character.

Mixing olives, herbs, and essences into whole butter is easy and will juice up your barbecue table this summer.

Some butter-flavor combinations are classic, like Maitre d' butter with shallots, lemon, and parsley.

Use high quality unsalted butter at room temperature when making compound butters. Mix by hand or machine. Some barbecue chefs like to melt a little compound butter and brush it onto the food while it's on the grill. This adds additional flavor, but can bring up excessive flame and smoke from the coals, which can give the food an off taste.

Garlic and Basil Butter

4 ounces (1 stick) butter, room
temperature
2 cloves garlic, finely minced
Salt and pepper
½ cup fresh basil leaves, washed

1. Cream the butter in a 2-quart mixing bowl with a wooden spoon until smooth. Work in the minced garlic, and salt and pepper to taste.
2. With a very sharp knife, gently chop the basil leaves and stir them into the butter. Spread or spoon onto grilled polenta or vegetables as they come off the grill. This butter is best used the day it is made.

Rosemary-Lemon Butter

3 lush sprigs fresh rosemary, leaves
only
1 large lemon
8 ounces (2 sticks) butter, room
temperature, cut into ½-inch slices
Salt and pepper

1. Chop the rosemary leaves finely.
2. Zest lemon with fine side of grater, then squeeze juice and reserve.
3. In a food processor or by hand, mix the butter until smooth, work in the rosemary and lemon zest, then the juice.

Black Olive Butter

⅓ cup Kalamata, niçoise, **or** other
   black olives, pitted
8 ounces (2 sticks) unsalted butter,
   room temperature
1 tablespoon freshly squeezed lemon
   juice
Pinch of crushed red pepper flakes
   (optional)

1. In a food processor, pulse olives until they are finely chopped, but not puréed.
2. With the processor running, gradually add the butter, then the lemon juice and red pepper flakes. Scrape down the sides of the bowl with a rubber spatula and mix a little by hand.
3. Turn out onto a piece of plastic food wrap and roll into a log, about 1 inch in diameter, twisting the ends of the plastic wrap to tighten the roll. Chill or freeze, and cut crosswise into "coins" when needed.

Maitre d' Butter
(excellent on bread or crackers)

4 ounces (1 stick) butter
1 tablespoon freshly squeezed lemon
   juice
2–3 tablespoons chopped parsley
1 tablespoon finely minced shallot
   or scallion
Salt and pepper

1. Beat the butter in a 2-quart mixing bowl with a wooden spoon, adding the lemon juice a little at a time until it is incorporated. Stir in the parsley, shallot or scallion, and salt and pepper to taste.
2. Spread or spoon-drop soft butter over each vegetable as it comes off the grill. Or shape it into a stick on a piece of plastic wrap, and roll it up for later use. Chill it, then cut small "coins" of compound butter to use at any time. It can be frozen for up to 3 months.

Chili-Orange Butter for Grilled Bread

8 ounces butter, room temperature
1 teaspoon orange juice concentrate
2 teaspoons dark honey
2 teaspoons New Mexico chili
   powder, **or** other chili powder
Pinch of salt

1. Pulse butter in a food processor until smooth. With machine running, add orange juice concentrate, honey, chili powder, and salt.
2. Spread or spoon onto grilled country bread.

Pumpkin Bread

Don't you dare use canned pumpkin for this bread! If you can't steal one of your kids' jack-o'-lanterns, use butternut squash instead! This is a recipe from Todd K. Snyder, a chef with whom I studied at the Culinary Institute of America.

Yields 1 loaf—about 10 slices

2 cups boiled and mashed pumpkin
1 cup sugar
1 cup brown sugar
½ cup oil
1 egg
2½ cups flour
½ teaspoon salt
½ teaspoon cinnamon
½ teaspoon cloves
¼ teaspoon nutmeg
2 teaspoons baking soda
1 cup chopped walnuts

1. Combine pumpkin, sugar, oil, and egg. Mix well.
2. Combine remaining ingredients, except nuts. Add to pumpkin mixture. Stir in nuts.
3. Bake in greased loaf pan at 350 degrees for 1 hour. Test periodically by inserting a toothpick into the center of the loaf; when the toothpick comes out clean, the bread is done.

Making Your Own Cinnamon Ice Cream

If commercially made cinnamon ice cream is unavailable, allow 1 pint of vanilla ice cream to soften but not totally melt, and then work 1 teaspoon of ground cinnamon into it with a wooden spoon. Refreeze for at least one hour before serving.

Apple Walnut Upside-Down Pie

This is the first restaurant-style dessert I made myself, so it holds a special place in my heart. Guaranteed: No one will ever forget this pie.

Serves 8

1 recipe Basic Pie Dough (page 92)

Caramel-Walnut Topping:

1 cup light brown sugar   *1 cup toasted walnut pieces, roughly chopped*
4 ounces (1 stick) unsalted butter   *Pinch of salt*

1. Melt brown sugar and butter together in a heavy-bottomed skillet, over medium-high heat, until smooth and bubbling. Cook 5 minutes. Stir in walnuts and remove from heat.
2. Spread into bottom of 9-inch pie pan.

Apple Filling:

8 or 9 Granny Smith apples, peeled,   *1½ teaspoons ground cinnamon*
   cored, and diced into 1-inch slices   *½ teaspoon ground allspice*
½ cup sugar (give or take,   *¼ teaspoon ground cloves*
   depending on sweetness of   *¼ cup flour*
   apples)   *Pinch of salt*

1. Preheat oven to 375 degrees. Roll out bottom crust very thin (¼-inch) and drape over caramel/walnut-lined pie pan. Mix filling ingredients and fill the pie, mounding somewhat in the center.
2. Roll out top crust (¼ inch thick). Brush rim of bottom crust with a little water to seal the crusts together, and cover the pie loosely with the top. Crimp the edges. Make several vents, using a fork or the tip of a knife.
3. Bake 375 degrees for 1 hour, until filling is bubbling. Cool, then reheat quickly in a hot oven before inverting and unmolding. Serve with cinnamon ice cream.

Scones

Tender and buttery, these delicate tinless muffins are traditionally served with fine marmalades and jams and thick English "clotted" cream at teatime. This recipe was taught to me by Todd K. Snyder, a classmate at the Culinary Institute of America, who made them for the elegant tearoom at Saks Fifth Avenue's flagship store in Manhattan. If you don't have cake flour, use 100 percent all-purpose flour.

Yields 12 scones

2 cups cake flour
2 cups all-purpose flour
1 ½ teaspoons baking powder
1 teaspoon salt
½ cup sugar
4 ounces (1 stick) butter, cut into
*   pieces the size of a hazelnut*

4 ounces (1 stick) margarine, cut
*   into pieces the size of a hazelnut*
¾ cup currants or raisins (optional)
2 eggs
About ½ cup milk

1. Heat oven to 350 degrees. Whisk together the cake flour, all-purpose flour, baking powder, salt, and sugar in a bowl until fluffy. Add the butter and margarine; mix with your hands, pinching together the flour between your fingers to coat it. Continue mixing until the flour has taken on the color of the butter, and it clumps, but there should still be some nuggets of butter/margarine. Add currants, if using.
2. In a separate bowl, whisk together the eggs and milk. Add egg mixture to the flour mixture, and mix with your hands or a wooden spoon just until combined. Do not overmix, as it will make the batter tough. The consistency should be like oatmeal. Add additional milk if necessary.
3. Drop the batter into 12 scones on an oiled sheet pan. Bake until set, about 20 minutes, on top shelf of the oven. For extra color, flash under the broiler for a moment to brown the tops.

Tarte Tatin

Serves 8

8 tablespoons butter, room temperature
1 cup sugar
6 medium Gala **or** Golden Delicious
  apples, peeled, cored, and cut
  into quarters

1 thin (⅛ inch) sheet store-bought
  puff pastry **or** Basic Pie Dough
  (page 92), cut into a circle
  12 inches in diameter

1. Heat oven to 350 degrees. Spread the butter evenly into a 10-inch tarte Tatin mold or heavy, 10-inch nonstick ovenproof skillet. Evenly spread sugar on sides and bottom of the pan. Starting at the edge of the pan, arrange apples, peeled side down, in concentric circles, fitting apples closely together.
2. Place pan over high heat, and cook without stirring until sugar caramelizes and turns dark golden brown, 15–20 minutes. Remove from heat, and gently press the apples closer together with a wooden spoon, eliminating any gaps. Cover the apples with the puff pastry. The dough will overlap the rim of the pan. Bake until pastry is golden brown, about 30 minutes.
3. Remove from oven and rest it for 5 minutes. Place a large serving plate on top, and rapidly invert the tart; remove the pan. Serve warm.

The Many Faces of Puff

Store-bought puff pastry dough saves you the inelegant task of repeated rolling and resting required to manufacture the stuff yourself. This frees you to use the dough whenever you want, which may be plenty often, once you discover its advantages. Here are just a few examples: Chop and sugar some apples, wrap them in puff pastry, seal with egg wash, and bake for instant apple turnovers. Cut disks, spoon in mashed potatoes and leftover curry vegetables: Voila! Instant Indian Pakoras. Try some cheese and black bean chili in a puff pastry pouch. Bake them off and they're Mexican *empanadas*. Even a small wheel of French Camembert cheese, or Brie, wrapped in puff pastry dough and baked until golden is a quickie elegant *fromage en croute* hors d'oeuvre. Cut disks, bake them between two baking sheets, and garnish with sauce and cheese for mini pizzas. Cut into strips, sprinkle with grated Parmesan, pinch in the center, and bake for "Parmesan Bowties." The possibilities are endless.

Simple Cloverleaf Dinner Rolls

Nothing brings a more comforting aroma to the house than baking rolls. The dough can be made and rolled in advance, then frozen. Just thaw and rise before baking.

Serves 12

1 envelope active dry yeast
1 cup milk, lukewarm (about 110 degrees)
6 tablespoons butter, divided
3 tablespoons sugar
1 large egg
1 teaspoon salt
3½ to 4 cups all-purpose flour

1. In a large mixing bowl, combine yeast with 3 tablespoons of lukewarm water. Let stand 5 minutes. Add milk, 4 tablespoons butter, sugar, egg, and salt; mix well with a wooden spoon. Gradually add 2 cups of flour; mix 1 minute. Gradually mix in 1½ to 2 cups more flour, until dough is moist but not sticky. Knead 10 minutes, until it's smooth and elastic. Form into a ball and place in a mixing bowl with a few drops of oil; toss to coat. Cover bowl with plastic wrap; allow to rise in a warm place until double in size, about 1 to 1½ hours. Knead dough 1 minute; cover and refrigerate 30 minutes.

2. Form into 36 tight, round balls, rolling them against an unfloured surface. In a buttered muffin tin, place 3 balls in each muffin cup; cover loosely with greased plastic wrap. Allow to rise in a warm place until double in size, about 1 to 1½ hours.

3. Heat oven to 375 degrees. Melt remaining butter, and brush it onto the rolls. Bake 25–30 minutes, until golden brown.

Chocolate Mousse

While not exactly diet food, this mousse contains no egg yolks, making it lighter in both taste and fat than French chocolate mousse.

Serves 8

1½ tablespoons Kirshwasser **or**
    cherry brandy
1½ tablespoons dark rum (such as
    Meyer's)
1 tablespoon vanilla extract, plus a
    few drops
6 ounces dark chocolate
    (bittersweet)

1½ cups heavy cream
2½ tablespoons confectioners' sugar
6 egg whites, whipped to medium-
    soft peaks, refrigerated
Additional whipped cream and
    chocolate shavings to garnish
    (optional)

1. Chill eight (8-ounce) wineglasses. Combine cherry brandy, dark rum, 1 tablespoon vanilla extract, and chocolate in a double boiler (or a steel mixing bowl set over a pot of simmering water). Warm, stirring occasionally, until melted and smooth. Whip together the cream, confectioners' sugar, and a few drops of vanilla until it forms soft peaks when the whisk is lifted from it.

2. Gently fold ⅓ of the whipped cream into the chocolate mixture. Fold the chocolate mixture back into the rest of the whipped cream, mixing only as much as is necessary to incorporate it most of the way (a few streaks of chocolate are okay). Fold the whipped egg whites very gently into the chocolate cream mixture, just barely enough to incorporate. Fill the mousse into a pastry bag with a star tip (or a plastic bag with a corner cut out), and pipe it into 8 chilled wineglasses. Cover the glasses individually with plastic wrap and chill for at least 6 hours, until set. Garnish with a spoonful of whipped cream and chocolate shavings if desired.

Old-Fashioned Baked Apples

Serve these delicious apples warm after an autumn day outside. They'll warm you right up. They can be made in the microwave (see below).

Serves 4

*4 baking apples (Romes **or** Cortlands are good)*
8 whole cloves
2 ounces butter (½ stick)
⅓ cup light brown sugar
½ teaspoon ground cinnamon

1. Wash and dry apples thoroughly. Using a small knife, cut a divot from the top of the apples, leaving the stem intact. This "cover" will be replaced when baking. Scoop out the seeds and core with a melon-baller or small spoon. Drop 2 cloves into each apple.
2. Knead together the butter and brown sugar, along with the cinnamon, until it is a paste. Divide equally over the scooped apples, leaving enough space to replace the tops.
3. Place apples in a baking dish, with ½ cup of water on the bottom. Bake 350 degrees for 1 hour. Sprinkle with cinnamon or powdered sugar before serving.

Microwave Option

This dish works in the microwave oven, though the flavor develops better in the conventional oven. To microwave, follow steps one and two, then score the apples one inch from the bottom, cover, and cook on high for five minutes per apple.

Cinnamon-Apple Cobbler with Rome Beauty Apples

This dessert is an American favorite, and it makes a beautiful presentation at a picnic.

Serves 8

Filling:
8 or 9 Rome Beauty apples, peeled,
   cored, and diced into 1-inch pieces
Pinch of salt
¼ teaspoon ground nutmeg
1 capful of vanilla extract
1½ teaspoons ground cinnamon
½ cup sugar
¼ cup flour
Juice of ½ lemon

Biscuit Topping:
3 cups flour
½ teaspoon salt
2 teaspoons baking powder
2 eggs
½ cup sugar
⅔ cup milk
6 ounces melted butter

1. Make the filling: Preheat oven to 375 degrees. Mix together the apples, pinch of salt, nutmeg, vanilla, cinnamon, ½ cup sugar, ¼ cup flour, and lemon juice. Place in a 6" × 10" baking dish.
2. Make the topping: Sift together the flour, salt, and baking powder. In a separate bowl, combine the eggs, sugar, milk, and melted butter.
3. Add the wet ingredients to the dry, mixing only until they are well combined. Do not overmix. Batter should have consistency of thick oatmeal. Adjust with milk if necessary.
4. Spread batter over fruit filling, as evenly as possible with your hands. Some holes are natural, and will make for a more attractive presentation.
5. Bake on bottom shelf of 375-degree oven for 90 minutes, turning halfway through, and checking after 1 hour. Fruit should be bubbling thoroughly, and biscuit topping should be nicely browned. Allow to cool at least 15 minutes before serving with vanilla ice cream and a sprig of fresh mint.

Pink McIntosh Applesauce
with Cranberry Chutney

Do not peel the apples before making Mac Applesauce. Cooking the Macs and Delicious apples with the skins on gives this sauce its distinctive pink color.

Mac Applesauce

Serves 6

*1 cinnamon stick, about 2 inches
    long
8 McIntosh and 2 Red Delicious
    apples, washed and quartered
¼ cup sugar
¼ cup water
1 recipe Cranberry Chutney*

1. Warm the cinnamon stick, dry, in a heavy-bottomed pot large enough to hold all the apples. Reduce flame to low and add the apples, sugar, and water. Cover tightly.
2. Simmer gently for 40 minutes, then uncover and simmer 10 minutes more.
3. Strain through a Foley food mill or push through a strainer with a flexible spatula. Cool and serve with a dollop of cranberry chutney.

Cranberry Chutney

Serves 2–3

*2 cups fresh or frozen cranberries
¼ cup very finely diced red onion
1 cup sugar
6 whole cloves
¼ cup water*

Combine all ingredients in a small, heavy-bottomed saucepot. Simmer 10 to 15 minutes, until all cranberries are broken, and have a saucy consistency.

Golden Delicious Apple-Strawberry Crisp

Tailor this to suit your tastes and what's available—other berries, different nuts, etc.

Serves 8

8 or 9 Golden Delicious apples,
  peeled, cored, and cut into 1-inch
  cubes
3 tablespoons granulated sugar
¼ teaspoon ground cloves
½ teaspoon ground cinnamon
Juice of ½ lemon

1 cup plus 2 tablespoons all-purpose flour
1 cup almonds, toasted and roughly
  chopped
1 cup light brown sugar
⅛ teaspoon salt
4 ounces (1 stick) unsalted butter,
  cold, cut into pea-sized pieces

1. Preheat oven to 350 degrees. Toss the apples with granulated sugar, spices, lemon juice, and 2 tablespoons flour. Fill into a 6" × 10" baking dish.
2. Toast almonds lightly in moderate oven at about 300 degrees. Cool.
3. Using your hands, rub together 1 cup flour, brown sugar, salt, and butter until mixture clumps. Add toasted nuts and cover the fruit evenly with this topping. Bake on bottom shelf of 350-degree oven for 1 hour, until fruit is bubbling and topping is crisp. Serve with vanilla whipped cream or vanilla ice cream.

Toasting Nuts for Fresher Flavor and Crispness

Nuts aren't truly "ready to eat" right out of the bag or can. They're asleep. To wake up their natural flavor, and to ensure that they're crisp and delicious, not chewy and flat, heat them on the stovetop or in the oven for a few moments. It improves the quality of very fresh nuts, and it's the way to liven up nuts that may not be completely fresh.

For the stovetop, spread the nuts into a dry skillet, and heat over a medium flame until their natural oils come to the surface, giving them a sheen. For the oven, spread the nuts into a single layer on a baking sheet, and toast for five to ten minutes at 350 degrees, until the oils are visible. Cool nuts to just above room temperature before serving.

Nuts are perishable, and should be kept in the freezer if not being used within a week of purchase. When nuts get too old they become rancid, and will have an odor like wet cardboard. Their flavor will be flat, oily, and unpleasant.

Banana Nut Bread

For fun, you can make this recipe into banana nut cupcakes or minimuffins by baking them for half the time in muffin tins. It freezes well.

Yields 1 loaf

1¼ cups all-purpose flour
1 teaspoon baking soda
¼ teaspoon baking powder
½ teaspoon cinnamon
½ teaspoon salt
1 cup sugar
2 large eggs (see note following)

½ cup oil
3 medium overripe bananas, mashed (1¼ cups)
1 teaspoon vanilla extract
¾ cup coarsely chopped walnuts, toasted lightly in a dry pan until fragrant

1. Heat oven to 350 degrees. Butter a 9" × 5" loaf pan. In a mixing bowl, whisk together the flour, baking soda, baking powder, cinnamon, and salt. In a separate bowl, whisk together the sugar, eggs, and oil; whip vigorously until creamy and light in color, about 5 minutes. Add mashed bananas and vanilla extract to the egg mixture. Add the flour mixture to the wet ingredients in 3 additions, mixing only as much as necessary to incorporate the ingredients, since overmixing will toughen the batter. Stir in the nuts, and pour batter into prepared pan.
2. Bake in center of oven until the top is springy, and a toothpick inserted in the center comes out clean, about 50 to 60 minutes. Allow to cool for 10 minutes; transfer to a rack to cool completely before slicing.

How Large Is a Large Egg?

"Large" eggs connote an actual measurement, not a rough estimate. Buy eggs labeled "large" when they're specified in a recipe.

Spicy Southwestern Cornbread

This smoky cornbread is a specialty at the Bright Food Shop, a Mexican/ Southeast Asian "fusion" cuisine restaurant in New York City. Chef/owners Dona Abramson and Stuart Tarabour, both devoted vegetarians themselves, taught me the enormous value of chilies.

Yields 2 loaves

4½ cups fine cornmeal
1 cup sugar
2 cups flour
4 tablespoons baking powder
1 tablespoon baking soda
4 teaspoons table salt
3½ cups buttermilk
1 cup oil

1 cup (2 sticks) melted butter
6 eggs
1½ tablespoons chopped jalapeño peppers
2 tablespoons puréed chipotle in adobo (see "¡Hola! I Must Be Going: Mexican Specialty Foods" page 61)

1. Heat oven to 400 degrees. In a large mixing bowl, combine the cornmeal, sugar, flour, baking powder, baking soda, and salt. Mix thoroughly with a stiff wire whisk or spoon to combine well and break up any lumps. In a separate mixing bowl, mix the buttermilk, oil, melted butter, eggs, jalapeños, and chipotle; whisk well to combine. Fold the cornmeal mixture into the buttermilk mixture in 3 additions, mixing only as much as necessary to combine ingredients. Pour the batter into two 9" × 5" loaf pans, or one 9" × 13" baking dish. It is not necessary to grease the pans.

2. Bake until the top springs back when pressed, and a toothpick comes out clean when inserted into the center. Cook 10 minutes before turning onto a rack to cool completely.

Corny Polenta Breakfast Pancakes

These unforgettable pancakes come from Dona Abramson of New York's Bright Food Shop. If you have leftover polenta from another dish, you can omit the first step in this recipe, and substitute three cups of cooked polenta.

Serves 8

1 cup coarse yellow cornmeal
2 cups boiling water
1¼ cups flour
1¼ teaspoons table salt
2½ tablespoons sugar
4½ tablespoons baking powder
¾ cup milk
2 eggs plus 1 egg white, beaten
5 ounces (1¼ sticks) melted butter

1. Make the polenta by whisking the cornmeal directly into the boiling water. It should quickly thicken to a paste. Transfer immediately to a platter or pan to cool.
2. Sift together flour, salt, sugar, and baking powder. In a separate bowl, whisk together milk, eggs, and melted butter. Whisk flour mixture into egg mixture, mixing only as much as is necessary to combine. Overmixing will toughen the cakes. Crumble the cooled polenta into the batter, breaking up large pieces between your fingers. Adjust consistency of the batter with additional milk, if necessary, to achieve the consistency of thick oatmeal.
3. Cook on a hot buttered griddle, cast-iron skillet, or nonstick pan, forming 3–4 inch pancakes, cooking thoroughly on both sides. Serve with pure maple syrup.

Tiramisu

Now that this adult dessert of espresso and Italian cream cheese (a.k.a. mascarpone) has become ubiquitous in restaurants, it's time to make the very best version at home.

Serves 12

9 egg yolks
1 cup quick-dissolving sugar
3 teaspoons vanilla extract
750 grams (a little more than 1½ pounds) mascarpone (Italian cream cheese)
1 tablespoon sweet Marsala wine
3 cups cream, whipped to medium-soft peaks

One package (about 60 pieces) lady fingers (a.k.a. savoiardi)
2 cups espresso **or** very strong brewed coffee
2 tablespoons dark rum (such as Meyer's)
Cocoa powder

1. Over a bath of warm water, stir together sugar, yolks, and vanilla until sugar dissolves. In an electric mixer, or by hand, whip the yolks to medium-hard peaks; fold in the mascarpone and Marsala. Fold in the whipped cream.
2. Combine the coffee and rum. Quickly dip ¾ of the lady fingers into the coffee mixture, and use them to line the bottom and sides of a 10-inch springform pan or deep cake pan. Pour half of the cream mixture into the cookie-lined pan; dust thoroughly with cocoa powder. Dip remaining lady fingers in coffee mixture, and layer them into the pan. Top that with the remaining cream.
3. Cover with plastic wrap and refrigerate overnight. Dust top with cocoa powder before cutting into 12 portions, with a hot, wet knife, and serving garnished with mint sprigs.

Mascarpone: It Ain't Philly

Italian cream cheese, known as mascarpone, is the key ingredient in the wildly popular dessert, tiramisu. It's also the perfect rich, creamy accompaniment to fresh figs, or August Georgia peaches. Think yogurt without the tang. It's smooth and unsalted. Buy it at specialty gourmet shops, Italian food stores, and the dairy sections of most modern supermarkets.

Créme Caramel

Silky smooth texture and complex flavor belie this classic French custard's simplicity. When unmolded, the caramel becomes its own natural sauce. Todd Snyder taught me this recipe.

Serves 8

1½ cups sugar, divided
3 cups heavy cream
6 egg yolks
1 teaspoon vanilla extract

1. Heat oven to 350 degrees. In a small, heavy-bottomed skillet, combine ¾ cup sugar with ½ cup water. Bring to a boil over medium-high heat and cook until sugar caramelizes into a deep orange brown. Watch the sugar closely when it begins to color, swirling the pan to keep it evenly colored. Pour immediately from the pan into the bottoms of eight 6-ounce custard cups or ramekins.
2. Bring cream and remaining ¾ cup sugar just to the boiling point, stirring to dissolve the sugar. Place egg yolks in a bowl, and pour the scalded cream mixture over them, whisking vigorously and constantly. Ladle this cream mixture into the caramel-lined molds. Set the molds into a deep roasting pan or casserole dish, and place on the center rack of the oven. Carefully pour water into the roasting pan, filling just past the cream and egg mixture in the molds. Bake for exactly 50 minutes. Remove from oven to cool to room temperature, then refrigerate at least 8 hours or overnight.
3. Unmold the créme caramels by loosening the edges of the custard with a small knife, then inverting the molds onto a plate.

Sour Cream Butter Cake

Frost this cake with homemade Butter-Cream Frosting (page 321), or a store-bought favorite. The cake is rich and moist, so serve it in very thin slices.

Serves 12

4 egg yolks
⅔ cup sour cream
1½ teaspoons vanilla
2 cups sifted cake flour
1 cup sugar

½ teaspoon baking powder
½ teaspoon baking soda
½ teaspoon salt
6 ounces (1½ sticks) unsalted butter,
   softened to room temperature

1. Heat oven to 350 degrees. Grease a 9-inch cake pan, dust it with flour, and line the bottom with waxed paper. In a bowl, whisk together the yolks, ¼ of the sour cream, and the vanilla. In a large, separate bowl, mix the flour, sugar, baking powder, baking soda, and salt; whisk vigorously to combine.
2. Add the butter and remaining sour cream to the flour mixture, and mix well until flour is completely moistened. Add the egg mixture to the flour mixture in 3 separate additions, mixing between each addition. Pour into prepared cake pan.
3. Bake in the middle of the oven until a toothpick inserted in the center comes out clean, usually about 35 to 40 minutes. Start checking at 25 minutes, since oven temperatures and ingredient characteristics vary, and it might be done quicker. Cool 10 minutes, then take out of pan and cool completely on a wire rack.
4. To frost, cut laterally in half and frost both sections, then stack smooth sides, and refrigerate to set.

It Takes a Tender Hand to Make a Tender Cake

Any stirring, kneading, mixing, or working of a batter or dough causes gluten, a natural protein in wheat flour, to develop strands. This makes cakes tough, muffins leathery, and scones basically unfriendly. When a recipe says, "stir or knead only as much as necessary to combine the ingredients," it's telling you that you should avoid developing the gluten in this recipe, lest your product becomes tough as nails. Who eats nails?

Flourless Chocolate Cake

Luxury incarnate, this voluptuous chocolate cake is a vehicle for fine chocolate, so use the best you can get. Chocolate is high in heart-healthy antioxidants.

Serves 12

8 large eggs
1 pound semisweet chocolate
8 ounces (2 sticks) unsalted butter, cut into pieces the size of a hazelnut
¼ cup strong brewed coffee (optional)

1. Heat oven to 325 degrees. Grease an 8- or 9-inch springform pan and line the bottom with waxed paper. Wrap the outside of the pan in foil to prevent leaks. Prepare a pot of boiling water.

2. Using a handheld or standing electric mixer, beat the eggs until double in volume (about 1 quart), about 5 minutes. Melt the chocolate, butter, and coffee in a double boiler or microwave until very smooth, stirring occasionally. Fold in the whipped eggs in 3 additions, mixing only enough as is necessary to incorporate them. Pour into prepared springform pan.

3. Place springform into a deep roasting pan, and place on the lower middle rack of the oven. Pour enough boiling water into the roasting pan to come about halfway up on the sides of the cake. Bake about 25 minutes, until the cake rises slightly, has a thin, wispy crust, and reads 140 degrees on an instant-read thermometer inserted in the center. Transfer springform to a wire rack and cool to room temperature. Refrigerate overnight. Warm sides of springform with a hot, wet towel to loosen, then pop open, cut with a hot, wet knife, and serve dusted with confectioners' sugar and/or cocoa powder.

Butter-Cream Frosting

For chocolate butter-cream, add four ounces of melted chocolate to this recipe at the end. It's excellent with milk chocolate.

Yields enough to frost 1 (9-inch) cake

1½ cups sugar
½ cup water
2 large eggs plus 4 egg yolks
1 pound unsalted butter, softened to room temperature
2 teaspoons vanilla extract

1. Boil the sugar and water together without stirring until slightly thick and between 234 and 240 degrees on a candy thermometer (this is called the "soft ball" stage—a thin ribbon should fall with the last drops off a spoon). Whisk together eggs and yolks in a double boiler or steel bowl atop a pot of simmering water. Gradually whisk in the hot sugar syrup; heat, whisking constantly, until the mixture is hot to the touch, thick, and ribbony. Remove bowl from heat, and continue whisking until cool, about 5 minutes more.
2. In a mixer or bowl, beat the butter until it is fluffy and light. Gradually beat the whipped butter into the egg mixture, adding it in tablespoon-fuls. Add the vanilla, and whisk to incorporate. If desired, flavor by adding melted chocolate, fruit liqueur, or espresso. Cool over an ice water bath until it reaches a comfortable consistency for spreading. Keeps in the refrigerator for up to 1 week.

Chocolate Curls

Use a swivel vegetable peeler to make attractive shavings and curls from a block of chocolate. Just start with a large flat surface of chocolate, like the edge of a bar or the side of a hunk, and shave away from yourself, letting the curls fall onto whatever food you're garnishing. Don't try to pick them up with your fingers, though, because they melt faster than butter.

Blondies

Chewy butterscotch-flavored chocolate-chunk brownies are called blondies, and taste great out of the icebox.

Yields 36 pieces

1½ cups flour
½ teaspoon baking powder
½ teaspoon salt
6 ounces (1½ sticks) unsalted butter, at room temperature

Generous 1¾ cups brown sugar
2 teaspoons vanilla extract
3 large eggs
6 ounces (about 1 cup) semisweet chocolate chunks or chips

1. Heat oven to 350 degrees. Butter a 9-inch baking pan. In a medium bowl, using a stiff wire whisk, whisk together the flour, baking powder, and salt. Separately, combine the butter, brown sugar, and vanilla, and cream together using an electric mixer or by hand, until light and fluffy (about 2 minutes). Gradually beat in the eggs, working each 1 in completely before adding the next. Scrape down mixing bowl; add the flour mixture. Beat just long enough to incorporate. Mix in chocolate chunks. Transfer the batter into the prepared baking pan, and smooth with a spatula.

2. Bake until a toothpick inserted in the center comes out clean, about 30 to 35 minutes. Cool at room temperature at least 1 hour. Cut into 36 pieces. Will keep refrigerated for 1 week, or in freezer for up to 6 weeks.

Dessert Smoothies

Make your own fruity cooler. For a banana shake: Blend together one banana, one tablespoon sugar, one cup of milk, one-fourth teaspoon vanilla extract, and seven ice cubes until very, very smooth. Add blueberries or strawberries to the mix, if desired. A cup of chilled coffee, with a drop of almond extract, a tablespoon of sugar, a half-dozen ice cubes, and a splash of cream also blends up into a righteous quencher.

Pears Poached in White Wine with Strawberry Sauce V

This simply beautiful dessert is perfect in any season. It's light, contains no cholesterol, and finishes an elegant dinner or an everyday lunch with a touch of class.

Serves 8

*1 bottle (750 ml) white wine (chardonnay **or** Riesling are both excellent for this)*
Zest of 1 lemon, shaved off with a vegetable peeler in strips
8 whole cloves
2 whole cinnamon sticks
1 cup sugar, divided
4 Bosc pears, peeled, halved lengthwise, seeds scooped out
1 pint strawberries, hulled and halved
1 teaspoon vanilla
8 sprigs fresh mint

1. Combine the wine, lemon zest, cloves, cinnamon sticks, and ½ cup sugar in a large (4–5 quart) pot; bring to a boil. Reduce heat to a simmer and add the pears, arranging them so they are mostly submerged. Cover tightly and cook slowly for 5 minutes; remove from heat and leave to steep 20 minutes. Chill.

2. In a blender, combine the strawberries, remaining ½ cup sugar, and vanilla. Purée until smooth, adding a few drops of water if necessary to get things started.

3. Spoon the sauce onto dessert plates to form small pools midplate. Serve the pears cut-side down atop the sauce, garnished with mint sprigs at the stem end.

Chocolate Chip Cookies

Serves about 12

2½ cups all-purpose flour
1 teaspoon baking soda
1 teaspoon salt
1 cup (2 sticks) unsalted butter, softened
¾ cup sugar
¾ cup (packed) light brown sugar
1 teaspoon vanilla extract
2 large eggs
2 cups (12-ounce package) semisweet chocolate chips

1. Heat oven to 375 degrees. In a mixing bowl, whisk together flour, baking soda, and salt. In a separate bowl, cream together the butter, granulated sugar, brown sugar, and vanilla using a wooden spoon. Add the eggs 1 at a time, mixing until incorporated before adding the next one.

2. Add the flour in 3 additions, mixing just enough to incorporate after each addition. Stir in the chocolate chips. Drop the dough in tablespoon-size drops onto ungreased baking sheets. Bake until golden, about 10 minutes. Cool the pans for a few minutes before transferring the cookies to a wire rack to cool completely.

Appendix A

Resources

Jewish Ethnic Products

- *www.manischewitz.com*
- *www.hagalil.com/shop/kosher/*

Best for Mexican and Southeast Asian Specialties

Kitchen Market
218 Eighth Avenue
New York, NY 10011
(888) HOT-4433
www.kitchenmarket.com

Asian Vegetables

Indian Rock Produce
530 California Road
Box 317
Quakertown, PA 18951
(800) 882-0512
www.indianrockproduce.com
Will FedEx orders of any size to anywhere.

Japan California Products, Inc.
544 Stanford Avenue
Los Angeles, CA 90013
(213) 622-6386
Top U.S. grower of Asian vegetables; will ship any item anywhere overnight.

Specialty Ethnic Ingredients

- *www.ethnicgrocer.com*
- *www.epicurious.com*

Cheeses

Ideal Cheese Shop Ltd.
942 1st Avenue (at 52nd Street)
New York, NY 10022
(800) 382-0109   Fax (212) 223-1245
www.idealcheese.com

Natura: The Ninth Avenue Cheese Market
615 Ninth Avenue
New York, NY 10036
(212) 397-4700

Zabar's
2245 Broadway
New York, NY 10024
(212) 787-4477
Be prepared for real New York attitude when you call, but they have everything, and the prices are good.

Wild Rice

- *www.christmaspoint.com*

Kasha and Buckwheat

LifeField Buckwheat Products
847A Second Avenue, Suite 181
New York, NY 10017
✆ (516) 487-2262

Wolff's

P.O. Box 440
Penn Yan, NY 14527
✆ (315) 536-3311
✑ www.thebirkettmills.com

Specialty Mushrooms

East Coast Exotic Mushrooms
Box 468
Toughkenamon, PA 19374
✆ (610) 268-5009 or (800) 282-9399
✑ http://members.dca.net/westmj/
mushrooms

Balducci's
424 Avenue of the Americas
New York, NY 10014
✆ (212) 673-2600
All exotic produce and wild mushrooms

Delftree Corp.
234 Union Street
North Adams, MA 01247
✆ (413) 664-4907
Cultivated exotic mushrooms

Grains, Beans, and Seeds

Purity Foods
2871 West Jolly Road
Okemos, MI 48864
✆ (517) 351-9231 Fax: (517) 351-9391
✑ www.purityfoods.com

Dean and DeLuca
560 Broadway
New York, NY 10012
✆ (212) 226-6800 or (800) 221-7714

Spices, Nuts, Dried Fruits, Grains, Beans, Middle Eastern Ingredients

Kalustyan's
123 Lexington Avenue
New York, NY 10016
✆ (212) 685-3451 Fax: (212) 683-8458
✑ www.kalustyans.com

Foods of India
121 Lexington Avenue
New York, NY 10016
✆ (212) 683-4419

Dowel Quality Products Inc.
91 First Avenue
New York, NY 10009
✆ (212) 979-6045

Spice House
99 First Avenue
New York, NY 10009
✆ (212) 387-7812

Appendix B

The Vegetarian Cook's Essentials

Equipment for a Vegetarian's Kitchen

While the only tools a cook needs to make most of the dishes in this book are a sharp, solid knife (such as an 8" "French" or "Chef's" knife) and a good cutting board, the following items will make certain jobs much easier and more professional looking.

MANDOLIN	See the sidebar on page 132 to find out why this cutting/julienne device can revolutionize your cooking style.
GREENS SPINNER	Dressings adhere to dry lettuce leaves, and run off wet ones. An inexpensive lettuce spinner gyrates away excess water, making your salads more intensely flavored.
WIRE WHISK	A 10" "balloon whisk" has fine wires which incorporate air into foods, lightening their texture. This tool is also essential for making dressings and sauces where insoluble ingredients like oil and vinegar are combined.
STANDING ELECTRIC MIXER	This one is an investment for life. They run about $300, but make baking 300% easier, kneading dough, whipping cream, softening butter . . .
FOOD PROCESSOR	Anytime I'm chopping more than four cloves of garlic, I chop them in a processor. It's faster. Dips and dressings practically make themselves, and some of the recipes in this book are meant to be made in one.
BLENDER	Not to be used in place of a food processor or vice-versa. Blenders yield smooth, velvety purees that most processors just can't do. See the sidebar on page 69 comparing use of blenders and food processors.
STOVETOP GRILL PAN	Easier, healthier and more eco-friendly than charcoal or gas grills, a cast-iron or coated alloy pan with ridged surfaces for indoor grilling is incredibly useful. Good cast-iron ones go for under $20.
SPICE GRINDER	Basically, any small coffee grinder can be used as a spice grinder. Since the best flavor comes from spices that are toasted as whole seeds in a dry pan, then ground just before use, having one of these $10 devices, about the size of a can of pineapple, in your cabinet is a good idea. You can use the same one for coffee if you clean it out really well between uses.

The Basic Pantry

Beyond the usual bottles of ketchup, cans of DelMonte fruit cocktail and emergency corn most of us keep in the closet, the following items can make your vegetarian cooking the best it can be, and should be around the house at all times:

- ☐ Extra-virgin Olive Oil *(see sidebar, page 3)*
- ☐ Dijon-style Mustard
- ☐ Kosher (Coarse) Salt *(see sidebar, page 51)*
- ☐ Japanese Rice Vinegar
- ☐ Pickled Jalapeno Peppers
- ☐ Assorted Dried Beans *(see sidebar, "Bean There . . ." page 16)*
- ☐ Dried Mushrooms *(such as Chinese Black Mushrooms or Shiitakes)*
- ☐ Vegetable Bouillon Cubes *(in case you can't make stock)*
- ☐ Wild Rice
- ☐ Dry Sherry *(for use in any dish calling for white wine—it keeps for years)*

General Index

Vegan Index

We Have
EVERYTHING!

Everything® **After College Book**
$12.95, 1-55850-847-3

Everything® **American History Book**
$12.95, 1-58062-531-2

Everything® **Angels Book**
$12.95, 1-58062-398-0

Everything® **Anti-Aging Book**
$12.95, 1-58062-565-7

Everything® **Astrology Book**
$12.95, 1-58062-062-0

Everything® **Baby Names Book**
$12.95, 1-55850-655-1

Everything® **Baby Shower Book**
$12.95, 1-58062-305-0

Everything® **Baby's First Food Book**
$12.95, 1-58062-512-6

Everything® **Baby's First Year Book**
$12.95, 1-58062-581-9

Everything® **Barbeque Cookbook**
$12.95, 1-58062-316-6

Everything® **Bartender's Book**
$9.95, 1-55850-536-9

Everything® **Bedtime Story Book**
$12.95, 1-58062-147-3

Everything® **Bicycle Book**
$12.00, 1-55850-706-X

Everything® **Breastfeeding Book**
$12.95, 1-58062-582-7

Everything® **Build Your Own Home Page**
$12.95, 1-58062-339-5

Everything® **Business Planning Book**
$12.95, 1-58062-491-X

Everything® **Candlemaking Book**
$12.95, 1-58062-623-8

Everything® **Casino Gambling Book**
$12.95, 1-55850-762-0

Everything® **Cat Book**
$12.95, 1-55850-710-8

Everything® **Chocolate Cookbook**
$12.95, 1-58062-405-7

Everything® **Christmas Book**
$15.00, 1-55850-697-7

Everything® **Civil War Book**
$12.95, 1-58062-366-2

Everything® **Classical Mythology Book**
$12.95, 1-58062-653-X

Everything® **Collectibles Book**
$12.95, 1-58062-645-9

Everything® **College Survival Book**
$12.95, 1-55850-720-5

Everything® **Computer Book**
$12.95, 1-58062-401-4

Everything® **Cookbook**
$14.95, 1-58062-400-6

Everything® **Cover Letter Book**
$12.95, 1-58062-312-3

Everything® **Creative Writing Book**
$12.95, 1-58062-647-5

Everything® **Crossword and Puzzle Book**
$12.95, 1-55850-764-7

Everything® **Dating Book**
$12.95, 1-58062-185-6

Everything® **Dessert Book**
$12.95, 1-55850-717-5

Everything® **Digital Photography Book**
$12.95, 1-58062-574-6

Everything® **Dog Book**
$12.95, 1-58062-144-9

Everything® **Dreams Book**
$12.95, 1-55850-806-6

Everything® **Etiquette Book**
$12.95, 1-55850-807-4

Everything® **Fairy Tales Book**
$12.95, 1-58062-546-0

Everything® **Family Tree Book**
$12.95, 1-55850-763-9

Everything® **Feng Shui Book**
$12.95, 1-58062-587-8

Everything® **Fly-Fishing Book**
$12.95, 1-58062-148-1

Everything® **Games Book**
$12.95, 1-55850-643-8

Everything® **Get-A-Job Book**
$12.95, 1-58062-223-2

Everything® **Get Out of Debt Book**
$12.95, 1-58062-588-6

Everything® **Get Published Book**
$12.95, 1-58062-315-8

Everything® **Get Ready for Baby Book**
$12.95, 1-55850-844-9

Everything® **Get Rich Book**
$12.95, 1-58062-670-X

Everything® **Ghost Book**
$12.95, 1-58062-533-9

Everything® **Golf Book**
$12.95, 1-55850-814-7

Everything® **Grammar and Style Book**
$12.95, 1-58062-573-8

Everything® **Guide to Las Vegas**
$12.95, 1-58062-438-3

Everything® **Guide to New England**
$12.95, 1-58062-589-4

Everything® **Guide to New York City**
$12.95, 1-58062-314-X

Everything® **Guide to Walt Disney World®,
Universal Studios®, and
Greater Orlando, 2nd Edition**
$12.95, 1-58062-404-9

Everything® **Guide to Washington D.C.**
$12.95, 1-58062-313-1

Everything® **Guitar Book**
$12.95, 1-58062-555-X

Everything® **Herbal Remedies Book**
$12.95, 1-58062-331-X

Everything® **Home-Based Business Book**
$12.95, 1-58062-364-6

Everything® **Homebuying Book**
$12.95, 1-58062-074-4

Everything® **Homeselling Book**
$12.95, 1-58062-304-2

Everything® **Horse Book**
$12.95, 1-58062-564-9

Everything® **Hot Careers Book**
$12.95, 1-58062-486-3

Everything® **Internet Book**
$12.95, 1-58062-073-6

Everything® **Investing Book**
$12.95, 1-58062-149-X

Everything® **Jewish Wedding Book**
$12.95, 1-55850-801-5

Everything® **Job Interview Book**
$12.95, 1-58062-493-6

Everything® **Lawn Care Book**
$12.95, 1-58062-487-1

Everything® **Leadership Book**
$12.95, 1-58062-513-4

Everything® **Learning French Book**
$12.95, 1-58062-649-1

Everything® **Learning Spanish Book**
$12.95, 1-58062-575-4

Everything® **Low-Fat High-Flavor
Cookbook**
$12.95, 1-55850-802-3

Everything® **Magic Book**
$12.95, 1-58062-418-9

Everything® **Managing People Book**
$12.95, 1-58062-577-0

Everything® **Microsoft® Word 2000 Book**
$12.95, 1-58062-306-9

Everything® **Money Book**
$12.95, 1-58062-145-7

Everything® **Mother Goose Book**
$12.95, 1-58062-490-1

Everything® **Motorcycle Book**
$12.95, 1-58062-554-1

Everything® **Mutual Funds Book**
$12.95, 1-58062-419-7

Everything® **One-Pot Cookbook**
$12.95, 1-58062-186-4

Everything® **Online Business Book**
$12.95, 1-58062-320-4

Everything® **Online Genealogy Book**
$12.95, 1-58062-402-2

Everything® **Online Investing Book**
$12.95, 1-58062-338-7

Everything® **Online Job Search Book**
$12.95, 1-58062-365-4

Everything® **Organize Your Home Book**
$12.95, 1-58062-617-3

Everything® **Pasta Book**
$12.95, 1-55850-719-1

Everything® **Philosophy Book**
$12.95, 1-58062-644-0

Everything® **Playing Piano and Key-
boards Book**
$12.95, 1-58062-651-3

Everything® **Pregnancy Book**
$12.95, 1-58062-146-5

Everything® **Pregnancy Organizer**
$15.00, 1-58062-336-0

Everything® **Project Management Book**
$12.95, 1-58062-583-5

Everything® **Puppy Book**
$12.95, 1-58062-576-2

Everything® **Quick Meals Cookbook**
$12.95, 1-58062-488-X

Everything® **Resume Book**
$12.95, 1-58062-311-5

Everything® **Romance Book**
$12.95, 1-58062-566-5

Everything® **Running Book**
$12.95, 1-58062-618-1

Everything® **Sailing Book, 2nd Edition**
$12.95, 1-58062-671-8

Everything® **Saints Book**
$12.95, 1-58062-534-7

Everything® **Selling Book**
$12.95, 1-58062-319-0

Everything® **Shakespeare Book**
$12.95, 1-58062-591-6

Everything® **Spells and Charms Book**
$12.95, 1-58062-532-0

Everything® **Start Your Own Business Book**
$12.95, 1-58062-650-5

Everything® **Stress Management Book**
$12.95, 1-58062-578-9

Everything® **Study Book**
$12.95, 1-55850-615-2

Everything® **Tai Chi and QiGong Book**
$12.95, 1-58062-646-7

Everything® **Tall Tales, Legends, and
Outrageous Lies Book**
$12.95, 1-58062-514-2

Everything® **Tarot Book**
$12.95, 1-58062-191-0

Everything® **Time Management Book**
$12.95, 1-58062-492-8

Everything® **Toasts Book**
$12.95, 1-58062-189-9

Everything® **Toddler Book**
$12.95, 1-58062-592-4

Everything® **Total Fitness Book**
$12.95, 1-58062-318-2

Everything® **Trivia Book**
$12.95, 1-58062-143-0

Everything® **Tropical Fish Book**
$12.95, 1-58062-343-3

Everything® **Vegetarian Cookbook**
$12.95, 1-58062-640-8

Everything® **Vitamins, Minerals,
and Nutritional Supple-
ments Book**
$12.95, 1-58062-496-0

Everything® **Wedding Book, 2nd Edition**
$12.95, 1-58062-190-2

Everything® **Wedding Checklist**
$7.95, 1-58062-456-1

Everything® **Wedding Etiquette Book**
$7.95, 1-58062-454-5

Everything® **Wedding Organizer**
$15.00, 1-55850-828-7

Everything® **Wedding Shower Book**
$7.95, 1-58062-188-0

Everything® **Wedding Vows Book**
$7.95, 1-58062-455-3

Everything® **Weight Training Book**
$12.95, 1-58062-593-2

Everything® **Wine Book**
$12.95, 1-55850-808-2

Everything® **World War II Book**
$12.95, 1-58062-572-X

Everything® **World's Religions Book**
$12.95, 1-58062-648-3

Everything® **Yoga Book**
$12.95, 1-58062-594-0

Visit us at everything.com

Everything® is a registered trademark of Adams Media Corporation.

EVERYTHING

Trade Paperback, $12.95
1-58062-488-X, 352 pages

The Everything® Quick Meals Cookbook

By Barbara Doyen

The Everything® Quick Meals Cookbook features 300 easy-to-follow recipes for cooks with gourmet tastes and limited time. You'll learn to prepare delicious and nutritious meals faster and easier than ever before. From a one-course dinner for the family to an elaborate feast for special guests, this book provides mouth-watering recipes that will satisfy any appetite. It also features dozens of valuable time-saving tips, and complete instructions so that your favorite meals turn out perfect every time.

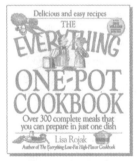

Trade Paperback, $12.95
1-58062-186-4, 288 pages

The Everything® One-Pot Cookbook

By Lisa Rojak

What could be easier than cooking an entire meal using just one pot? One-pot cuisine is characterized by hearty, satisfying dishes that can be prepared using only one of a variety of conventional cooking techniques: a single baking pan, skillet, crock pot, or conventional stovetop pot. *The Everything® One-Pot Cookbook* features hundreds of exciting recipes that are guaranteed crowd pleasers, with minimal mess. From appetizers to entrees and even desserts, these one-pot meals are quick, simple, and delicious.